LOAN WORKOUTS AND DEBT FOR EQUITY SWAPS

A Framework for Successful Corporate Rescues

By

Subhrendu Chatterji and Paul Hedges

JOHN WILEY & SONS, LTD

Chichester • New York • Weinheim • Brisbane • Singapore • Toronto

Other Wiley Editorial Offices

John Wiley & Sons, Inc., 605 Third Avenue,
New York, NY 10158-0012, USA

Wiley-VCH Verlag GmbH, Pappelallee 3,
D-69469 Weinheim, Germany

John Wiley & Sons Australia, Ltd, 33 Park Road, Milton,
Queensland 4064, Australia

John Wiley & Sons (Asia) Pte Ltd, 2 Clementi Loop #02-01,
Jin Xing Distripark, Singapore 129809

John Wiley & Sons (Canada) Ltd, 22 Worcester Road,
Rexdale, Ontario M9W 1L1, Canada

Library of Congress Cataloging-in-Publication Data

Chatterji, Subhrendu.
    Loan workouts and debt for equity swaps: a framework for successful corporate
rescues/by Subhrendu Chatterji and Paul Hedges.
       p.cm. — (Wiley finance)
    Includes index.
    ISBN 0-471-89339-0
    1. Corporate turnarounds. 2. Corporations–Finance. 3. Corporate debt. 4. Corporate
reorganizations. I. Hedges, Paul. II. Title. III. Wiley finance series.

    HG4028.R4 C46 2001
    658.15—dc21
                                                              00-068517
British Library Cataloguing in Publication Data

A catalogue record for this book is available from the British Library

ISBN 0-471-893390

Typeset in 10/12pt by Laser Words, Chennai, India
Printed and bound by CPI Antony Rowe, Eastbourne

LOAN WORKOUTS AND DEBT FOR EQUITY SWAPS

To a banker, his wife, their daughter-in-law and her son

—SC

To Coelho

—PJH

CONTENTS

FOREWORD

When I was approached to provide a foreword to this book I was enthusiastic for two reasons.

Firstly, I have known the authors personally for many years, having worked with them on major cross-border reconstructions which of necessity involved working into the early hours of the morning in crisis situations. Such was the desire and commitment to achieve a beneficial outcome for all stakeholders outside insolvency. The authors have extensive knowledge of the strategies and techniques required to achieve equitable and successful workouts, and these are shared in this book.

Secondly, although workouts cannot be too prescriptive, I have long believed that a book of this nature was needed in the market place, outlining the principles of voluntary problem debt standstills and associated restructurings and documenting the methodologies which have been established by experienced practitioners over the years.

Although the recessions of the 1970s and early 1980s saw instances where corporates entered insolvency proceedings or were involved in rescue operations mounted by their bankers, subsequent UK recessions have seen an unprecedented level of problems in terms of the number of cases, the magnitude of debt and the degree of complexity involved. Despite high profile collapses, in the vast majority of cases a successful recovery has been engineered to the benefit of all the stakeholders involved in each business.

Many lessons have been learned and re-learned during this period. At the same time, whilst standard procedures have arisen to deal with most cases, the level of general expertise required and flexibility necessary to produce solutions has, of necessity, increased to a considerable degree.

The rescue or 'workout' process will in most instances broadly encompass the various phases outlined below. It has been consistently proven that the earlier a problem is identified/predicted, particularly if this can happen whilst relative stability still exists, then the quicker and, in all likelihood, the more successful the turnaround will be.

These steps effectively cover a three-way process:

- The identification/early warning of distress and an initial assessment of viability.
- The support operation encompassing standstill principles and including, as necessary, a full financial restructuring.
- The recovery process and the commercial measures needed to achieve a turnaround/ rescue.

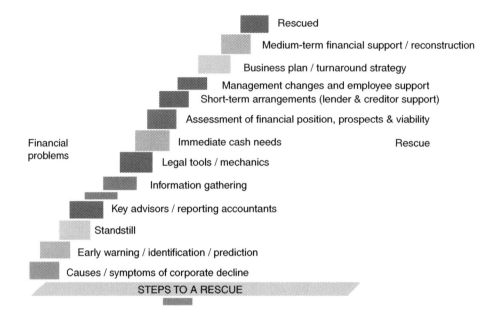

Rescued

Medium-term financial support / reconstruction

Business plan / turnaround strategy

Management changes and employee support

Short-term arrangements (lender & creditor support)

Assessment of financial position, prospects & viability

Financial problems   Immediate cash needs   Rescue

Legal tools / mechanics

Information gathering

Key advisors / reporting accountants

Standstill

Early warning / identification / prediction

Causes / symptoms of corporate decline

STEPS TO A RESCUE

From an overview of major corporate distress seen in the market place, over the years, there is a clear commonality of some factors.

The root often starts with the quality of executive management and their entrepreneurial propensity to grow the business, together with the inability of the supporting team to cope with an expanded empire. Aggressive acquisitions and diversification programmes, especially into unknown overseas markets, supported by increased debt has crippled many companies. Often these companies have been headed by dominant individuals and/or there has been founder/family involvement.

The problems have then frequently been compounded by poor cash management and deficient internal controls and management reporting, a general trading downturn of the core businesses (particularly in a recessionary environment) and a collapse in property values.

In addition, creative accounting techniques can send up a smoke screen which delays the identification of problem situations. Indeed this can end up as gross misrepresentation and/or fraudulent activities, and there have been some high profile cases which illustrate this.

However, even in these situations there can be a viable underlying business or part of a group worth rescuing outside insolvency.

It would be amiss not to mention the important role of non-executive directors in providing a truly effective, independent counterbalance both strategically and operationally (for example in ensuring that adequate management reporting and audit systems are in place), with a view to helping avoid the characteristics seen in corporates in difficulties.

Ultimately, the effect of the problems referred to is to render debt unserviceable with breaches or impending breaches of covenants, cash flow shortfalls and a heavy write down of asset values against net worth. The bottom line to an impending collapse is that the company eventually and simply runs out of cash.

The general scenario of cause and effect and solution can be summarised as follows:

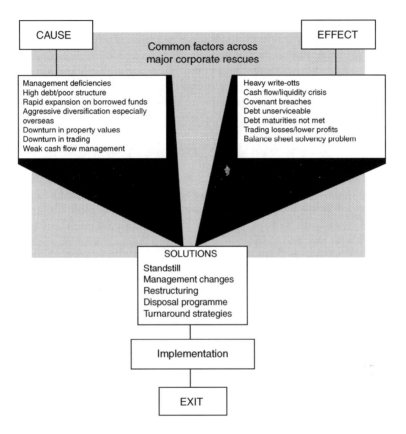

Whilst any voluntary approach requires flexibility on a case-by-case basis, there are clearly defined parameters which need to be adopted to achieve a successful result where time is of the essence, and this book helps to enshrine the tried and tested approaches which have developed over time.

Fundamentally, a workout emerges from the general premise that voluntary support for a distressed multinational corporate is likely to be better than insolvency to preserve value, and accordingly there needs to be a high level of co-operation and communication amongst lenders on a cross-border basis.

This voluntary approach has been encapsulated in a formalised statement by the INSOL Lenders Group:

> In the event of financial difficulties being experienced by a multinational corporate the major financial creditors should act in a co-ordinated manner to facilitate short-term viability and stability whilst confirmation of the present position of the debtor and relative positions of the creditors is obtained in a timely and cost effective manner enabling the available options to be presented, assessed and a way forward agreed upon.

Put another way, a rescue culture on which this book is based can be defined as the spirit of co-operation, understanding, support and commonality of approach of lenders on a cross-border basis outside formal insolvency or court rehabilitation processes that facilitates an attempt to preserve value for all stakeholders where a commercially viable multinational corporate enterprise is confronting financial difficulties.

Importantly, lenders need to avoid failure of potentially viable businesses for want of reconciling competing creditors' interests.

Apart from a company addressing its underlying commercial trading problems a critical area of any workout is the complexity of inter-creditor priorities.

Lenders will need trust and confidence in a rescue process and this will include the experience and abilities of the co-ordinator or leader as well as the adoption of established principles on a consistent basis.

More specific issues which will need to be addressed include:

- *Identification of key participants and their relative contributions to a restructuring.* The increasing diversity of financial instruments available and markets accessible to corporates inevitably leads to an equally wide variety of providers. Therefore, whilst historically there may have been a fairly narrow group of participants in workouts this is no longer the case, with a far wider range of creditors who now have the right to become involved. For example, high yield bonds are an increasingly common feature in the European market. However, this brings certain obligations for them to participate in the process. Indeed in any workout it is appropriate that all major financial creditors/creditor groups whose rights are likely to be affected be involved in the support operations.

- *Moratorium or standstill/stay.* Given the fact that a corporate has reached the position where it is in need of a support operation from its creditors, this suggests that matters have become or are close to becoming critical (the likelihood is that the directors will have tried everything they can to avoid having to enter a workout). This is likely to mean that willing and unilateral support has been tried and failed and as such the overall situation is highly unstable. To give time to assess the position and the options open to lenders and the corporate it is essential that a stable environment is established. At the broadest level this will involve a moratorium (standstill/stay), but there are a number of associated issues that will arise in the context of achieving such a state, particularly where the corporate operates across national boundaries.

- *Sufficient and reliable information to enable judgements to be made.* Information must be shared and produced in a timely manner. The need to make decisions on an informed basis is fundamental to any credit assessment process. This is particularly important in the case of potentially highly complex multinational corporates with multiple operations and creditor arrangements. It is essential to obtain a sound information base both in the context of the status and prospects of the corporate and creditor relativities and to provide the base for decisions on the provision of new money and the overall restructuring.

- *Independent professional review of the financial position, viability and options.* It is essential to obtain independent advice for the benefit of the lender group and this may need to be accountant, lawyer and investment banking advice.

- *Appointment of a co-ordinator or leader.* Experience shows that there is a need to approach support/workout situations in a co-ordinated and timely manner, particularly where a corporate has a broad range of financial creditors and/or operations (be that type or jurisdiction). This is important on a number of fronts to ensure that:
  - Inter-creditor relativities are maintained.
  - The corporate and its advisors have a main point of contact for dealing with creditors. This provides the reassurance the directors may need to satisfy themselves they can continue rather than seeking the protection of the relevant court procedure.
  - The potentially scarce resources of the corporate are focused on finding a solution rather than 'fire-fighting' with creditors, which should save costs and may provide a swifter solution. This also focuses on the need for the co-ordinator to possess the appropriate skills, experience and resources to chair the committee, take responsibility for overall co-ordination and drive for a solution.

- *Usually provision of short-term liquidity and/or continuation of existing facilities.* The cash position of a group has to be established as an absolute priority. In order to achieve stability and allow time to obtain information to make a decision on the way ahead, some form of short-term liquidity needs to be achieved, usually involving new money and/or the release of headroom in facilities and/or disposal of surplus unencumbered assets and/or deferment of interest.

- *Understanding and acknowledgement of the relative strength of differing claims.* This is often referred to as entity priority positions and is vital for drawing up a notional liquidation model and for preparing the restructuring plan and facility agreement.

- *Understanding local jurisdiction issues.* In order to devise appropriate workout strategies some knowledge is required of local jurisdiction issues relating to group operations in those countries. For example, the relevant local voluntary rescue cultures and processes, rehabilitation and insolvency legislation will impact on a rescue plan.

- *Voting structures.* Voting structures will need to cover issues requiring either all-lender agreement, majority lender or individual agreement. There is clearly a need to reach agreement on a number of issues relating to a workout, and these range from covenanting aspects (e.g., restrictive covenants on capex, inter-company trading/loans, etc.) through to matters of more fundamental lender rights (e.g., term, pricing, new money, etc.). Whilst understandably all affected parties will want to have a say in these issues, it is clear that unless agreement can be reached the attempt to achieve a workout/rescue will fail. Therefore this is a critical area for debate which necessarily impacts directly on all other areas of a workout. Importantly, no approach outside legislation can remove the rights of a lender, and therefore any understanding reached on voting will be purely voluntary and not mandatory.

These above mentioned ingredients will all be needed to lead to the ultimate objective of a successful restructuring plan.

International debt problems have been around for decades, but there have been new developments driving a more sophisticated and consistent approach, namely:

- Increasing complexity of financial structures both in types of facilities and diversity of global credit providers and, for example, capital market instruments.
- Evidence of increased internationalisation of corporate borrowers with complex legal structures.
- Emergence of a more active debt trading market beyond that established in the US, which has brought new players into the equation who may have a different agenda depending on their entry price and exit objectives.
- Timescales for workout periods have tended to lengthen as a result of increased complexity.
- More active use and acceptance of debt to equity conversions in restructuring solutions.

Arguably this has further endorsed the need for a strong co-operative rescue culture.

Indeed realistically we cannot look to any global harmonisation of insolvency laws in the short- or even medium-term which would at least give a uniform backdrop for a rescue. This to me wholeheartedly endorses the importance placed on voluntary approaches and the methodology required in these cases.

In one of my previous roles as Head of Credit Risk Management at Nat West Bank and as Chairman of the INSOL Lenders Group established to take a leadership role in encouraging and developing cross-border support, co-operation and communication, I have been a strong advocate of a rescue culture approach and standardisation as far as possible of the principles involved whilst retaining some flexibility on a case-by-case basis.

These views also transcend into the need for corporates themselves to seek appropriate independent financial advice at the earliest signs of distress or impending financial problems. These need to be competent professionals who understand all the issues on both sides of the table (debtor and creditor related) for an equitable and timely solution for all stakeholders.

This book covers all the issues I have mentioned above, and more, detailing how workouts can be achieved in practice taking into account all the many variables and including an insight into ways of running a workout department.

I commend it to readers whether they be new or more experienced practitioners.

David Wilson Havelock
Chairman-Corporate Restructuring Group
Close Brothers Corporate Finance
Formerly Director of
Credit Management and
head of workouts at
National Westminster Bank
and Chairman of the
INSOL Lenders Group

ABOUT THE AUTHORS

Subhrendu Chatterji

Subhrendu Chatterji is a consultant specialising in corporate and financial restructurings. He also advises on financial sector and banking strategy. He has advised UK banks on a large number of loan workouts, with a particular emphasis on debt for equity swap aspects of transactions. In addition, he has lived and worked in Central Europe for over four years, directing consultancy projects and advising banks on organising loan workout departments and on their non-performing loan resolution strategies. He also advised local banks on the financial restructurings of their large clients. In addition to the United Kingdom, Subhrendu's country experience includes Australia, China, Poland, Romania, Tanzania and Turkey. He has organised and participated in a number of seminars on commercial, investment banking and financial stability issues and has published articles on corporate restructurings in professional journals.

Prior to becoming a consultant, Subhrendu was with NatWest Markets, an investment bank, and worked on corporate acquisitions, disposals, flotations and fund-raisings. He is a Fellow of the Institute of Chartered Accountants in England and Wales, a qualified Corporate Treasurer and has an MBA from Oxford University.

Subhrendu is currently the Chief Executive of Consulting Base, an exchange for consultants working in the emerging markets and developing countries.

Paul Hedges

Paul Hedges is a Senior Manager with the Royal Bank of Scotland. His career with NatWest Bank, prior to its takeover by the Royal Bank of Scotland, spans twenty years, primarily in corporate banking and more specifically since 1989 in the credit risk and debt workout areas. During the early 1990s' recession in the UK, Paul was closely involved with a number of loan workouts involving large corporates, particularly those involving multiple banks. His focus is particularly on the structuring aspects and inter-creditor issues involved in senior debt moratoriums and restructurings.

In the early 1990s, Paul spent two years living in Poland advising a major Polish bank on creating and managing a debt workout department and on individual company restructurings.

Since returning to the UK Paul has worked in NatWest's and the Royal Bank of Scotland's senior credit functions with responsibility for approving and reviewing many of the bank's largest corporate, leveraged and mezzanine exposures as well as maintaining a close working relationship with the bank's loan workouts department.

Paul is an Associate of the Chartered Institute of Bankers and has written a number of articles on loan workouts for a national professional journal in Poland.

PART I

INTRODUCTION
AND
BACKGROUND

1

INTRODUCTION

The onset of a loan workout is typically characterised by chaos, confusion and a sense of crisis. There is considerable instability surrounding the company's affairs. The management team feels helpless, demotivated, and at best, distracted from running the company. The company's staff are affected by considerable uncertainty about the future. They may not have been paid for some time. Morale is low. Rumours about the company's problems will be undermining customers' confidence, and they will be increasingly reluctant to enter into commitments. The problems will be exacerbated by suppliers, who will frequently be reluctant to deliver products or services other than on a strictly cash basis.

However, perhaps the greatest problems for a company in a financial crisis come from its financial creditors. These principally tend to be banks and their immediate objective is to get repaid. They will be withdrawing credit lines, and threatening to enforce their security or to petition for bankruptcy. The complexity of the situation is considerably heightened if a number of lenders are involved. They will have different lengths of association and depths of relationship with the company. Their priorities and outlook will differ, particularly if they come from different countries. The tensions created as the financial creditors seek to strengthen their respective positions can by themselves trigger a new wave of crisis. These problems will be multiplied if the company is in fact a group operating through different subsidiaries, perhaps in a number of countries. Inter-relationships of borrowing arrangements will infect even financially healthy subsidiaries elsewhere in the group.

The challenge is to reverse this downward spiral and to set up a process whereby each step builds on the previous one, to gradually strengthen the company. Stability is a prerequisite if a company is to be rescued, with decisions taken on the basis of a robust information base, which may take many months to develop. Stability requires patience from the company's stakeholders in general, and its financial creditors in particular. They will only be prepared to exercise restraint if they are confident their positions will not deteriorate as a result. Trust, which will have been greatly damaged, will need to be re-established in the company's management and between its stakeholders. Moreover, once the necessary information has been examined, alternative solutions to the company's problems will need to be explored and their relative merits evaluated. It is only at this point that the complexities associated with negotiating and restructuring a company's finances can be addressed.

Successful loan workouts address all these issues effectively. They ensure that the company continues to operate in a stable environment during the workout. They seek to create an atmosphere in which the participants in the transaction work together, in a trusting relationship, on achieving a common objective. A successful loan workout addresses the company's underlying business and financial problems, not just the symptoms. The solutions arrived at are based on a detailed exploration of alternatives. Although they employ the latest, sophisticated structuring techniques, designers of such transactions aim to deliver the simplest possible transaction that meets the interests of the participants, whilst acknowledging the constraints facing the company. Ultimately, a successful loan workout provides a sustainable solution to a company's problems, not one that will need to be revisited repeatedly every few years.

In writing this book, our aim is to provide corporate rescue specialists world-wide with a roadmap to navigate themselves through the complexities of loan workouts and deliver successful transactions.

The environment for loan workouts

The demand for loan workout skills has never been greater. The fallout from the 1997 Asian crisis continues to sustain the need for financial restructuring expertise from around the world. This need is also reflected in other regions, such as the transition economies in Central and Eastern Europe and many of the countries in Latin America, where enterprise and financial restructuring is at the heart of their economic modernisation programmes. The liberalisation of economies in many developing countries, including the largest, India and China, will also require resolving bad debt problems at state-owned banks and the financial restructuring of their client state-owned enterprises. In many of these countries, commercially-oriented loan workout units will have to be established for the first time.

Equally importantly, banks in developed countries continue to need significant loan workout expertise. Although risk management techniques have seen considerable advances over the last decade, non-performing loans remain an unavoidable by-product of the business of banking. The quality of banks' loans remains susceptible to economic downturns. Even a strong economy does not guarantee a problem-free credit portfolio. Moreover, there are no convincing signals that the periodic banking crises caused by bad debts in countries with more advanced banking systems will abate in the near future. Japan, the Nordic countries, the United Kingdom and the United States are all but a small proportion of the developed countries that have experienced systemic bad debt crises over the last two decades.

Thus, loan workouts are likely to remain an important, albeit undesired, component of lending activity. Nevertheless, there are a number of underlying trends that are expected to have a significant impact on its practice in the future. As a result, whereas loan workout has often been traditionally considered merely an extension of day-to-day credit control activity, changes in the industry now demand considerably more specialist skills. The most influential trends in this regard are:

- Increased complexity of transactions.
- A more unstable workout environment.
- Globalisation.
- Development of a more pronounced rescue culture.

These issues are discussed in more detail below.

Increased complexity

Greater complexity in loan workouts is a result of increased diversity, both in the participants involved in financing companies and in the nature of financial claims. Traditional bilateral banking relationships are being replaced by more transaction-based financing arrangements, including the direct access to investors in the capital markets. As a result, when corporate distress occurs, there is a very wide range of institutions that become involved in support operations. Potentially conflicting objectives from a wide spectrum of financiers, including venture capitalists, credit insurers, institutional and retail bondholders and vulture funds, can be difficult to reconcile. At the same time, the complexity of companies' legal structures and financial management activities results in a loss of transparency. Considerable effort is required to unravel financing arrangements if such companies encounter difficulties. The process of determining the prioritisation and negotiating strengths of the different claims on a company's assets is hampered, causing uncertainty among the participants.

Greater instability

An increasingly competitive banking industry and a more critical focus on return on capital, is shortening the decision-making horizon. There is less willingness to become drawn into complex and time-consuming loan workouts. As a result, practices such as the sale of distressed debt are becoming more common. A more competitive environment for companies means that if their financial problems are publicised, it can have a severe impact on their prospects for survival. Increasingly stringent disclosure requirements, for example for stock exchange quoted companies, exacerbate this problem. All these factors contribute to considerable instability in a workout transaction. The diverse range of interests represented in a workout add to this instability. Consequently, the time available to develop and negotiate a restructuring is curtailed.

Globalisation

As markets become international, companies serving them have been expanding geographically. Even small- and medium-sized enterprises need an international presence today. In addition to multiplying the impact of many of the factors under discussion, global corporate rescues bring unique challenges. Perhaps most importantly the activities of a group can become subject to the incompatible insolvency rules and regulations of different countries. The internationalisation of banking and capital markets has meant that lenders may also face different local constraints, for example, in the areas of loan loss provisioning, taxation and lender liability. The impact of variations in formal rules and regulations is exacerbated by different local traditions, cultures and practices.

Although globalisation is adding to the complexity of loan workouts, it also brings many benefits. International banks are exporting best practice in this area to new countries. The adoption of variants of the London Approach in many South-east Asian countries is an example of this. Moreover, a cadre of industry professionals comprising bankers, accountants, lawyers and consultants are now working globally. Their activities are considerably improving the technical skills of local participants in loan workouts.

Rescue culture

Although there are new pressures on lenders to focus on short-term results, there is also a growing realisation that it is commercially desirable to support potentially viable businesses in their turnaround efforts. The direct and indirect costs associated with failed businesses can be considerable. In addition to the financial impact this has on their operations, banks are more sensitive to the increasing social responsibility being placed on large organisations to behave as good corporate citizens. As loan workouts become more common, previous successes demonstrate their benefits. This reinforces the rescue culture.

Objectives of this book

The principal objective of this book is to present a systematic approach to loan workouts that meets the demands of a complex, sophisticated and global environment. To yield sustainable results, a loan workout transaction needs to be approached methodically. The framework presented in this book seeks to highlight the importance of each of the stages in a loan workout, their key objectives and their implications for the transaction as a whole. Similarly, detailed restructuring techniques are explained with reference to their underlying principles and objectives, so that they can be adapted to the circumstances of a transaction.

In order to adopt a systematic approach for loan workouts, an institution needs to ensure that each transaction is an integral part of an effective strategy for its entire non-performing loans portfolio. Such a strategy needs to be supported by the appropriate organisation, systems and resources. Some of these institutional prerequisites for achieving optimum results at the level of individual transactions are highlighted in this book. Moreover, given that loan workouts are essentially renegotiations of interests in a company among its various stakeholders, it is important to understand their likely objectives and attitudes. This book therefore aims to highlight the characteristics and motivations of the major interest groups that usually participate in such transactions.

The fact that differences in legal, regulatory, cultural and banking practices between countries can influence the approach to loan workouts has already been stressed. Nevertheless, the extra-statutory nature of such transactions provides considerable flexibility. The framework and techniques proposed in this book draw on a philosophy that aims to deliver a sustainable solution based on fairness, which can be applied universally. Nevertheless, some of the approaches proposed in this book may require adaptation to the local environment. It follows that we have had to make various generalisations and undoubtedly some exceptions to the cases highlighted will exist.

The focus of this book is on the financial aspects of loan workouts. Nevertheless, financial and business restructurings are closely inter-linked. An outline of the more important business restructuring-related issues is provided, but an exhaustive treatment of that subject is beyond the scope of this book. Moreover, this book approaches loan workouts from a lender's perspective. One aimed principally at other stakeholders, for example the company's management or its shareholders, will emphasise different aspects of such transactions.

The INSOL Lenders Group is currently working on developing universally accepted standards on multinational loan workouts. We hope that this work will make a positive contribution to their deliberations.

This book is not designed to be an operational manual for executing loan workout transactions. Nor should it be seen as a substitute for specialist professional advice on the various areas covered. Issues are explored at a strategic level, with an emphasis on the objectives for each action or approach, and the underlying principles that should be adhered to.

Intended audience

This book is principally aimed at bankers and other financiers involved in loan workouts. Given that this is a specialised area of lending activity that builds on core credit skills, some prior experience of banking and finance matters is assumed. Our detailed treatment of transactions involving diversified groups of companies, multiple lenders and debt for equity swaps will be of particular interest to financiers involved in such transactions. It is hoped that this book also offers consultants, accountants, lawyers, investment bankers and other professionals advising on loan workouts a unique insight into this complex field from a bankers' perspective. Finally, company managers involved in corporate turnarounds will also find many of the areas covered in this book valuable.

Our aim is to present a comprehensive treatment of loan workouts and associated institutional arrangements. As such, this book can be used in two ways. Firstly, it will be a valuable introduction to the subject for those who are new to this field. More experienced practitioners will find it a useful source for updating their knowledge of the subject. Secondly, specialists in this area will find the more technical issues about restructuring debt and debt for equity swaps a valuable reference source when approaching complex transactions.

Structure of the book

The book is divided into four parts. Part I provides the background and context to loan workouts. Part II highlights the strategic and organisational aspects of managing loan workouts. It also introduces the participants typically involved, and presents a framework for approaching and implementing such transactions. More technical aspects of financial restructurings are explored in Part III. Finally, Part IV presents a

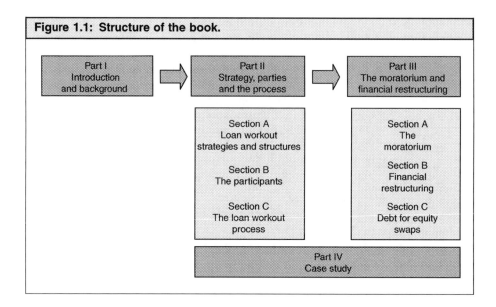

Figure 1.1: Structure of the book.

case study to illustrate many of the concepts covered in this book. Figure 1.1 summarises the book's structure.

Chapter 2 aims to set loan workouts in the context of statutory frameworks for addressing corporate distress. The role and limitations of statutory and voluntary insolvency frameworks are highlighted, along with the key factors affecting their effectiveness. We also define the nature and scope of a loan workout and highlight some of its key components.

Section A of Part II takes a detailed look at the strategic, organisational and operational issues involved in effectively managing a loan workout portfolio in a financial institution. It is important that loan workouts are seen as an integrated component of the institution's overall risk management activities. The importance of prevention, control and timely action is stressed in Chapter 3. It also stresses the need for adopting a portfolio-oriented approach to workouts, rather than viewing each transaction in isolation. Chapter 4 goes on to explore organisational and systemic matters, such as the role, objectives, structure and resourcing of loan workout units and their relationships with other parts of the bank. The nature and importance of early warning systems are also examined. Structures for addressing bad debts portfolios outside the bank, such as asset management companies, are also discussed. Finally, more procedural matters such as the importance of developing appropriate communications frameworks, the issues involved in maintaining transaction momentum and cost control are outlined in Chapter 5.

In developing a strategy for loan workouts, it is crucial to be aware of the objectives and motivations of the main participants in such transactions. Section B of Part II provides an overview of the nature of the relationship between the major stakeholder groups in a company and how these are affected during the workout. Chapter 6 introduces the subject from the perspective of the company and highlights the role and objectives of stakeholders such as the management team, shareholders and the company's employees. It also presents some of the features of companies particularly suitable for loan workouts. Chapter 7 explores how a company's bankers might organise themselves in approaching a restructuring where a number of lenders are involved, including the roles and objectives of the co-ordinator, steering committee and other members of the bank group. Other participants in loan workouts, including non-bank financial creditors, debt traders and suppliers, are discussed in Chapter 8. Professional advisors such as reporting accountants, lawyers and investment bankers can make a significant contribution to the success of a workout and the importance of their independent advice, together with their roles and responsibilities, are highlighted in Chapter 9.

The process involved in implementing financial restructuring transactions is presented in Section C. Chapter 10 highlights the interaction between business and financial restructurings and introduces the principal stages involved in a loan workout transaction. Many of these stages are explored in greater detail in Chapters 12 to 15. Chapter 11 outlines some of the key principles and processes involved in business turnarounds, including the most common internal and external problems that lead to corporate decline, and the role of various corporate distress prediction models. The critical stage of information gathering and review is dealt with in Chapter 12, which discusses the various steps involved in this process and the nature of information required to provide a robust foundation for any restructuring plan. Chapter 13 presents the various short-, medium- and long-term options which can be used to formulate restructuring plans, whilst the following chapter presents techniques for evaluating such plans with reference to their risk and return characteristics. The key factors that should be considered in developing loan workout proposals are also presented in this chapter. Chapter 15 highlights the principles involved in developing an effective negotiation strategy, and the likely stance of the various interest groups involved in negotiating loan workouts. It also examines the steps involved in completing such transactions, including the nature and contents of loan workout information memorandums.

Part III of the book deals with many of the important technical issues involved in restructuring debt. Section A focuses on moratoriums. Chapter 16 provides an introduction to moratoriums, their principal features and their advantages and short-comings. The principles involved in structuring them and issues relating to their documentation are also highlighted. The choice of participants for a moratorium arrangement can have a critical impact on its success, and Chapter 17 outlines the characteristics of different financial creditors that should be taken into account when making this decision. Different types of facilities and the key considerations about their inclusion in moratoriums are explored in the following chapter. The concept of loss-sharing is introduced in Chapter 19. Its importance in maintaining parity between lenders in a moratorium is highlighted and various concepts such as equalisation, ringfencing and treatment of priorities are explained. Chapter 20 deals with the particular complexities that arise in moratoriums involving debt denominated in more than one currency.

Section B of Part III focuses on financial restructurings. Chapter 21 introduces some of the underlying concepts involved in restructuring debt facilities. In particular, issues relating to restructuring the finances of multi-subsidiary groups are explored. Ringfence and entity priority structures, the treatment of new finance and issues connected with the taking of security are also covered. Chapter 22 relates to the restructuring of financial arrangements between the lenders involved in a loan workout. Matters such as priority rankings, pre-enforcement distributions, loss-sharing, indemnities and voting arrangements are addressed in this chapter. The following chapter covers various other provisions of financial restructuring agreements. In particular, the use of undertakings and covenants to maintain control over the company over the turnaround period is highlighted.

Section C deals with the various matters relating to loan workouts involving debt for equity swaps. Chapter 24 introduces the concept, provides a definition of such transactions and highlights their principal advantages and drawbacks. The key parameters for structuring debt for equity swaps are also overviewed. The following chapter points out the unique characteristics of debt for equity swap transactions relating to their implementation, with particular reference to the methodology for loan workouts outlined earlier in the book. Chapters 26 and 27 deal with the key parameters of such transactions, including the characteristics and appropriateness of using different forms of equity instruments, the determination of the magnitude of debt to be converted into equity and the proportion of the company's enlarged equity base that lenders might seek to negotiate. Finally, Chapter 28 overviews some of the more important accounting, taxation, legal and regulatory issues that will arise in debt for equity swap transactions.

Part IV of this book, which comprises Chapter 29, presents a case study of a loan workout transaction involving a debt for equity swap.

Terminology used

As with any other text dealing with a complex, technical issue spanning various countries, it is difficult to arrive at a consistent set of terminology that applies everywhere. We have generally adopted expressions used in the United Kingdom but where appropriate, more internationally recognised terms have been used.

Unless the context dictates otherwise, the words 'lenders' and 'bankers' have been used interchangeably. Similarly, the terms 'loans', 'debt', 'finance' and 'facilities' should be regarded as having the same meaning unless the context warrants otherwise. References to a 'company' may apply to a group of companies, although the distinction has been explicitly made where appropriate. The term 'moratorium' has been used in much of the book, although in some countries, the word is used specifically with reference to sovereign debt. Moratoriums relating to companies are described as 'standstills' in these countries. The event of 'liquidation', used generally throughout the book, is more commonly referred to as 'bankruptcy' in many jurisdictions. 'Liquidation' and 'insolvency' have been used in their general usage meanings rather than their strict legal interpretations.

Acknowledgements

This work builds on our experience of loan workout transactions over many years. It is impossible to thank individually all the bankers, professional advisors and company managers in various countries who, in working with us, provided their insights and opinions that have helped us to develop our philosophy and approach for loan workouts. Nevertheless, we feel that certain individuals have played a critical role.

Our particular thanks go to Pawel Gierynski, currently the Chief Executive of Armada Fund Managers in Poland, who co-authored with us many articles that we have drawn on for a number of chapters of this book.[1-5] Nick Syson, Partner at Linklaters' Singapore office, provided his valuable insights into the various legal aspects of loan workouts. We also thank Paul Rex and David Havelock for their comments on earlier drafts of the book. Any errors or omissions are, of course, entirely our responsibility. We are also grateful to Sally Smith at John Wiley, our publishing editor, for her patience, support and encouragement without which this book would not have been possible.

Finally, but not least, our thanks go to our wives, Amanda Hedges and Lisa Chatterji, for their patience and tolerance over the many evenings and weekends they gave up over many months so that we could realise this ambition. Additional thanks go to Lisa for proof reading the various drafts of the manuscript.

---

[1] S. Chatterji et al., Restrukturyzacja finansowa Przedsiębiorstw—Podstawy (Financial restructuring of enterprises—an introduction), BANK, April 1994, 33–36 (published in Polish).

[2] S. Chatterji et al., Restrukturyzacja finansowa Przedsiębiorstw—Departament restrukturyzacji finansowej (Financial restructuring of enterprises—organising the loan workout department), BANK, June 1994, 44–49 (published in Polish).

[3] S. Chatterji et al., Restrukturyzacja finansowa Przedsiębiorstw—Realizacja transakcji: Przygotowanie i określenie strategii (Financial restructuring of enterprises—executing transactions: formulating strategy), BANK, July 1994, 19–24 (published in Polish).

[4] S. Chatterji et al., Restrukturyzacja finansowa Przedsiębiorstw—Realizacja transakcji (cz. 2): Zarządzanie, kontrolowanie i monitoring (Financial restructuring of enterprises—executing transactions (Part 2): managing, controlling and monitoring), BANK, August 1994, 43–49 (published in Polish).

[5] S. Chatterji et al., Restrukturyzacja finansowa Przedsiębiorstw—przygotowanie rozwiązania (Financial restructuring of enterprises—exploring solutions), BANK, January 1995, 25–39 (published in Polish).

2

LOAN WORKOUTS: WHAT THEY ARE AND WHY THEY ARE NEEDED

Introduction

Corporate financial distress is an inevitable consequence of a market-based economic system. The purpose of this chapter is to introduce the concept of loan workouts and their role in rescuing companies from corporate distress. The objectives of insolvency legislation and some of the factors that impede their effectiveness, and thereby create the need for workouts, are explored. Some countries promote voluntary rescue frameworks that facilitate loan workouts and the key features of such frameworks are outlined. Finally, we highlight the principal characteristics and components of loan workouts, and factors contributing to their success.

It should be stressed that the provisions of insolvency legislation vary considerably between countries. As a result, there are considerable risks in generalisation. Moreover, the laws and regulations in this area are being updated regularly around the world. The treatment of the subject in this chapter, which is intended to highlight general principles only, should therefore be considered in this context.

Background to statutory insolvency frameworks and loan workouts

There is normally considerable uncertainty and instability surrounding a company experiencing financial difficulties. This makes an accurate assessment of its position and prospects difficult. Reaching agreement on a course of action becomes problematic. Insolvency legislation is aimed at overcoming such problems. The key challenge for policy-makers in this area is to design a legal and regulatory framework that meets two key objectives:

- To identify and rescue those companies that can and should be rehabilitated.
- To liquidate efficiently those companies that do not have a viable future.

In reality, various shortcomings associated with statutory frameworks, highlighted later in this chapter, create difficulties in meeting these objectives. Rescuing commercially viable companies within a statutory framework can be particularly difficult. Failure of such companies causes unnecessary losses among their stakeholders and for the economy as a whole.

Many of the drawbacks of rescuing companies within a statutory framework can be avoided if a company's stakeholders, and in particular its creditors (who are usually the interest group most affected) can assess a company's commercial viability and agree a financial restructuring without recourse to the courts. Loan workouts, which are essentially financial restructurings agreed in an out-of-court process, can therefore be an effective tool for corporate rescues.

The need for corporate recovery and rescue frameworks

In a market-based economic system, a company in financial distress should be liquidated if the value realised as a result is greater than its value as a going concern. This allows financial, physical and human resources to be released for more productive use in the economy. 'Recovery' in this context relates to the process of realising assets from an non-viable enterprise by following the mechanisms set out in a country's legislation. Conversely, if the value of a company as a going concern is greater than that which could be realised if it were liquidated, its stakeholders as a group, and the wider economy, would be better off if it could be 'rescued', or rehabilitated. This would be the case even if a company is technically insolvent. Also, there may be cases where parts of a company are suitable for rescue, whilst others need to be liquidated.

In practice, the various stakeholders in a company often find it difficult to determine accurately whether a company indeed has a viable future and should therefore be rescued, or whether liquidation is the superior option. This is partly because of the imbalance in information available. For example, the management of a company will usually have access to better quality information than the other stakeholders. However, they are often in a position where liquidation is against their interests, even though it may be the more appropriate course to follow. As a result, there is considerable uncertainty among, in particular, external stakeholders when a company has financial difficulties.

This 'information asymmetry' problem is compounded by what is described as the 'common pool' problem. Other than in very narrowly defined circumstances, the interests of stakeholders in a company are pooled together, and cannot be identified separately. As a consequence, if there is any uncertainty about a company's prospects, and therefore a possibility that a stakeholder, or a group, will suffer a shortfall, it is in their interest to withdraw their stake from a company. There would be an incentive to do so even if one stakeholder believes that the company's prospects are viable, because the pre-emptive action of other stakeholders might precipitate a crisis. This fear of being left with nothing, or very little, can create a competition among stakeholders to extract as many assets out of the company as they can, causing an otherwise viable business to fail.

Finally, stakeholder groups rank differently in bearing losses if a company is liquidated. For example, unsecured creditors rank behind secured ones, and are therefore likely to bear a greater burden of losses. The resulting divergence in risk and reward positions influences the courses of action different groups wish to pursue.

Corporate rescue and recovery frameworks aim to prevent such situations by providing rules and mechanisms that reduce uncertainty and protect stakeholders' interests. They thereby allow the most appropriate choice to be made about a company's future. Where necessary, they provide for an orderly realisation and distribution of assets to stakeholders in accordance with an agreed priority of claims. Alternatively, they create a stable environment to enable stakeholders to re-contract with a company on the basis of a better understanding of its current situation and future prospects.

Statutory and voluntary frameworks for corporate distress

Frameworks that facilitate corporate rescues or recoveries can be:

- Based on a country's insolvency legislation.
- Voluntary and not backed by statute.

Figure 2.1 below highlights some of these frameworks.

Figure 2.1: Statutory and voluntary frameworks for corporate rescues and recovery.

Rescue (or rehabilitation)

Voluntary	UK London Approach The Framework for Corporate Debt Restructuring in Thailand

Statutory (outside insolvency)	US Chapter 11 France 'redressement judiciaire' Poland Enterprise and Bank Restructing Act
(on insolvency)	Germany 'Vergleich'

Recovery (or liquidation)

Statutory	Bankruptcy or liquidation

Thus, statutory insolvency procedures can provide for both rescue and recovery, whilst voluntary frameworks apply to corporate rescues only. The nature of these frameworks is explored below.

Statutory insolvency frameworks

Statutory insolvency frameworks provide the rules and mechanisms for the realisation and distribution among stakeholders of the assets of insolvent companies. If the value of a company as a going concern is greater than if it were to be liquidated, such frameworks also enable the preservation of the enterprise of the company so that, if appropriate, it can be rehabilitated. If necessary, this can be under a different ownership. Also, the procedures provide for changes in control once insolvency is established or expected.[1]

Statutory insolvency frameworks aimed at the recovery of assets from a non-viable business are prevalent in all countries around the world, although they vary considerably in their effectiveness. They generally provide for a trustee or other official appointed by a court (or other body empowered by legislation) to realise the assets of an enterprise and distribute them to the various stakeholders of the company in accordance with priority rules. In many jurisdictions, they also provide for the prevention of preferential treatment of a party or interest group in the period leading up to a financial crisis. Insolvency procedures aimed at rehabilitation are also common, providing for the stabilisation and, usually, sale of the business to new owners, under the supervision of a specialist appointed under the provisions of a statute.

Statutory frameworks aimed at rescuing or rehabilitating businesses outside insolvency are rarer. The most widely-known procedure that belongs to this category is the US Chapter 11 procedure, which, although part of the US Bankruptcy Code, enables companies to be restructured by their management under the temporary protection of the court from the company's creditors. In other situations, temporary statutes may be legislated to address specific incidences of systemic bad debts. An example of this being The Enterprise and Bank Restructuring Act of 1992 in Poland, which gave temporary powers to banks to negotiate debt resolution agreements with the creditors of mainly state-owned enterprises outside the country's court system.

Factors affecting the effectiveness of statutory frameworks

An effective framework for resolving corporate distress should be able to reliably distinguish between the candidates for recovery or rescue, and implement the desired outcome for the minimum possible time and cost. In reality, very few statutory frameworks fulfil this definition of effectiveness. Very often, bankruptcy or liquidation procedures take a considerable time. In some developing countries, for example, periods of up to 10 years are not uncommon. The process itself can lack transparency, substantially increasing the uncertainty over its outcome. Moreover, the system can have ingrained biases that can discriminate against particular stakeholder groups. Figure 2.2 below highlights some of the key influences on the effectiveness of statutory insolvency frameworks.

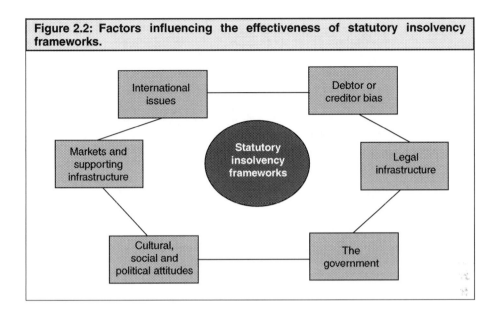

Figure 2.2: Factors influencing the effectiveness of statutory insolvency frameworks.

Creditor- and debtor-friendly insolvency regimes

Statutory frameworks can be broadly categorised into those that are 'creditor-friendly' or 'debtor-friendly'. In a strict creditor-friendly insolvency regime, the control over all the assets and businesses of a company is taken away from its management and shareholders upon entering into formal procedures. Responsibility for managing and realising the assets passes to a trustee or administrator, who does so on behalf of all, or the secured, creditors. Also, the country's priority rules are followed strictly when proceeds are distributed among creditors. Countries with English law tradition, such as England, Ireland, Malaysia and Australia, are considered as having strongly pro-creditor insolvency regimes. Scandinavian countries and those with German law traditions also have creditor-friendly regimes, although less so than the first group.

Insolvency under debtor-friendly regimes tends to encourage some form of debt forgiveness or forbearance as part of the financial restructuring. Also, the company is generally allowed to continue operating, either in the hands of its existing management, or a trustee. The creditors have a relatively passive role in the restructuring process. Debtor-friendly insolvency procedures are found in the United States, France and, to a lesser extent, in parts of Central and South America. The lenders' influence over the outcome of statutory insolvency proceedings is considerably weaker in debtor-friendly regimes.

Some countries without a corporate tradition, such as Islamic jurisdictions, tend to be neutral in this area.

Figure 2.3 provides an overview of various countries' positions in the spectrum of debtor- and creditor-friendly regimes.

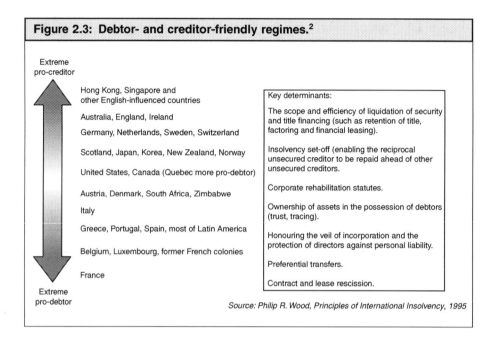

Figure 2.3: Debtor- and creditor-friendly regimes.[2]

Extreme pro-creditor

Hong Kong, Singapore and other English-influenced countries

Australia, England, Ireland

Germany, Netherlands, Sweden, Switzerland

Scotland, Japan, Korea, New Zealand, Norway

United States, Canada (Quebec more pro-debtor)

Austria, Denmark, South Africa, Zimbabwe

Italy

Greece, Portugal, Spain, most of Latin America

Belgium, Luxembourg, former French colonies

France

Extreme pro-debtor

Key determinants:

The scope and efficiency of liquidation of security and title financing (such as retention of title, factoring and financial leasing).

Insolvency set-off (enabling the reciprocal unsecured creditor to be repaid ahead of other unsecured creditors.

Corporate rehabilitation statutes.

Ownership of assets in the possession of debtors (trust, tracing).

Honouring the veil of incorporation and the protection of directors against personal liability.

Preferential transfers.

Contract and lease rescission.

Source: Philip R. Wood, Principles of International Insolvency, 1995

The judiciary and supporting infrastructure

To maximise effectiveness, matters relating to insolvency should be dealt with in specialised courts, supervised by judges trained in commercial issues. Additionally, there needs to be adequate capacity in the court system to process cases as they arise. Moreover, there is a need for an infrastructure of trained, professional insolvency practitioners who can implement the actions required under the law.

Very often, however, some, or all of these needs are lacking, particularly in countries with less developed legal systems. For example, inadequate capacity in the court system, partly caused by a shortage of trained judges, can result in considerable delay. Lack of professional standards can result in corruption and biases toward particular interest groups. These factors can create uncertainty and tie up resources, substantially increasing the cost associated with the insolvency process.

The role of the government

Despite the prevailing trend towards economic liberalisation, in some parts of the world the government continues to exercise considerable influence over the country's economic affairs. In many countries, the government is the owner of both the banks and their client enterprises. As a result, principles wider than pursuing profits, or returns on capital, may override the statutory insolvency procedures. For example, as is the case in China at present, there may be considerable pressure on state-owned banks to support non-viable enterprises to avoid the social consequences of mass lay-offs. A bankruptcy code, even though it may exist, is ineffective in such circumstances. Additionally, governments may also intervene to bail-out large privately owned enterprises in more developed economies, to avoid negative social or political consequences. These situations typically arise in traditional, labour-intensive industries.

Cultural, political and other influences

Cultural and political influences can also impact on the effectiveness of a country's statutory insolvency framework. This can be partially reflected in the nature of the insolvency regime, but also in the relationship between the company and its bankers. For example, in some countries with a tradition of private family ownership of companies, such as in Thailand, there is a tradition of secrecy that can create difficulties for external stakeholders to exercise corporate governance, or to evaluate a company's prospects effectively. Certain companies or industries, most notably agriculture and heavy industries that generate considerable employment, may exercise strong political influence in particular countries. As a result, it may not be possible to enforce insolvency proceedings effectively in these cases.

Markets and supporting infrastructure

The valuation of assets and businesses is a critical component of the decision-making process involved in insolvency procedures. Also, ultimately, assets and businesses need to be disposed of to realise cash for distribution to the stakeholders as part of the insolvency process. Efficient and liquid markets in assets and businesses are therefore important prerequisites. In many countries, an absence of such markets can prolong the insolvency process as it takes a long time to dispose of potentially viable businesses at reasonable valuations. Moreover, the lack of a liquid market impairs the ability to value assets and businesses accurately.

Cross-border insolvency

Insolvency regimes in different jurisdictions often show strong variations. As a result, when a group of companies with international operations becomes insolvent, particular difficulties can arise. For example, a potentially viable foreign subsidiary of an insolvent parent company may be forced into bankruptcy to comply with its home-country laws. Similarly, considerations related to lender-liability may cause the withdrawal of finance from a potentially viable foreign subsidiary if another, albeit unrelated subsidiary of the group, enters insolvency procedures.

Work is currently being carried out to overcome these problems. In particular, the United Nations Commission for International Trade Law (UNCITRAL) and INSOL International, the world-wide association of insolvency practitioners have been working for a number of years to harmonise insolvency practices around the world. Nevertheless, this will not be easy, given the unique influences that impact on a country's insolvency law and, more importantly, its implementation.

Statutory frameworks can suffer from various drawbacks, therefore. In many countries, these shortcomings can hamper the rescue of potentially viable enterprises. Factors such as the time taken and the negative cultural and competitive implications of being part of a formal insolvency process can cause an otherwise viable business to fail.

Many of the disadvantages associated with rescuing a company through a statutory process can be overcome if the participants agree a financial restructuring voluntarily, without recourse to the courts. This task is considerably facilitated if principles or rules are available, subscribed to by the parties involved, that provide guidance on the methodology for implementing a rescue transaction. Voluntary rescue frameworks seek to meet this objective.

Voluntary rescue frameworks

A voluntary rescue framework can be defined as:

> A set of principles or guidelines that facilitate the rescue of commercially viable enterprises by providing a framework under which the stakeholders (principally financial creditors) can agree a mutually acceptable course of action, in a stable environment on the basis of full and reliable information, without recourse to the courts.

The earliest voluntary rescue framework was proposed by the Bank of England in the early 1990s. Known popularly as the London Approach, it provides a framework for multi-bank loan workouts in the United Kingdom. Variations of the London Approach have been adopted in various countries, most notably in South-east Asia after the 1997 currency crisis.[3]

Voluntary rescue frameworks aim to provide a stable environment in which all the participants involved in negotiating a company's rescue can do so, without any fear of their relative positions being worsened as a result. Such frameworks generally share a number of important features:

- *They tend to provide for principles or guidelines, rather than prescriptive rules.* The key objective is to retain flexibility so that the principles can be put into operation on a case-by-case basis.
- *Stress is placed on achieving stability in a company's business and, in particular, finances.* This is usually achieved by the major financial creditors (at the very least) agreeing to a moratorium, or standstill, so that a company's current situation and prospects can be ascertained.
- *The gathering and sharing of reliable information* about a company's financial situation and future prospects is seen as a critical prerequisite for developing a sustainable solution.
- *Risk-sharing.* The participants agree to share equitably in the risks and rewards of the process.
- *There is usually the need for an independent mediator* in the event of disagreements between the participants. For example, this role has traditionally been fulfilled by the Bank of England in the United Kingdom.

Thus, voluntary rescue frameworks provide the basis for participants involved in loan workouts to develop a consistent and co-ordinated approach. The common platform thereby created overcomes many of the drawbacks associated with out-of-court loan workouts outlined later in this chapter, whilst retaining many of their advantages.

Nevertheless, although such frameworks considerably facilitate the negotiation of loan workouts, they are not a prerequisite for such transactions.

Despite many of their advantages, however, voluntary frameworks ultimately rely on a robust statutory insolvency regime. A credible threat of insolvency as the only alternative to a voluntarily agreed settlement is often necessary to induce compromises.

The nature of loan workouts

Loan workouts are voluntary agreements to restructure a company's finances. The principal aim of such transactions is to improve a company's ability to service its debt. At its core, this requires one or more of the following:

- A reduction in the nominal or present value of the company's debts.
- An extension of the period over which its debts are serviced.
- The provision of new finance.
- The appropriate restructuring of the business of the enterprise.

A loan workout may be formally defined as:

> An out-of-court agreement between the stakeholders of a company on a mutually acceptable course of action, with the aim of rescuing an enterprise with a commercially viable future.

Loan workouts are entered into voluntarily by all the participants affected by their terms, without being compelled to do so by a court. There is also a distinction between the company (or the legal entity) and its business undertakings. The focus of a loan workout is on the latter. In certain circumstances, a business may be viable, whereas the company which owns it, may not be. In such circumstances, a loan workout may focus on the commercially viable parts of an enterprise (provided they are a relatively significant element of the group), whereas other parts may be subject to statutory insolvency procedures.

A typical loan workout involves three stages:

- The calling of a moratorium to achieve stability.
- A restructuring of the company's business and finances.
- A refinancing once the business has been turned around, or the implementation of other exit strategies by the company's lenders.

The benefits and disadvantages of loan workouts

Figure 2.4 below highlights the principal advantages and shortcomings of loan workouts.

Advantages

One of the major advantages of loan workouts is that negotiations can be conducted in private. In some situations, the entire process can be resolved without any publicity, thereby avoiding uncertainty among customers and suppliers, and any consequent instability to the business. Even in cases where the disclosure of a company's financial

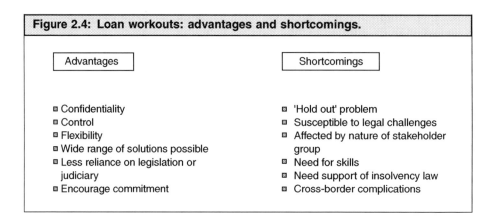

Figure 2.4: Loan workouts: advantages and shortcomings.

problems is unavoidable, for example to meet local stock exchange requirements for quoted companies, the parties involved are usually able to manage communication flows better outside a statutory process.

The participants in a loan workout are able to retain control over the transaction, rather than relinquishing it to the court. As a result, the final outcome more closely reflects the needs of the participants most affected by the company's problems. The ability to control the process also results in flexibility. Provided the needs of the participants are met, the process (for example, the timetable) can be varied to respond to the prevailing circumstances. This is often impossible under a court-administered process.

The range of solutions possible, for example, the use of innovative financial instruments, is often greater under an out-of-court process. Less reliance on the legislation and judiciary can overcome many of the other shortcomings associated with statutory processes highlighted previously in this chapter. For example, transactions can usually be completed quicker, and with more focus on commercial issues. The fact that it is up to the participants to agree a financial restructuring and ensure the rescue of a company, rather than delegating that responsibility to a third party, can also engender greater ownership and commitment to the process.

Disadvantages

Although there are many benefits associated with loan workouts, they can suffer from drawbacks that make them unsuitable for all cases of corporate distress.

The principal problem is that they need all the participants affected by the terms of a workout to agree to its terms. This can create a 'hold-out' problem, whereby one or more disgruntled creditor can demand disproportionately preferential terms in exchange for their consent. Similarly, parties not necessarily directly affected by the loan workout, for example trade creditors, may seek to improve their position by taking, or threatening to take, legal action to recover their exposures to a company. This can undermine the entire process.

In addition, the structure of the creditor group in a multi-creditor workout can have a considerable impact on its effectiveness. The larger this group is, and the more divergent its interests are, the more difficult and time-consuming the process of developing a consensus is likely to be. For example, a loan workout involving a significant number of banks, purchasers of distressed debt, bondholders and shareholders, with each group potentially having conflicting objectives, may not be possible to agree without some form of recourse to the courts.

A wide range of specialist expertise and resources is needed to implement loan workouts effectively. Such transactions can be highly complex and time-consuming, requiring skills relating to both managing the process, as well as to structuring any financial and business reorganisation effectively. Furthermore, a team approach is required, involving the company's management, its major lenders and their respective professional advisors. In many countries the availability of such a range of skills and resources is still limited.

Although loan workouts by their definition are unconnected with the courts, a strong and supportive statutory insolvency framework is nevertheless very helpful. For all the parties involved in such negotiations, a major incentive to reach a compromise voluntarily is the threat of considerable loss, or greater loss, from recourse to insolvency procedures. If the statutory system is ineffective, or, more importantly, is biased towards the interests of one party, reaching an equitable agreement will be difficult. A supportive judiciary would also discourage spurious litigation from participants seeking to improve their position at the expense of others.

A well-executed loan workout is likely to be a superior route to rescuing a company than through the courts. However, the risk remains that if it is not managed effectively, or there is a lack of commitment from some participants, control over the process will be lost.

Finally, where international companies are involved, the conduct of loan workouts can be additionally complicated by differences in insolvency legislation between jurisdictions.

Factors affecting the effectiveness of loan workouts

The process of negotiating and implementing loan workouts is considered in detail in Parts II and III of this book. Some of the common factors that contribute to their effectiveness are highlighted in Figure 2.5 below.

The company's management

The management team is probably the most critical single factor in a successful restructuring. A company with the most attractive product and the best market positioning may still underperform, or even fail, with weak management. Even the most conservative performance targets may not be achievable without a management team of sufficient calibre. Therefore, one of the first questions a banker facing a restructuring should ask is 'is this the right management team to deliver the agreed

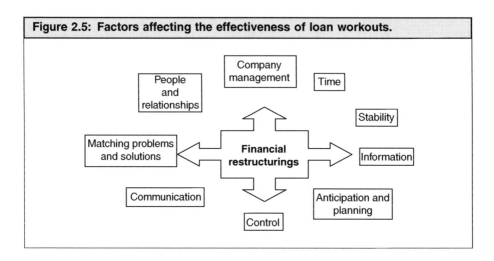

Figure 2.5: Factors affecting the effectiveness of loan workouts.

turnaround strategy?' Management changes are an almost inevitable consequence of a corporate rescue. A company's management can influence the success of a workout by acknowledging that there is a serious problem and co-operating with the lenders to resolve it.

Time

Time is one of the most valuable resources during a workout. Many restructurings fail simply because the company runs out of time before the relevant information has been evaluated and negotiations are completed. The time available to the company before it runs out of cash, or the confidence of its customers and suppliers evaporates, needs to be assessed early in the restructuring and every attempt should be made to deliver a solution within that period. As soon as it becomes apparent this may not be achievable, banks need to explore ways of extending the time available.

Stability

Corporate distress situations are characterised by uncertainty and instability. The key contributor to the crisis tends to be a 'liquidity crunch', whereby the company experiences severe cash shortages. This constrains the company's ability to carry on operating normally. An assessment of the company's short-term liquidity position, and meeting the cash needs identified, is necessary if stability is to be attained, so that the loan workout can be transacted effectively.

Information

A restructuring solution that is based on erroneous or unreliable information is unlikely to succeed. Every attempt should be made to establish the exact financial position of the company, as well as the credibility of any financial projections. Often this is very difficult and takes considerable time, partly because the lack of reliable information usually contributes to the company's problems in the first place. Banks must invest all the time that is necessary to obtain reliable information at the outset of the restructuring. It is usually necessary to verify any information produced by the company independently to achieve this. Also, the sharing of information amongst stakeholders promotes trust in the loan workout process.

Anticipation and planning

An experienced banker can anticipate problems and take corrective action before it becomes necessary. To be able to do so, the banker must have sufficient dedicated time and resources to consider all possible options and approach loan workouts in a methodical way. The planning process should also incorporate contingency plans to be implemented in the event of unexpected outcomes. Planning also enables a bank's resources to be deployed efficiently.

Control

Control is exercised by monitoring the company's performance against agreed targets. Control over the transaction enables momentum to be maintained to complete it both during the restructuring discussions and subsequently within a given time frame. It also gives the participating banks the ability to react to events quickly, and thereby address problems before they are too late. Control plays an important part within the bank as well, so that the transaction team works efficiently and effectively.

Communication

Communication should be present at all levels: within the workout team in a bank so that all members of the team know the exact position and status of the restructuring; within the loan workout unit of a bank so that a consistent approach is adopted by the institution in all its workouts; within the bank to enable knowledge transfer from the workout department to, in particular, the bank's credit function; with other creditors and the company during the restructuring so that all parties are kept informed of each other's positions, where appropriate; and communication should be maintained with the company after the restructuring is in place to ensure effective monitoring and control.

Matching problems and solutions

The sooner a company's problems can be identified, the easier they are to resolve. The company's most significant problems should be established before the process of developing a solution begins. Other problems that emerge during the transaction also need to be resolved effectively. Very often the eventual solution addresses only symptoms, or only some of the company's difficulties, with the consequence that a further restructuring is necessary soon afterwards. In more extreme cases, the company fails. In addition, the solution should be robust enough to withstand uncertainties and accommodate contingencies. Financial restructurings should be seen as 'once and for all' solutions.

People and relationships

Finally, but perhaps most importantly, the right people must be involved in a restructuring, and the right relationship exist between them, for a loan workout to succeed. Apart from the quality of the company's management, the calibre, experience and training of the bank staff involved in the workout, as well as those of the advisors, are also critical. This also includes the personal relationships between the company's management, the bankers and other creditors. A restructuring is unlikely to be successful without the confidence of all parties in each other's ability and integrity.

---

[1] Q. Hussain and C. Wihlborg, Corporate insolvency procedures and bank behaviour: A study of selected Asian economies, IMF Working Paper, International Monetary Fund, October 1999, p. 7.

[2] P. R. Wood, *Principles of International Insolvency*, Sweet and Maxwell, London, 1995, pp. 4–6.

[3] P. Kent, Corporate workouts—a UK perspective, 1997 (downloadable from www.bankofengland.co.uk/londapp.htm).

PART II

STRATEGY, PARTIES AND THE PROCESS

SECTION A

LOAN WORKOUT STRATEGIES AND STRUCTURES

3

A FRAMEWORK
FOR MANAGING
NON-PERFORMING
LOANS

Introduction

Many of the underlying causes of corporate distress are outside the direct control of banks. Nevertheless, the impact of losses from bad debts can be reduced by taking steps to minimise their occurrence in the first place. When they do arise, the institution's approach to loan workouts at the transaction level must be consistent with the strategy for its underperforming assets portfolio. This, in turn, will be dictated by the organisation's wider business strategy.

Thus, a bank's non-performing loan strategy must be closely integrated with its overall business and corporate strategy. Its risk management framework should have as a key objective the need to minimise the adverse consequences of bad debts. The institution's strategy should also provide for its philosophy and approach to problem debts, both in the long-term and for the portfolio in hand. The key issues arising in this area are addressed in this chapter. The organisational implications of the bank's strategy in this area are dealt with in Chapter 4.

This chapter focuses on the reasons why lending institutions need a comprehensive strategy for dealing with non-performing loans. The key elements of a framework for this purpose are outlined. The bank's wider risk strategy and credit processes are highlighted as an important starting point in the drive to prevent problems arising. The need to identify problem loans at an early stage is stressed as a critical factor. The value of taking decisive action when problems are identified is also emphasised. The case for transferring major problems to a specialist team is made. Finally, the chapter concludes by pointing out the benefits of maintaining effective communication channels between the various functions of the bank and building on feedback from each stage of the risk management process.

Elements of a non-performing loan strategy

Loan workout units fall into two basic categories. The first is created to address a specific set of circumstances. This unit has a finite life and its task is similar to a project or assignment. Typically, this might be to deal with a historical legacy, such as in the transition countries in Central and Eastern Europe. It might arise following the insolvency of a financial institution and the need to liquidate its loan portfolio. Alternatively, the objective may be to manage out a specific portfolio of assets following an acquisition, or a decision to close an operation. In these cases the primary objective will be to exit the non-performing loan portfolio quickly and surgically.

The second category of workout units constitutes an integral part of a bank's operations. The workout department will exist on an on-going basis throughout the business cycle, albeit expanding and contracting in line with the scale of the bank's underperforming assets at any particular time. In this case the bank's non-performing loan strategy needs to consider not only resolving the existing stock of problem loans, but also the prevention of a flow of new bad debts being created.

Elements of the loan workout strategy explored in this chapter, and elsewhere in the book, relate primarily to the latter case. Nevertheless, many of the components of such a strategy are equally applicable to those focused on short-term exit.

The key elements of an effective non-performing loan strategy can be compared to the various components of a healthcare programme. Figure 3.1 illustrates the concept. Just as in the medical analogy outlined below, the management of non-performing loans has as much to do with prevention as with cure. An effective framework for addressing problem loans needs to operate as an integrated process across the various parts of a bank. It should seek to start confronting the problems at source and go on

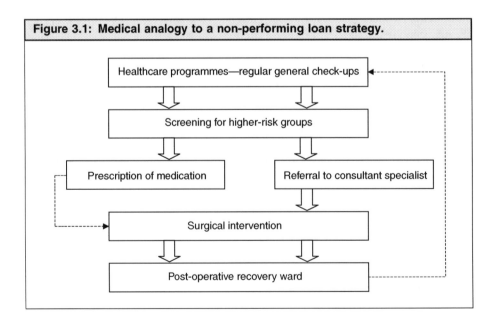

Figure 3.1: Medical analogy to a non-performing loan strategy.

to select and deliver an appropriate treatment at each stage of deterioration thereafter. Crucially, the process should also generate its own capacity to evolve and improve.

The role of credit risk strategy

A bank needs to articulate a clear credit risk strategy. This should provide explicit guidelines on the quantity and quality of loans which the bank proposes to make. This enables the bank to achieve consistency in its decision-making across the economic cycle, with predictable levels of bad debts and sustainable levels of profitability. The credit risk strategy will draw on a combination of the bank's:

- Business plan.
- Risk appetite.
- Credit culture.
- Credit policies.

The credit risk strategy should also incorporate key financial targets, such as the Total Return on Capital Employed ('TROCE') and the Risk-Adjusted Return on Capital ('RAROC') to be achieved for each transaction or relationship.

A critical component of a bank's credit risk strategy is its risk management framework. This brings together its organisational structure, operating processes, and central risk management techniques. Key elements of this include:

- Management of the balance between assets held and distributed.
- Portfolio concentration levels.
- Credit controls and delegated authorities.
- The loan approval and regular review processes.
- Risk grading mechanisms.

The way in which this framework is developed and implemented has a significant bearing on the level of problem loans. The risk management framework is essentially the first line of defence against problem loans arising. It is important for a bank's overall strategic framework to be subject to periodic re-evaluation in order to assess the actual outcome against original aims. As a result, the credit risk strategy can be refined to influence the extent of the non-performing loan portfolio.

Prevention and control

The key objective for a bank is to minimise problem loans arising in the first place. However, in a mature and competitive market, the need to generate profits and meet asset-growth targets will often conflict with the desire to minimise risk. As a result, the bank will be unable always to avoid exposures that may develop into problem loans. The other principal determinants of problem loans are external factors over which a bank has little influence. These include:

- Vulnerability to the economic cycle.
- Unforeseen events impacting on its borrowers.

In order to manage problem loans within an acceptable level, a bank needs to employ robust credit rating and loan approval processes. The key elements of these are:

- Integrity of the credit grading systems.
- Independence of the credit function.
- Establishment of credit approval authorities on a risk-adjusted basis.
- Effective decision overview arrangements.

The principal role of an independent credit function is to provide an objective opinion on risk and to ensure minimum standards are maintained, both in terms of asset quality and the risk assessment process. The credit function should also have a central role in ensuring that the pricing of loans meets a minimum hurdle rate which covers the cost of risk.

A rigorous credit standard will have a positive influence on the incidence of bad debts. However, this needs to be balanced carefully since one potential drawback from an overly-cautious credit function is the risk of missing out on profitable business opportunities. An important factor in this equation lies in the decisions made in relation to the organisational structure. Put simply, a credit department can either be located within an operating division, reporting to the head of a business unit. Alternatively, it can be part of an independent risk function which reports separately to a head of group risk, or directly to the main Board of the bank. Where the credit department is located within a business unit the head of the unit will be required to perform a balancing role. By contrast, when the credit function forms part of an independent division, the balance is achieved through a process of natural tension and conflict resolution between two independent units. Various factors, including the risk-preference of the bank, the aggressiveness of its strategy, and its corporate culture will typically influence the choice between these alternatives.

Timely identification

An essential ingredient in the effective management of a non-performing loan portfolio lies in the early identification of problems. The advantages of this are that:

- There is more time to address problems.
- The range of available solutions is greater.
- The prospects of recovery are enhanced.
- The amount at risk is reduced.

Nevertheless, frequently a bank will only become aware of a problem loan when it has become relatively serious, and it is too late to take corrective action. This will either be because the bank was simply not aware that a problem existed at all, or because there is an attempt to play down the potential problems in the belief that the situation will improve by itself.

A bank may employ a number of techniques to identify problems early. These range from subjective assessments to statistical probability models which seek to predict corporate distress. The key issue is not to rely on any one methodology as each one has various shortcomings. Success in identifying problem loans early is a function of:

- Understanding why and when things go wrong.
- Building a network of objective triggers to identify emerging problems.
- Developing 'spotting' techniques.
- Interpreting events intelligently.
- Undertaking frequent and high-quality reviews.
- Being prompted to make further enquiries.
- Experience.

An effective early warning system is about the culture of the organisation and the combination of processes within the bank which draw attention to certain situations. One of the fundamental needs is for the credit and workout teams to work closely together and exchange experiences.

Protective steps and remedial actions

Even when a problem loan has been identified, the danger is that too little is done, or action is deferred. It can still be difficult to convince the management team of the company, or even the bank's own relationship managers, that corrective action needs to be taken. There is also a tendency to underestimate significantly the scale of the problem involved. This leads to an inadequate response to the problem, which in turn can result in a considerably worse position for the bank and the company. Competitive and personal factors often detract from the bank taking firm and decisive action at this early stage. Key elements of an effective approach in this respect centre on:

- Resolution of any conflicts of interest within the bank.
- Agreement with the company on a timetable and specific milestones.
- Close, frequent attention.

In the meantime, the bank can usefully use this period to evaluate how best to protect its interests and reduce the risk of loss in the event of default by the borrower. This might involve reducing any headroom in the company's facilities, or taking additional security.
   The advantages of taking a firm stance are that:

- All parties understand that there is a potential problem.
- Full and proper consideration is given to the alternatives available.
- The prospects of a more serious problem being averted are increased.

The danger is that the business relationship is strained. This may result in the company immediately moving its banking business elsewhere, if it is able to. Alternatively, and in many ways even worse, it may decide to do so once its fortunes have been restored. Obviously, the communications process has to be handled very sensitively.

The role of specialist teams

In many cases a company's problems will be too severe to be dealt with by the bank's relationship officers, despite preventative steps. In such situations, it is likely that a fundamental review of the company's operations will be required. A turnaround strategy will need to be developed, accompanied by some form of financial restructuring. Where the company is a multinational group with a large panel of banks, this will introduce a further dimension of complexity. The immediate requirements are for:

- Time.
- Stability.
- Information.

At this point it is essential that the responsibility for the case is passed to specialists with experience of similar situations. Since it is inevitable that at least a small percentage of a bank's risk assets will always be underperforming at any one point in time, most banks will find it worthwhile establishing a dedicated team to manage problem loans as part of their on-going operations. This team will be responsible for an effective methodology for implementing loan workout solutions. The methodology also needs to recognise the need to provide intensive care and to monitor underperforming credits closely until the objectives of a financial restructuring are met. The advantages of a workout unit are that:

- Dedicated staff are made available for what can be a resource-intensive process.
- Specialist knowledge and expertise are introduced.
- The bank is seen to take control of the process.
- The focus shifts firmly towards protecting the bank's capital rather than the relationship with the client, if there is any conflict between these objectives.
- The case benefits from an independent and objective perspective.

There are a number of strategic decisions that need to be made in relation to the formation and *modus operandi* of a workout department, which have a direct bearing on its operating philosophy, and therefore its role within the problem loan management framework. The key factors are:

- Location within the organisation.
- Reporting lines.
- Business objectives.
- Mechanics governing the transfer of responsibility for a case.

Decisions will need to be taken on the workout department's location within the organisation. One choice is for it to be located within the credit function. In this case it is likely to be established as an overhead which charges out its costs to the relationship teams. Alternatively, it can be formed as a business unit. In this case it can either be required to recharge its costs to the relationship teams, or it can be established as a profit centre which buys in problem loans at an agreed price. The structure chosen will have a significant effect on the way in which the department operates. This issue is explored further in the next chapter.

Communication channels and feedback loops

By far the greatest drawback of creating a separate debt workout department lies in the removal of what is a natural (if infrequent) occurrence in banking from the day-to-day activities of credit officers and relationship teams. Managing problem loans, raising loan-loss provisions, and writing-off bad debts should be an integral element of a credit officer's training and work experience. It reinforces the understanding of the risks involved when extending credit. Also, the credit officers and relationship managers miss out on gaining experience in recognising the warning signals of impending difficulties. Shortcomings in this area can be addressed if provisions are made for:

- Effective communication channels.
- Rotation of staff between the workout department and other functions.
- The workout team to work with other departments.
- Lessons learnt from workouts to be recycled.
- The workout team and the credit function to have input into the institution's business planning process.
- The potential for systems modifications and enhancements to be captured and developed.

A further area that needs to be avoided is that of the workout department either becoming used as, or being perceived to be, a judge of credit officers' lending decisions. This is undesirable as it creates friction between the workout team and staff from other parts of the bank. At the very least, this would result in a greater level of distrust and reduced co-operation. Almost certainly, it would inhibit the bank's credit officers from approaching the workout unit staff at an early stage.

Impact of the bank's wider strategy

The approach taken on loan workouts must be consistent with the bank's wider strategy. Although decisions taken at the transaction level will be determined primarily by the circumstances of a case, the institution's wider interests will also need to be incorporated in the process.

Perhaps the key consideration in this area is the institution's wider business philosophy and the role it sees itself fulfilling in the local economy. This is partly influenced by the local culture and traditions. Nevertheless, a bank which focuses on near-term profitability will be more inclined to pursue a more aggressive, short-term recovery-oriented workout approach than one which focuses on a longer-term horizon.

The institution's longer-term objectives in a particular market or sector will also influence its strategy for workouts. For example, a bank intending to withdraw from a market (say, a country) will seek a quick exit from its exposure, even if there are costs associated with this approach.

The scale of the bank's problems in this area and the resources available to address it will be additional determining factors. An institution with a relatively large non-performing loans portfolio will focus on eliminating the problems as a priority, so that it can focus on its on-going activities. A lack of adequate resources to monitor and nurse companies will reinforce this bias.

The timing of a transaction in relation to the economic cycle will also influence the approach taken. Non-performing loans are a lagging indicator of the economic cycle. Banks are more likely to contemplate longer-term workouts if an economic upturn is anticipated in the near future.

The institution's own financial health can at times be a decisive factor in loan workouts. A financially strong organisation will be more able to pursue riskier strategies than others. Perversely, an organisation that is very weak might also do so, with the objective of deferring loan-loss provisions and with the hope that the strategy will pay-off.

Finally, as indicated earlier although financial institutions traditionally approach loan workouts as a 'cost centre' activity, there is a growing realisation that the resources and skills deployed in resolving the bank's problems can be leveraged to generate profits. A loan workout unit that is motivated by maximising profits from transactions will have different priorities from others.

4

ORGANISATION AND SYSTEMS RELATING TO NON-PERFORMING LOANS

Introduction

An effective strategy for dealing with non-performing loans needs the support of robust organisational structures and systems. These enable the institution's objectives to be translated into action at the transaction level. Organisational issues relating to a bank's non-performing loan strategy revolve around the positioning and structure of the specialist unit responsible for implementing the bank's workouts, and the systems supporting it.

The options available for positioning a loan workout unit, within a bank's structure are considered in this chapter. Alternative operating arrangements for the workout unit and different mechanisms for transferring cases from the relationship teams are also debated. The impact of different structures and systems on a bank's strategic objectives and its approach to problem loans is highlighted. Additionally, the key elements of the structure of a workout department and its resource needs are outlined.

The chapter goes on to examine some key non-performing loan-related operating systems. The essential components of an early warning system are reviewed. Different parameters for portfolio segmentation and classification are also outlined. Finally, considerations relating to establishing special-purpose vehicles for resolving problem loans are overviewed.

Positioning the loan workout unit

A workout unit can be located within one of three broad areas of a bank's organisational structure:

- The credit control function.
- The business area.
- On a standalone basis.

Each of these options yields different strategic implications for the institution.

The most commonly employed approach positions the workout unit within the bank's credit control function. The logic for this is straightforward. The activities of a workout department are an integral element of the institution's overall risk management framework. The credit function is responsible for approving, monitoring and managing the risks incurred through counterparty credit exposures. The mandate of the workout unit involves the active management and monitoring of risk in a particular segment of the loan portfolio.

The immediate advantages of locating a workout unit within a bank's credit control function include:

- Independence from the business units and relationship teams.
- A seamless process, with closer working arrangements between the workout and credit control units.
- Greater flexibility in resource management, given the relevant skills available in the bank's wider credit control function.
- Continued involvement and motivation for the head of the bank's credit control function, who can be given greater responsibility for managing the allocation of the bank's capital.

In our opinion, where the scale of the non-performing loan portfolio and availability of resources permit, it is preferable for a workout unit to be established as an independent entity within a bank's credit control function. This enables the immediate reporting lines and decision-making processes of the workout and credit control teams to be kept separate. The autonomy achieved thereby allows the workout unit to exercise greater focus and objectivity in pursuit of specific objectives.

Figure 4.1 illustrates the positioning of a workout unit within the credit control function of a bank.

In the example illustrated, the workout unit has been separated into two teams to manage different elements of the bank's problem loan portfolio. The unit operates separately from the business unit responsible for the organisation's normal banking relationships with clients. Total responsibility for individual problem loans is transferred to the workout unit. The unit is also independent of the bank's mainstream loan approval process, although it firmly remains a part of its credit control function. The team responsible for large workouts also reports directly to the main Board of the bank, most probably to the director responsible for risk management. This reflects the importance of its activities for the organisation, and often the need to make significant decisions at short notice.

An alternative option provides for the loan workout function to remain within the business area of the bank. Figure 4.2 illustrates this approach.

In this structure, responsibility for individual problem loan exposures is still passed to a separate workout team. However, the credit control function only becomes involved

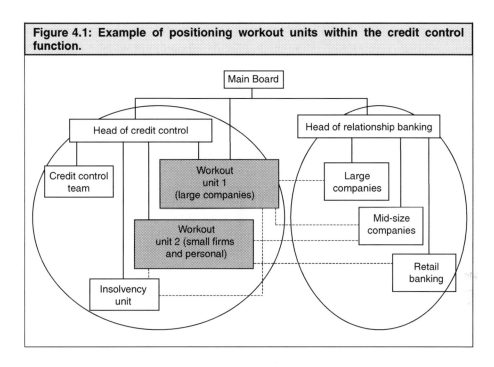

Figure 4.1: **Example of positioning workout units within the credit control function.**

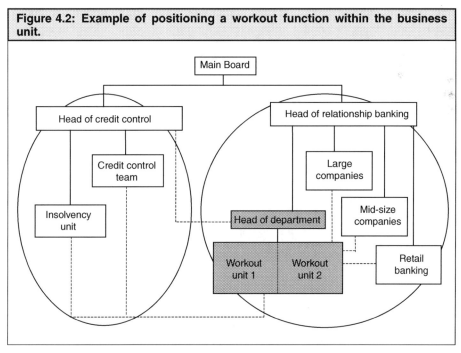

Figure 4.2: **Example of positioning a workout function within the business unit.**

in the process when decisions about increased facilities or loan-loss provisions are required. In this case, the workout unit is expected to operate as a business in its own right, with its own performance targets. In principle, such a unit would be willing to leverage its specialist resources to manage other banks' problem loans for commercial gain. This is in direct contrast to the first structure, which emphasises the protection and recovery of the bank's loan exposure on a case-by-case basis.

A third option involves a standalone loan workout function, whereby the unit reports directly to the main Board of a bank. This structure would be most likely to be adopted in emergency cases, where the scale of problem loans represents a material proportion of the bank's risk assets. An extreme example of this approach is an asset management company established to manage a bank's problem loan portfolio.

The choice between these options will be dictated by the scale and nature of the bank's problem loans portfolio, and its overall strategy for dealing with it.

Responsibility and authority

It is important that an operating mandate for a workout unit is agreed at the outset. This should provide for a clear and unequivocal allocation of responsibilities, authority and control for the unit. Three key areas need to be addressed in this regard.

Operational responsibility within the overall risk management framework

The primary responsibility of a loan workout unit is to manage individual problem loans. Nevertheless, its remit may be extended into a number of related areas. Under the most narrowly-drawn brief, a workout unit would only be responsible for managing larger problem loans up to a point short of insolvency action. At the other extreme, the workout unit would be responsible for all non-performing loans, early warning systems, formal insolvency and debt recovery. In practice, the scope of such a unit lies somewhere between the two extremes, and the unit shares some of the wider responsibilities with other parts of the institution. Nevertheless, the extent of the unit's authority needs to be clearly defined in areas such as:

- Risk reviews of business units.
- Early identification of problem loans.
- Shadowing and monitoring of underperforming loans.
- Loan-loss provisions and write-offs.
- Enforcement and security realisations.
- Insolvencies, receiverships and liquidations.

Larger banks will usually have a separate unit catering for cases subject to statutory insolvency proceedings, or companies that are being liquidated. There is limited scope to influence the outcome of these cases, with the process being very much driven by the prevailing statute. Legal and procedural, rather than banking expertise is more effectively deployed in these situations. Furthermore, each insolvency can potentially take many months to complete. Continued involvement in these cases can limit a workout unit's capacity to focus on its main aim, of trying to save companies.

Authority in relation to problem loans cases

Once the responsibility for a client relationship has passed to the loan workout unit, the team responsible for the transactions must be authorised to assume full control of all aspects of the case. New channels of communication between the bank and the client, or other interested parties, must be created, with the workout unit at its centre. Equally importantly, the unit must be seen to have the full backing of the bank's senior management for its decisions.

Delegated credit authority

The workout unit will frequently need to make credit-related decisions, often at short notice and at inconvenient times. Operational efficiency is enhanced if a clear and meaningful level of authority is delegated to the unit, both in respect of increases in facilities and changes in documentation.

Transfer of responsibility for cases

It is important to establish a system for identifying the point at which the responsibility for a problem loan case is passed to the workout unit. Equally, the point at which a case should be returned to the bank's mainstream credit control and relationship functions needs to be objectively determinable. Obviously, it is not possible to legislate for all circumstances and there is a need for flexibility. Nevertheless, a broad framework of trigger points should be established, which enable shifts in responsibility for a case between units to be determined. The bank's loan classification process and early warning systems can be used for this purpose.

In addition to the responsibility for a case, there is the need to agree whether the ownership of loan assets is transferred between the units. There are essentially two options:

- The ownership of the risk assets is transferred to and from the workout unit at negotiated or otherwise agreed prices.
- The workout unit charges a management fee to the relevant business units for its services.

These different systems can have a significant influence on the attitude to problem loan management in an organisation. The asset transfer methodology is more likely to be employed where the intention is to adopt a business-oriented approach to the unit's activities. In contrast, where the bank's primary objective is to minimise loan-losses, the workout unit would operate as a central business overhead and thus follow the second option.

The advantages of the ownership transfer method are that:

- It results in an unambiguous transfer of responsibility and decision-making authority.
- The workout unit is not seen as a burden whose costs need to be met by the business units of the organisation.
- It encourages solutions to be found quickly and pragmatically.
- The workout unit is encouraged to be more commercially-focused.

The disadvantages of the ownership transfer system include:

- The workout department is less sensitive to the longer-term and wider impact of its solutions.
- The price at which it acquires an asset may encourage short-term strategies which do not maximise the potential long-term returns for the bank.
- The workout department may be reluctant to take on cases which do not suit its business objectives.

The ownership-transfer system is also frequently used to measure the workout unit's performance and incentivise its staff.

Loan workout unit structure and resources

The structure of the workout unit will depend on the scope of its responsibilities. At its heart, the unit's structure will be determined by the profile of the problem loans portfolio under its control. The key parameters of the portfolio which will influence the unit's structure include:

- Size of individual exposures and the volume of cases.
- Nature of (corporate or personal) customer base.
- Single bank exposure or multiple-bank involvement.
- Loan classification.
- Geographic location.

The size and complexity of individual exposures are important factors in allocating staff within a workout unit. In Figure 4.3 below, each member of staff averages almost 2000 retail or personal accounts in a year, with just under 200 each for small- and medium-sized companies. On the other hand, the largest corporate exposures which require intensive, tailored treatment, see staff handling an average of less than two cases in a year.

Figure 4.3: Impact of size of exposure on workout unit structure.			
	Large	Small/medium firms	Small firms/ cards
No. of accounts	27	88 000	482 000
Av. debt/account	£37m	£40 000	£1500
Staff	14	462	261

Source: UK commercial bank 1992 information

There would therefore be one or more teams that are dedicated to a small number of large loan exposures that are commercially and strategically important to the bank. It is impossible to plan carefully for the workload involved with these cases, as each one will be unique and may take many months to resolve. Teams specialising in particular types of transactions may also be created. Most commonly, these would centre on either a specialist area such as leveraged transactions, or a vector, or those cases involving multiple financial creditors. Teams will also be established to address the smaller cases. These teams may also have a regional or sectoral focus. Sometimes the location of teams handling smaller workouts may be devolved to regional centres of the bank.

Figure 4.4 below illustrates a simple structure for a unit dealing with loan workouts.

Normally, a workout unit will be headed by a senior member of the bank's management team, perhaps even a main Board director. The seniority of the head of the unit usually reflects its importance. The head of the unit will usually only become involved in individual restructurings when they are either highly sensitive, or involve a significant exposure. For the most part, this involvement is on a 'case of need' basis. Senior managers are placed in charge of each team. In the case of the teams dealing with large exposures and multi-banked transactions, each team may comprise a senior manager and three or four junior staff.

For certain less serious situations, the workout unit may leave day-to-day control of the case with the bank's relationship team. In these cases the unit will only monitor the progress of the transaction and its staff may attend key meetings relating to the case alongside the relationship manager. A specific team would also be allocated responsibility for shadowing cases that are left with the bank's branches.

Effective workout units tend to use small teams within a relatively flat structure, thus providing for very short reporting lines. This, along with the relative seniority of

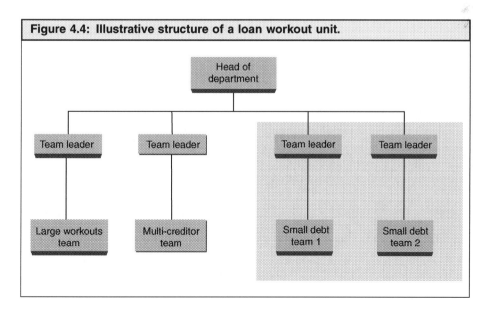

Figure 4.4: Illustrative structure of a loan workout unit.

the personnel involved, permits a considerable degree of authority to be delegated to the teams. It thereby allows the unit to react quickly to events as they develop.

In order to operate effectively, it is vital that:

- The senior staff of a workout unit are authorised to make important decisions.
- Internal reporting and approval requirements are kept to the minimum necessary.
- Necessary approval procedures operate in a timely manner.

All aspects of a loan workout should be dealt with by the same team from beginning to completion. Workout transactions should not be processed by different specialists sequentially, acting on their own. Each team should be multi-functional and capable of dealing with all aspects of a specific transaction, where necessary with the support of professional advisors.

Resources

For the most part, the staff of a workout department will be drawn from the bank's existing personnel. Given the importance of the work and the wide range of skills required, personnel tend to be from the upper quartile of the bank's staff in respect of calibre.

The key competencies required of workout unit staff include strong inter-personal skills. Since the unit is essentially concerned with assessing corporate viability and risk, a strong track record in lending is also important. Staff will be expected to develop a comprehensive knowledge of banking and insolvency law. They will also be required to acquire strong negotiation and resource management skills, be energetic, determined and realistic. Figure 4.5 illustrates the key competencies required in a workout unit.

Early warning systems

An effective early warning system is essential to minimise losses from problem loans. It is an integrated framework of procedures and systems which combine to provide a

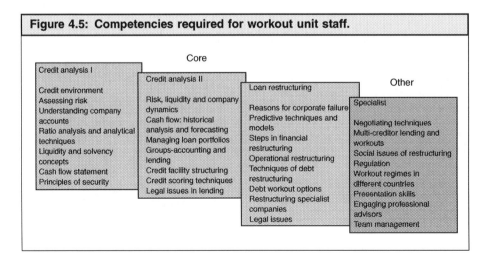

Figure 4.5: Competencies required for workout unit staff.

Core

Credit analysis I

Credit environment
Assessing risk
Understanding company accounts
Ratio analysis and analytical techniques
Liquidity and solvency concepts
Cash flow statement
Principles of security

Credit analysis II

Risk, liquidity and company dynamics
Cash flow: historical analysis and forecasting
Managing loan portfolios
Groups-accounting and lending
Credit facility structuring
Credit scoring techniques
Legal issues in lending

Loan restructuring

Reasons for corporate failure
Predictive techniques and models
Steps in financial restructuring
Operational restructuring
Techniques of debt restructuring
Debt workout options
Restructuring specialist companies
Legal issues

Other

Specialist

Negotiating techniques
Multi-creditor lending and workouts
Social issues of restructuring
Regulation
Workout regimes in different countries
Presentation skills
Engaging professional advisors
Team management

comprehensive network of triggers and warnings. Most such systems are an amalgam of various processes developed by an institution over time, which are designed to focus on particular segments of the loan portfolio, or on specific events.

The key elements of an effective early warning system are summarised below.

Segmentation of the high risk component of the loan portfolio

The bank must focus its attention on those areas where problems are most likely to arise. The higher risk loans are identified by a combination of traditional analysis allied to the use of risk grading systems and default probability models. The higher risk element of the loan book will need to pass more rigorous analysis and stress testing. Once a loan is advanced, this segment is subject to more frequent and through reviews. The bank will insist on a greater quantity, quality and frequency of management information with which to monitor the performance of such exposures.

Effective identification of declining performance

This is achieved by establishing minimum monitoring standards within a regular review process. Periodic reports must be submitted to an independent credit function. Financial information is analysed and data is fed into a variety of corporate failure prediction models. The bank seeks to identify those cases where adverse trends are being registered. Where these are in evidence, the bank will reclassify the loan as appropriate. The most serious cases may be included on a watch list. The workout unit may become involved in overviewing the cases within predetermined risk classifications, or following a given slippage in grade. The unit will need to work closely with the bank's credit control units in this area.

Internal audit review process

A bank will operate regular inspections of its various departments and business units to ensure that procedures are being complied with and no systemic failures exist. Amongst other benefits, these reviews help to ensure that there are no undisclosed facts which could affect the assessment of a client's risk profile. Additional reviews may be called for following a specific risk of loss, or the departure of a relationship manager. In these cases the bank would seek to confirm that there are no other problem loans in a particular relationship manager's portfolio, or originating from a particular business introducer.

Intelligence gathering and interpretation

Banks are in a relatively privileged position with considerable access to information. Much of this comes directly from customers and is confidential. The key is to harness and analyse all the data and interpret the messages accurately.

Warning signs

There are a number of features which are commonly found in companies with trading difficulties. Banks must learn to recognise these features and incorporate them into their monitoring regimes. The following table lists the common features of the companies vulnerable to corporate distress:

Management	Autocratic chairman and chief executive
	Narrow spread of skills
	Owner manager
	No succession planning
Business strategy	Rapid growth
	Numerous acquisitions
	Overseas expansion
	Diversification into new, unrelated areas
	Reliance on one product, customer, or supplier
Liquidity	No headroom in facilities
	Concentrated loan maturity profile
	Over-use of short-term uncommitted loans
Financial profile	Superficial planning and forecasting
	High gearing
	Overtrading
	Complex tax-driven borrowing structures

Similarly, companies which are either in, or are near to, financial difficulty will often exhibit one or more of the following symptoms:

- Unapproved facility excesses.
- Covenant waiver and amendment requests.
- Change of management.
- Change of auditor or inappropriate experience or size of auditor.
- Change of year-end.
- Changes in accounting policies.
- Late filing of accounts.
- Material fall in share price.
- Repeated requests for increases in facility.
- Withdrawal of loans by other banks.
- Delays in provision of financial information.

By itself, any of these indicators is not necessarily a cause of concern. However, a persistent display of a combination of these symptoms should trigger further investigation.

Corporate distress symptoms are considered further in Chapter 11.

Problem loan classification

A typical problem loans portfolio displays Pareto characteristics. A small number of cases will tend to account for a significant proportion of exposure. Segmentation of the portfolio by size enables a loan workout unit to focus more resources on the larger cases, where the financial impact of its work can be greatest.

Similarly, the portfolio can be classified with respect to the viability and turnaround prospects of the underlying companies. This will assist in focusing efforts on the cases where the prospects of recovery are the greatest.

Essentially, cases would be positioned in a matrix with reference to their size and prospects of recovery or, conversely, the risk of loss. This will enable the unit to prioritise and allocate resources to transactions most effectively.

This technique is particularly valuable as a strategic tool where a unit is established to deal with an existing portfolio of problem loans. Nevertheless, it is also extremely valuable as a monitoring tool for workout units with a continuous flow of cases.

The workout unit therefore needs to establish a problem loan database and develop a loan classification system. The aim of the classification exercise is to provide an analysis of the composition of the portfolio according to a range of chosen measures. This can be used to:

- Provide a profile of the problem loan portfolio.
- Help manage the workload.
- Prioritise resources.
- Assist with the unit's reporting and decision-making processes.
- Monitor progress in the unit's activities.

The framework for classifying problem loans can be augmented to develop a more comprehensive reporting system for the unit. This will incorporate information relating to each case that will enable portfolio-level information to be gathered with respect to:

- Type of solution being pursued.
- Anticipated loss at the event of default level.
- New money requirements.
- Cause of trading difficulty.
- Sectoral breakdown of portfolio.
- Major trends.

Asset management companies

Asset management companies ('AMCs') are special-purpose vehicles established to resolve a large portfolio of non-performing loans. They are normally established in countries experiencing chronic problems in this area. A number of structural variations exist, but they can be broadly divided into those that are:

- *Centralised.* Under this model, one or more AMCs are established to acquire and resolve distressed assets from a number of banks in the country. Countries such as the United States, Spain and the Czech Republic have pursued this approach.

- *Decentralised.* These institutions follow the same *modus operandi* as centralised AMCs, but their activities tend to be linked with the assets of a specific bank.

AMCs have a number of characteristics:

- *They are project-specific.* They are established to resolve a specific problem loans portfolio. As a result they usually have a finite life.

- *Their objective is to resolve a 'stock' of problem loans.* Many of the preventative systems and procedures highlighted in this chapter, that are aimed at reducing the 'flow' of problem loans, do not apply to them.
- *They have a short-term focus.* Loan workouts undertaken by AMCs have a short-term bias. The emphasis is on achieving quick exits.

Advantages and disadvantages of AMCs

AMCs are extremely effective in directing attention on a problem debt portfolio. The bank originating the problem loan can refocus its attention on developing its operations after the problem loans are transferred out. Given their *raison d'etre* is to resolve non-performing loans, staff are not detracted by other activities. Their independence from the originating institution enables them to take difficult decisions more easily. Moreover, a finite life places a premium on decisive action, which is often beneficial for all the participants in a workout.

Nevertheless, AMCs are not suitable for all circumstances. Certain types of businesses, for example property companies, are more amenable to quick exits. AMCs find it more difficult to deal with enterprises that require restructuring and turnaround before they can be sold. Also, there is a need for a liquid market in assets and businesses, and the availability of capital, for the exit strategies to be implemented. This does not exist in many countries. Moreover, AMCs' focus on the 'stock' problem risks institutions that originated the problem loans in the first place continuing their previous practices, but with a new capacity to create bad debts. Many of the lessons learnt from resolving problem loans, which if tapped could help the banks strengthen their credit operations, are lost.

5

MANAGING LOAN WORKOUT TRANSACTIONS

Introduction

Once initiated, most loan workout transactions fail because the company runs out of time before the participants can agree a solution, not because a technical solution is not available. Various factors inherent in such transactions contribute to delays. For example, persuading the company's management team that there may be a serious problem takes time. Maintaining stability, fire-fighting, and dealing with recalcitrant creditors diverts resources that should be engaged in working out the company's problems. Gathering reliable and relevant information can take a considerable time.

Effective management is an essential ingredient of successful loan workout transactions. At its core lies a robust methodology for approaching such transactions. This is covered later in the book. However, such a methodology can only be adopted consistently by a workout unit if certain prerequisites are met. The purpose of this chapter is to highlight these key issues relating to managing loan workouts effectively.

The chapter explores the factors that contribute to the development of a consistent workout philosophy. The various components of transaction management are highlighted, along with the issues involved in managing individual loan workouts. Finally, some steps that can be taken to control transaction costs, an important issue in workouts, are presented.

Business philosophy and integrity

When developing a strategy for a debt workout function, the rules of engagement need to be established from the outset. These will form the basis for the unit's culture and values system and they need to be articulated explicitly to its staff. These principles are moulded into a general business philosophy. Such a philosophy should address the areas set out below.

Protect reputation

Although a company's bankers must act to protect the interests of their depositors and shareholders, they should also recognise that they have:

- Wider responsibilities, where they are at the centre of a national or local economy.
- A vested interest in the health of the markets in which they operate.
- A potentially valuable role in supporting businesses that are in financial difficulty.
- A reputation to protect.
- A relationship with other banks to consider.

Like any other business, financial institutions have a duty to look after their own shareholders' interests. Clearly, the objectives of the debt workout unit and its strategy will need to be consistent with that overriding duty to shareholders. In deciding upon a business philosophy, a financial institution will also need to make conscious choices in relation to its reputation and how this impacts upon its relationship with other banks, regulatory authorities and, most importantly, its customers.

By and large, bankers wish to avoid a charge of being 'fair weather lenders'. They accept that some of their customers will occasionally encounter difficulties and that they have a role to play in establishing conditions that facilitate their rehabilitation. The objective should be to create a set of circumstances which will lead to an improvement in the company's fortunes.

Make consistent and impartial decisions

One of the key factors in multi-bank loan workouts is trust. In order to gain the confidence of other banks, the workout team must maintain a consistent and impartial approach. Each debt workout unit needs to decide what it considers to be the appropriate approach to a variety of technical issues, and then adhere to them. The workout units of different banks deal with each other regularly, and it will soon be apparent if one bank regularly alters its position to suit its own interests. This issue is particularly important for co-ordinating banks and members of steering committees.

Take a portfolio perspective

In order to achieve its overall business objective, a workout unit must adopt a total portfolio perspective. The overall composition of the portfolio and business strategy should be communicated to the workout team. Decisions in relation to individual workouts should always take into consideration the strategy for the whole portfolio. This is in order to allow:

- Workloads to be prioritised.
- Resources to be utilised effectively.
- Conflicts of interest to be avoided.
- Overall targets to be met.

A balance needs to be maintained between the individual circumstances of each transaction and the overall interests of the bank's shareholders. Decisions that create short-term losses in transactions may yield substantial benefits for the bank elsewhere.

Develop lasting solutions

Badly undertaken loan workouts often lose banks more than their original exposure, both in terms of the opportunity costs of resources invested, as well as the increases in financial exposure from new lending to the restructured companies.

The bank's workout team needs to focus on those cases which have a viable underlying business and which can be restructured and realistically financed. The success of a workout unit should not be measured by the number of financial restructurings apparently completed, but rather by the amount of provision which is permanently avoided as a result of the unit's activities. Our experience suggests that many corporate rescues undertaken in haste, either need further work very soon afterwards or, more seriously, collapse altogether.

Where a loan workout is considered appropriate, it is vital for the business to be provided with adequate finance as part of the restructuring, otherwise the business remains extremely vulnerable to shocks.

Establish a transaction framework

The transaction framework establishes the key relationships between the transaction team, the company's management and other participants in a workout. The successful completion of a transaction is considerably facilitated if all its participants commit to a common approach and informal operating rules at an early stage.

Build effective relationships

A successful loan workout is the product of a partnership between the company and its financial stakeholders. In most restructurings, this key relationship is likely to be very difficult to establish in the early stages. A company's management often resents the intrusion of its bankers into what is perceived to be its area of responsibility. Frequently, they will be very defensive as they may have been involved in decisions that have contributed to the company's difficulties. For their part, the banks are usually uncertain about the true extent of the company's problems. They will therefore wish to reserve their rights whilst imposing various restrictions on the company's activities. There is likely to be considerable mistrust about each other's motives. Every attempt therefore needs to be made to establish a positive relationship between the banks' loan workout teams (the co-ordinating bank in particular) and the company's management as soon as possible. Both sides will need time to gain confidence in each other's abilities and motives.

Agree lines of communication

Another important area that needs addressing at the outset is the manner in which parties will communicate with each other. This is essential to control the loan workout transaction and ensure that all the participants are making decisions based on the same, reliable information base.

Establish controls over the company

The banks will insist upon imposing strong controls over certain elements of a company's day-to-day activities in exchange for providing time, and sometimes additional finance. These controls need to be balanced by a recognition that the management team remains primarily responsible for managing and running the business during the transaction. In some jurisdictions the imposition of effective external control is made difficult by the existence of the legal concept of 'shadow directorship', whereby bank officers can be made personally liable for company debts. The areas that are likely to be reviewed or controlled by the bank include:

- Cash and bank accounts.
- Raising new finance.
- Giving guarantees or collateral.
- Acquisitions or disposals of material assets.
- Capital expenditure plans generally.
- Payment of dividends.
- Making public statements.
- Access to information.

Clarify authority and initial responsibilities

The banks and the company will need to agree a division of responsibilities and duties during the initial stages of the transaction. Usually, the company is charged with focusing upon:

- Managing its non-financial creditors, both in respect of maintaining communications and managing liquidity.
- Keeping certain financial creditors informed. This will be as agreed with the co-ordinating bank and usually relates to local relationship banks in other jurisdictions when a decision is made not to include them in a loan workout.
- Reassuring the company's principal customers.
- Managing the employees and middle management of the company.
- Managing the media. The preferred position is to maintain a news blackout, but where this is not possible the company will need to keep journalists, analysts and brokers informed. All such communication should ideally be agreed with the co-ordinator in advance.
- Complying with stock exchange and other regulatory requirements.
- Gathering and providing information to the banks' reporting accountants.
- Identifying and containing the cause of the company's difficulties, beginning a review of the company's strategic focus and considering the options available.
- Considering the legal position of the directors under the relevant insolvency frameworks.

The co-ordinator will initially be responsible for:

- Convening a meeting of the group's bankers and obtaining their agreement to some form of moratorium.
- Providing for the company's short-term liquidity requirements.
- Appointing external advisors to undertake a full review of the company's affairs.
- Maintaining control over cash through agreeing short-term, say weekly, cash flow budgets and monitoring performance against these.
- In addition, practical steps such as sending bank employees to company premises to protect cash and other assets, or directing that customer payments be made directly to the bank, may become necessary.

Transaction management

Workout units need to develop a methodical approach to deal with each problem loan. This is especially true when managing a large portfolio. The routine in a workout unit is inevitably hectic. A vast amount of information needs to be processed and a large proportion of the workload is time critical. Without a disciplined approach, the risks of overlooking important issues or losing control of a transaction are very high.

These transactions are very difficult to control because of the number of different parties involved, the different objectives being pursued and the volume of issues which need to be dealt with. Many of the developments will be outside the immediate control of the parties and therefore planning can only be on a best efforts basis. To compensate for this volatile environment, the workout team needs to work to a proven method which maximises the prospects of success. The key factors underpinning successful transaction management are illustrated in Figure 5.1 and examined in detail below.

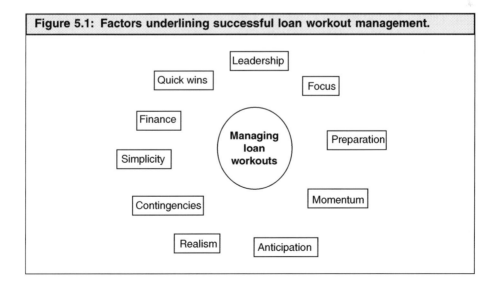

Figure 5.1: Factors underlining successful loan workout management.

Firm leadership

It is important to listen to the concerns and opinions of all the participants in a transaction. The co-ordinating bank will need to balance the desire to accommodate individual requirements with the interests of the wider creditor group and the company. This will require difficult decisions to be made from time to time. The co-ordinator will need to exert strong leadership at these times.

Focus

At the outset, the participants in a workout will be dealing with an uncertain situation. Progress may be halting. Frequently, as the banks and their advisors begin to assemble information, the number of problems appear to multiply. The co-ordinator will need to remain focused on the fundamental objective of the exercise, which is to find an acceptable long-term solution for the company's problems.

Thorough preparation

Maintaining confidence is an important requirement in loan workouts. That requires the co-ordinator to be one step ahead. There is little room for any errors, or for items to be overlooked. It is useful to make sure all the issues are addressed by maintaining a concise agenda of action points and following them up. At the end of each day, achievements should be reviewed and a new action plan developed for the following day.

Momentum

This is crucial. One of the key features of many large loan workouts is the amount of time that they take to be concluded. This adds significantly to the risk of failure. Delays in signing up to an agreement will arise for three main reasons:

- Continual requests for further information.
- Inability to reach a mutually acceptable agreement between the banks.
- Continued deterioration in the company's position leading to a need to re-evaluate the basis of a solution.

The co-ordinator will need to ensure that momentum is not lost. To minimise drift in a transaction, a timetable should be agreed containing clear milestones and deadlines. Progress should be monitored against them.

Anticipation

Experience of previous transactions is extremely valuable. Each case will have its own unique features, but it should be possible to anticipate challenges. An experienced team will be able to identify problems early, analyse the options and develop strategies to address the issues.

Realism

It is possible to lose sight of the objectives and practicalities involved when working exclusively on one transaction. It is important to retain a sense of proportion and be able to exercise sound judgements which stand independent scrutiny. The prospects of delivering a successful restructuring may diminish to a point where it is not worthwhile investing further resources. The co-ordinator must continuously judge whether it is worth pursuing a transaction, independently of the resources invested in it to date.

Contingency planning

Given the inherent uncertainties associated with loan workouts, contingency planning should be an integral component of such transactions.

Simplicity

The simplest remedies often have the greatest prospect of success. A complex refinancing structure or operating plan may be technically superior, but if it is not understood, supported or capable of being delivered for lack of expertise, then it is worthless.

Minimising the new money requirement

By far the most emotive aspect of loan workouts for many banks is the requirement to advance additional facilities. They are far more likely to agree to a financial restructuring that does not require them to inject new funds into an ailing company.

Quick wins

Psychology plays an important role in these transactions. It is helpful if the term of the facility restructuring can be kept relatively short and for the restructuring plan to include a few quick wins which evidence tangible progress at an early stage.

Controlling transaction-related costs

Apart from the fees paid to the banks as part of the transaction, those payable to professional advisors form the principal costs of a workout and are often the subject of much debate.

The reluctance to pay fees to secure high-quality professional advice is often misplaced. The fees should not be viewed in isolation but should be measured in the context of the potential benefits that may accrue. Often a very small percentage improvement in the financial outcome of the restructuring due to decisions taken on the basis of quality advice more than compensates for the costs of employing advisors.

Equally importantly, a failed restructuring will cost the banks many times the cost of employing professionals.

The question of who should meet the banks' advisors' costs is a sensitive area. Generally speaking, it is the company's responsibility to pay for the banks' advisors and this should be expressly provided for in both their terms of reference and any formal documentation. The underlying principle is that the company borrowed from the bank(s) on the condition that it would comply with the terms of the loan or facility. It follows that it is the company's responsibility to propose an alternative solution that will be acceptable to its bankers or creditors who would otherwise take enforcement action to recover their loans. The banks' advisors assist them to evaluate the management's proposal. The latter should therefore meet the associated costs. Otherwise the company's other creditors and shareholders will benefit disproportionately at the expense of the banks.

Until a turnaround has been successfully executed, the costs of a workout will ultimately fall on the creditors in terms of a reduced recovery in the event of liquidation. Often the banks have to make available additional facilities in order to meet the costs. Depending on how serious a company's position is, it is possible that the advisors will only undertake an assignment if they are either paid regularly or in advance, or their fees are guaranteed by third parties (such as the banks) in some way. To this extent the banks have just as keen an interest as the company in managing the costs of a workout, even if they do not directly pay them.

Best practice for controlling costs includes:

- Active management of the process of tendering for advisors.
- Greater focus on purchasing techniques and understanding of buyer power.
- Regular itemised billing.
- More focused terms of reference for professional advisors.
- Standardised short-form reporting in summary format.
- Back-ended success fees.

In the longer-term, costs might be contained through a move to:

- Increased consensus on inter-creditor issues which minimises debate and conflict.
- Greater use of majority-based decisions, perhaps including the ability to compel minorities to accede to restructuring agreements.
- Standardised documentation for moratorium and restructuring agreements.
- Universal insolvency legislation.

It is also worth noting that companies themselves have a responsibility to help in the area of cost containment. A feature of many companies, particularly those that get into financial difficulty, is the poor standard of records held and the lack of consistency in their facility agreements. There could be greater compulsion on companies to maintain adequate records. Considerable time and expense is incurred in obtaining a proper understanding of:

- Group legal structures.
- Records of contingent liabilities—especially guarantees issued.

- Records of inter-company indebtedness.
- Records of facilities available from financial institutions.
- The variety of terms and conditions within bilateral facility agreements.
- Group indebtedness at any one point in time.
- Terms and conditions of legal documents and contracts entered into.

Considerable costs are often incurred in reconstructing information during a workout which should be easily available from the company.

SECTION B

THE
PARTICIPANTS

6

THE COMPANY

Introduction

The company is at the heart of any financial restructuring. Throughout this book, we refer to what needs to be done to a company, its business, or its finances to achieve a successful corporate turnaround. Nevertheless, the company is simply a legal entity that brings together a number of stakeholder groups to carry out certain activities. When corporate distress occurs, and a financial restructuring becomes necessary, the basis of the relationship between a company and its lenders needs to be renegotiated. In reality, this involves a negotiation between the lenders and all the other stakeholders in a company. It is therefore important to know the objectives and motivations of the various stakeholders if a financial restructuring is to be approached effectively.

Each company will have a different corporate structure and operating profile. The features of a company that influence lenders' attitude to enter into a loan workout process are highlighted in this chapter. Also, the main stakeholder groups involved in a loan workout are outlined; and the different priorities and objectives of the company's management, its shareholders and its employees are explained.

Company features conducive to loan workouts

A loan workout becomes an option when a company is unable to meet its financial obligations in a timely manner. As such, it can be an appropriate way forward for all types of companies. However, the loan workout process can involve a significant investment of time, energy and resources, primarily on the part of the company's staff and its lenders. In practice therefore (other than in countries such as France and Germany where a company's directors have various legal obligations in this area) the decision on whether or not to pursue a workout primarily rests with the main financial creditors as their commitment is a prerequisite to a successful rescue. The other stakeholders in a company will normally wish to support a financial restructuring if this improves the prospects of the company or its business surviving.

There needs to be a commercial imperative to motivate a company's main financial creditors to undertake a financial restructuring in preference to recourse to the

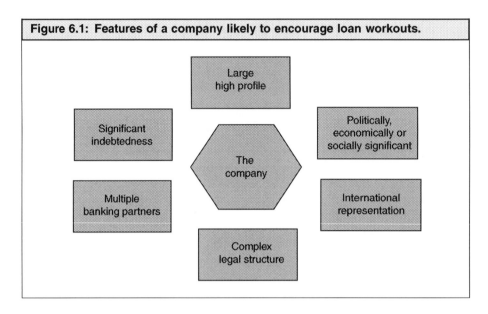

Figure 6.1: Features of a company likely to encourage loan workouts.

country's insolvency laws. Additionally, certain features about the company or its banking relationships may require a loan workout solution, rather than a relatively straightforward rescheduling. The decision between a loan workout and these other options would be taken based on non-financial as well as financial considerations, although it is unlikely that a restructuring would be pursued if it was demonstrably financially inferior to an alternative. Certain features of a company, or its relationship with its lenders, are likely to steer lenders toward a loan workout. Such features are highlighted in Figure 6.1 and are overviewed below:

- *Large or otherwise high-profile operations, or a stock exchange quotation.* In an increasingly competitive environment, lenders are keen to manage perceptions and avoid damaging publicity associated with company failures. The media is more likely to take an interest in events surrounding the larger, higher profile companies than very small individual private businesses.

- *Politically, economically or socially sensitive businesses.* Companies employing large workforces or providing socially necessary products and services fall within this category. Banks are increasingly conscious of their wider social obligations and responsibilities within the economy and local community and would wish to support such companies if feasible. Such sense of responsibility is likely to be enhanced by the attention these companies attract from the media, politicians and the general public.

- *International representation.* When a group contains subsidiaries in more than one country, the option of statutory proceedings is further complicated by differences in laws applying in the various jurisdictions. Such laws can conflict in key areas, such as the protections afforded to a company and its directors, as well as the rights and priorities of various classes of creditors. The inconsistencies created are such that the uncertainty of outcome, time and cost often argue for an out-of-court loan workout.

- *Complex corporate legal structures.* Larger businesses are likely to comprise a group with a parent company and a number of separate subsidiaries. In some cases, minority shareholders or joint venture partners may also be involved. Additionally, some of the group's interests may be held via associate companies where the group does not have management or voting control. Often these group structures are operationally inefficient, having evolved over a long period, or having been developed to maximise tax efficiency. Such complexity can dictate against simple debt reschedulings and necessitate a more complex loan workout.

- *Multiple banking partners.* The nature of a company's legal structure, operations and growth may well result in complex debt, capital and intra-group financing arrangements as well as the need for a wide range of banking relationships. This often results in a complicated mixture of different syndicated and bilateral bank facility agreements, each with different lenders, borrowers, guarantors and terms and conditions. In such cases, it is very difficult to establish with any accuracy the total indebtedness to, or rights of each creditor. This would preclude any easy agreement being reached between the creditors and the company and among the creditors themselves. A loan workout would be a more effective option. Nevertheless, if the complexity is such that a voluntary agreement between the company's stakeholders becomes impossible, statutory procedures may be required.

- *Significant level of indebtedness.* The absolute amount of debt and the level of estimated unprovided shortfall which would arise on insolvency will be an important consideration for the financial creditors. Companies with large exposures and which have not given collateral to financial creditors, or which have weak asset bases (such as companies in the services industries), are likely to be in a far stronger position to argue for a loan workout or other similar support from their bankers.

Key stakeholders involved in a loan workout

A loan workout can have a wide-ranging impact on the various stakeholders in a company. Being essentially a financial transaction, its principal impact is on the financial stakeholders in a company. These include the company's bankers, other creditors and shareholders. Other stakeholders are also affected because a company's business also tends to need restructuring as part of the process. Figure 6.2 highlights the key stakeholders in a company. Their involvement in loan workouts is explored in this chapter and in the remainder of this section of the book.

Directors and management

A company is a discrete legal entity acting through the medium of its directors, operational management and employees. In a financial restructuring the company will, in most cases, be represented by its main directors and their advisors. The directors are likely to be the only parties with sufficient authority to bind the company to a financial restructuring agreement. They also represent the interests of a number of other

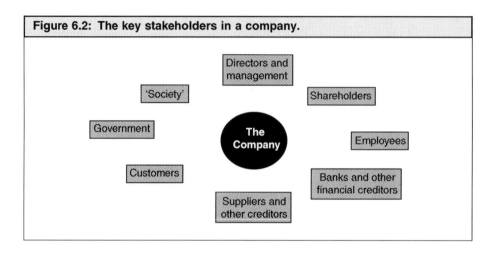

Figure 6.2: The key stakeholders in a company.

stakeholder groups. As a result, they wield considerable influence over the outcome of a restructuring transaction.

Background

The directors may be long-standing members of a company's Board, or they may have been appointed to their positions recently, perhaps as a result of the company's difficulties. They may have an executive capacity, directly managing the day-to-day business operations, or they may act in a non-executive role as members of a company's Supervisory Board, where it exists. The Chairman, Managing Director and Finance Director (or equivalent titles) will be most actively involved in loan workout-related discussions with the company's lenders.

A turnaround specialist may be engaged to lead the company through a financial and operational restructuring. Such a specialist may or may not be involved in the company in an executive capacity, depending on its particular circumstances, or the custom followed in the country. For example, he may wish to minimise the risks of personal liability imposed by local laws upon directors of failed companies. In many jurisdictions, however, the concept of a 'shadow director' would defeat such a step. Shadow directors are essentially persons in accordance with whose directions or instructions the directors of a company are accustomed to act.

Attitude of the directors

The directors of a large company are often successful, powerful people within their community. They will be used to exerting considerable authority. Almost certainly previous transactions with the company's bankers will have been negotiated from a position of relative strength.

The directors are often unable to cope easily with the feeling of failure, or the loss of control and power that accompanies many workouts. This is particularly so where the main directors are also the founders of the business, or are significant shareholders. Our experience suggests that overcoming the reluctance to accept the true magnitude of the crisis and securing the management's co-operation in developing a solution is a substantial threat to a loan workout in its early stages. One of the most important skills of a workout expert is to be able to convince directors that their company's future is in jeopardy, that the co-operation of the lenders is essential for its survival, and the basis of the relationship between the company and its lenders needs to change significantly.

The members of the lenders' workout team are unlikely to be the bankers the directors dealt with previously. The company's management team may itself have seen changes in the interim. As a result, an entirely new set of relationships will need to be established. This has the potential drawback of loss of corporate memory. A crucial advantage, however, is that the possibilities of building a forward-looking, constructive relationship are considerably enhanced. However, there may be considerable mistrust about each other's objectives. Conscious effort needs to be made by all parties to overcome such barriers.

Role and skills required

The early stages of a financial restructuring can be fraught with numerous, seemingly intractable, problems that demand solutions within impossible time constraints. At the same time, there is considerable uncertainty and confusion, both within and outside the company. Effective crisis management skills are essential in this situation. The existing directors may, or may not, have the right background, skills and balance to undertake such a task. The directors may be experienced in dealing with investors and clients, undertaking strategic reviews and making executive decisions. During a loan workout however, they will need the ability to deal with creditors, their information demands and the elements of micro-management and control that a workout entails, at least in the early stages.

In the medium-term, a wider range of specialist skills will be required of the company's directors. These include skills in business and asset disposals, cost reduction, negotiations with various stakeholders and communicating with the press.

A loan workout will inevitably be extremely time-consuming and the directors can easily feel that they are under siege from all sides. Directors of large companies often have other business interests and responsibilities and should consider carefully whether to relinquish such other duties, even if only temporarily. A loan workout will undoubtedly also place a heavy burden on the senior management as well as the financial and administrative personnel of a company. As a result, it is usually necessary for the company to engage a team of experienced advisors and establish a crisis management team to take responsibility for the restructuring on behalf of the company.

Legal responsibilities

The obligations imposed upon the directors of a company vary considerably between jurisdictions. Nevertheless, it is generally the case that their responsibilities shift dramatically during a financial restructuring.

Under the normal course of events, the directors are likely to be primarily accountable to the company's shareholders, although they also need to take into consideration the interests of other stakeholders to varying degrees, depending on the country concerned. Since the solvency of the company is likely to be threatened in a financial crisis, the country's insolvency laws will play a key role in dictating the actions of directors. As a result, the directors may suddenly find themselves required to pay particular attention to the interests of creditors. In many jurisdictions, insolvency legislation now imposes personal liability upon directors if they are found to have acted against the best interests of creditors, or not to have exercised due care and skill in discharging their obligations and duties.

Replacing the management team

One of the early judgements that will need to be made by lenders or shareholders is whether the directors of a company have the confidence of the various parties involved and the skills required to go forward. This will be considerably influenced by the particular circumstances and characters involved.

The fact that a company is in financial difficulty, or requires a financial restructuring, does not automatically indicate the need for a complete change in the management team. In many instances, this may not be desirable. It is vital for the business to continue to be run as smoothly as possible. Valuable corporate memory needs to be retained and important client, supplier and employee relationships will require careful handling, particularly if the company's difficulties are publicly known.

Nevertheless, this needs to be balanced with the need to deliver rapid change in the business. Existing management can be a barrier to this. Also, a new management team can signal a determination to change. Finally, lenders or shareholders may demand changes in management as a 'price' for continuing to support the company.

Engaging replacement management may not always be easy. The company's vulnerable financial position may detract candidates and reassurances may be required from lenders or shareholders that financial support will be forthcoming. In some countries, a dearth of candidates may also cause difficulties.

Shareholders

A company's shareholders will naturally be very interested in the progress and outcome of a loan workout. The extent to which shareholders may demand to be heard, or seek to influence proceedings directly, will depend on issues such as:

- The degree to which their financial and other interests are affected.
- The circumstances leading to the company's current operating or financial difficulties.
- The nature of shareholders involved.
- The extent to which ownership, and therefore power, is concentrated among a relatively small number of parties.

In the past, institutional investors have often tended to be very passive in discharging their roles as shareholders. Most countries, however, have recently seen more active shareholder participation in the major issues affecting a company. As a matter of course, shareholders do not become directly involved in the workout negotiations. The directors of the company are employed to manage matters for them in the best interests of the company and the long-term interests of the shareholders themselves.

Shareholders may become involved in a loan workout transaction if:

- A change in the composition of directors is sought.
- A significant asset disposal programme is planned.
- A capital raising exercise is proposed.
- The transaction affects the company's capital structure, for example through a debt for equity swap.
- A change in the company's statutes is required.
- The capital structure involves different classes of shareholders who may thereby need to negotiate between themselves.
- A given shareholder class benefits from terms governing share redemption or dividend rights.

Motivation of shareholders

When a company operates successfully, the interests of its shareholders and lenders are aligned. In corporate distress situations, however, potential conflicts of interest arise because shareholders have relatively little to lose in such situations. The value of their holdings is likely to have already been substantially eroded. As a result, they are likely to pursue riskier strategies, against the interests of the company's lenders and other creditors. Similarly, they will have relatively little incentive to invest more in the business, as most of the resulting benefit is likely to accrue to lenders. Finally, disputes may arise over the shareholders' and lenders' respective claims over the assets of the business. Loan workout negotiations between the shareholders and lenders must effectively address these issues if they are to succeed.

Family-owned companies

In many countries, particularly in Asia, large companies are traditionally owned and managed by families. In such circumstances, the conflicts of interest between the lenders and the shareholder-managers become particularly apparent. Negotiations can become emotive. Loan workouts can be very difficult to agree, particularly if there is a lack of experience in negotiating such transactions.

The government as a shareholder

When countries are liberalising their economies from state control and restructuring their banking sectors, systemic bad debts arise. Negotiating with the government as the shareholder of state-owned enterprises can be difficult, particularly if the lenders are also state-owned themselves. The government typically needs to take into account wider non-commercial considerations, such as the impact of any loan workouts on employment, and the provision of social services by the enterprise. Wider political considerations may also influence their perspectives. As a result, unless there is a strong commitment to change, the effectiveness of loan workouts involving the government can be impaired.

In some countries, the government may establish a special-purpose agency to restructure the enterprises and agree loan workouts with their lenders. The negotiating success of such initiatives tends to be inversely related to the degree of political influence such an agency or the banks are subjected to.

Employees and trade unions

The extent to which the employees of a company become directly involved in negotiating a loan workout depends considerably on the employment laws and culture of the country.

In countries where employee councils or trade unions have representation on the company's Management or Supervisory Board, it is more likely that employee representatives will be directly involved in a loan workout. At the very least the views of these bodies will be critical to any solution proposed.

In certain cases, irrespective of the legislative framework, it may be commercially essential to engage key employees of a company at an early stage of a restructuring, in order to stabilise the company's trading position and operations. This is particularly so for 'people' businesses, or in companies employing specialist workers, or in industries where there is intense competition for labour. These companies become particularly vulnerable to the loss of key employees during a restructuring as a result of uncertainty. If preventative action is not taken at an early stage, confidence in the company's future viability can be undermined by the departure of key personnel.

Trade unions and employee councils are often seen as a barrier to change and an impediment to a loan workout. This is not necessarily the case and the support of these institutions can considerably facilitate a restructuring. A key task of a company's management during a crisis is to keep representatives of these institutions informed of developments and secure their support for the changes that are agreed between the parties.

7

THE BANKS

Introduction

Banks tend to be amongst a company's largest creditors, both separately and as a group. Unlike other creditors, making loans is a core activity for banks. When a company faces financial difficulties, therefore, banks should be well-placed to respond effectively and take a proactive role in its rehabilitation.

Where a number of banks are involved in lending to a company, it is important that they unite in some way as a distinct class of creditors and take the initiative. If each bank negotiates independently, the risk is that the company will collapse before the banks' competing interests are reconciled. The effectiveness of the process is considerably enhanced if the banks can agree a restructuring proposal between them and conduct only one set of negotiations with the company.

Developing a robust structure and *modus operandi* for a bank group is critical if its members are to negotiate effectively on two fronts:

- Between themselves, so that the proposal ultimately negotiated with the company meets their needs.
- Between the bank group and the company, in a manner that reflects their collective interest.

The purpose of this chapter is to highlight the roles and characteristics of the key participants in a typical bank group involved in multi-bank workouts. Additionally, some of the key guiding principles for their effective operation are presented.

The bank group

There is no particular reason for a lender group to be distinguished from other financial or non-financial creditors. Usually, however, it is only the banks that seek to work together as a group. This is probably because other creditors do not wish to become involved in, or bound by, some of the 'obligations' that the bank group may agree to as part of a loan workout. For example, banks may agree to provide further credit, or

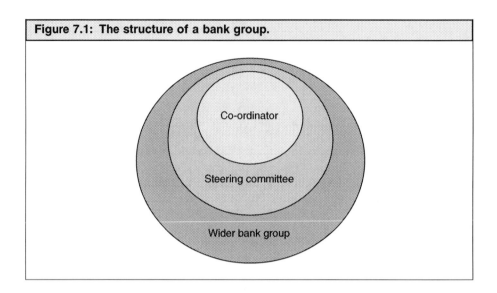

Figure 7.1: The structure of a bank group.

to enter into a debt for equity swap. Additionally, the complexities associated with seeking to include a large number of, say, trade creditors with relatively small exposures to a company can outweigh any benefits. As a result, non-bank creditors with relatively small exposures are normally excluded from a lender group and any negotiations that are appropriate are conducted with them by the company, usually on a bilateral basis. Depending on their relative exposures, however, a 'bank' group may include lessors, providers of performance bonds, or, increasingly, credit insurers.

The bank group will comprise those institutions with whom the company was transacting at the time it encountered financial difficulties. Accordingly, the bank 'group' can range in size from just one bank to, in the larger cases, over 100. The greater the number of banks involved and the more diverse their interests, the more likely it is that a formalised process will be required that manages their respective interests in an orderly manner. The structure of a bank group is shown in Figure 7.1.

When a company in financial difficulty reaches the point at which it needs to ask for the collective co-operation and support of its bankers, it is usual for a temporary moratorium to be called. One of the objectives of this is to gather all the banks together in a 'new' syndicate, be it formal or informal. In any traditional syndicated transaction, a lead bank is appointed, and for larger transactions an influential sub-underwriting group may also be created. In a similar way, where a workout is envisaged a co-ordinator is appointed to lead the bank group (normally this is one of the creditor banks involved) and for the larger transactions, one or more steering committees will be created.

The co-ordinator

The co-ordinator represents the bankers' interests, albeit not as a formal 'agent' of the banks, with the legal responsibilities that can entail in most jurisdictions. The appointment of the co-ordinator requires ratification by the bank group and the company. The company also has to agree matters such as renumeration for the co-ordinator and an indemnity.

The primary role of the co-ordinator is to lead the negotiations with the company on behalf of the bank group. This will involve:

- Stabilising the company's financial position in the short-term.
- Co-ordinating the activities of, and where relevant, appointing, the advisors to the bank group.
- Canvassing the views of the entire bank group.
- Collating and distributing information to the bank group.
- Mediating between different banks and other classes of creditors.
- Convening, reporting to and chairing meetings of the steering committee (of which it is also a member) and the wider bank group.
- Regularly engaging in dialogue, meetings and negotiations with the company and its advisors.
- Devising an appropriate restructing plan in conjunction with the company and the various advisors.

Figure 7.2 highlights the position of the co-ordinator in relation to other parties directly involved in a loan workout. Issues relating to the banks' and the company's professional advisors are covered in Chapter 9.

The role of the co-ordinator is difficult to fulfil, whilst keeping all participants in the transaction satisfied. Inevitably it is impossible to meet all parties' preferences but the co-ordinator needs to ensure that it, along with the rest of the bank group under its leadership, maintains its focus on the ultimate goal. This is to agree on a workable and fair solution to a company's problems and ensure that it is implemented.

The co-ordinator will often find itself having to balance the need to move the transaction forward, whilst ensuring it represents and takes into account a large number of often conflicting views. Frequently, this will require it to exercise its judgement and a measure of responsibility so that the wider interests and objectives of all parties are protected, sometimes at the expense of individual banks, including itself.

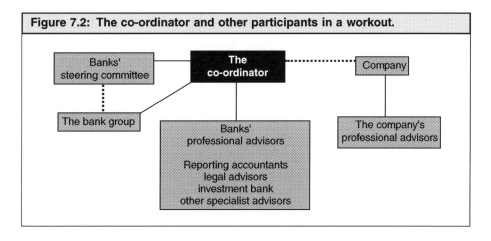

Figure 7.2: The co-ordinator and other participants in a workout.

An effective co-ordinator is:

- Fair.
- Trustworthy.
- Honest.
- Consistent.
- Professional.
- Efficient.

Selection and appointment

Although in most countries the role of the co-ordinator is fulfilled by a bank, it does not need to be one of the lenders to the company. Ultimately, the co-ordinator can be any party with the requisite skills to discharge the role effectively. In some jurisdictions the role is fulfilled by an independent party, such as the partner from a firm of accountants. The co-ordinator should have the necessary level of experience, in-depth understanding of how banks operate, and access to adequate resources in the relevant jurisdiction. Critically, the co-ordinator will need to command the support and confidence of all the key parties to a financial restructuring if it is to discharge its duties effectively.

In most case the co-ordinator is selected from the company's bank group, often being the bank with the largest exposure. This institution is also likely to be the company's main relationship bank. Whilst at the outset a company will tend to approach the banker to which it is closest, in practice the decision on who the co-ordinator will be, is usually made by the bankers themselves. In the natural order of things, the bank with the largest exposure tends to have a significant influence on the final decision. Ideally, however, the co-ordinator will be acceptable to all the major participants in the bank group, and should be able to represent the divergent interests within it.

For particularly large loan workouts, joint co-ordinators may be appointed. This could be because it is not entirely clear which bank has a combination of the largest and most vulnerable exposures, or because more than one bank with a large exposure strongly desires an influential role in the process. Sometimes, joint co-ordinators may be appointed for presentational or reputational reasons. Joint co-ordination of a bank group is easier in workouts where it is possible to have a clear separation of responsibilities, and the debt structure can be naturally divided, possibly along the lines of divergent or conflicting interests. Our experience suggests, however, that joint co-ordination of a bank group tends to be less effective. A single co-ordinator is preferable structurally, providing a clear focal point for all the parties, enabling better control of the bank group, and a more transparent allocation of responsibilities.

Independence

The continuing success of a co-ordinator will critically depend on its perceived fairness. Confidence in its decisions and guidance will depend on its ability to adopt and demonstrate a consistently even-handed, impartial and essentially fair approach to the treatment of specific issues and conflicts between the members of the bank group.

This is particularly important for members of the group who take a wider view of their entire problem loan portfolio and prefer a consistent approach being adopted in the treatment of issues, rather than an opportunistic, case-by-case method. A co-ordinator enjoying the full support and confidence of all the members of its bank group can concentrate on progressing the loan workout with the company, rather than dealing with disaffected or disruptive members. It can also negotiate from a stronger position.

Dissemination of information

A particularly difficult issue for the co-ordinator lies in disseminating information to the members of the bank group. What information should be provided to the rest of the bank group and at what time? Clearly, part of the role of the co-ordinator is to filter and communicate information so that the bank group is presented with the clearest possible picture as soon as is feasible. However, another important objective is to create and preserve stability, as this is essential for the overall success of the financial restructuring. The role of the co-ordinator will involve discussions with the advisors and the company's management, and access to sensitive documents. In the course of undertaking such a role, unfavourable information will frequently be received or problems identified. The co-ordinator has a duty to disclose and share information with the rest of the bank group. In complex transactions, the strategy for information sharing may need to be looked at flexibly in practice. An effective co-ordination role may necessitate the management of information flows to a degree, such that the bank group is presented with information on a coherent and considered basis.

Managing conflicts of interest

Where a co-ordinator is also a member of the bank group there is a potential for conflicts of interest to arise. In these cases it is crucial for the co-ordinator to be seen to be acting impartially and not pursuing its own interests, unless these happen to coincide with, or do not otherwise conflict with, the wishes of the majority of the bank group. The co-ordinator will need to balance carefully the natural desire to protect its own position and have its own views heard, with its responsibilities towards the rest of the bank group. This conflict is best overcome by preserving and strengthening its reputation for addressing issues in a consistent and transparent manner, based on clearly established principles. Indeed, the co-ordinator's success in this role will depend substantially on its reputation and integrity, achieved through the manner in which it has discharged its responsibilities in previous financial restructuring transactions.

The co-ordinator is often also the agent under an existing syndicated facility agreement for the company. As such, it has a duty of care to represent the views of its syndicate, which may form only a part of the bank group. The potential for wider conflicts of interest arises in these situations. Although the co-ordinator could arrange to relinquish any agency roles and pass these duties on to another member of the syndicate, such a move could exacerbate confusion and uncertainty. A possible solution for this problem is for the bank to establish a 'Chinese Wall' between the syndicated loan agency team and the team responsible for co-ordinating the financial restructuring. Alternatively, another member could be appointed to represent the syndicate's interests in the steering committee.

Another situation where there is often potential for disagreement arises at the outset of a loan workout. The prospective co-ordinator will inevitably find itself possessing privileged information in the period between holding initial discussions with the company and the time when arrangements can be made to bring together the remainder of the bank group and agree a moratorium. Where the co-ordinator is also a bank providing revolving credit or other fluctuating bank facilities, it will need to manage the position carefully and not actively seek to improve its position between the two dates. It is crucial to ensure that no lender is prejudiced by any delays in agreeing a moratorium, as retrospective adjustments are virtually impossible.

Other risks

In addition to the difficulties that arise in the course of performing the role of a co-ordinator in a loan workout, there are a number of risks associated with the position:

- *Reputational risk.* The co-ordinator will need to consider and address the reputational risks that it may become exposed to as a result of undertaking the role. The bank may potentially become the focus of adverse publicity from the media, the company's employees, or other banks.

- *Legal risk.* This can arise in a number of ways, depending on the relevant jurisdiction. Perhaps the most common areas relate to the duty of care commonly owed to the various other parties involved in the transaction. Lender liability-related considerations also apply in some countries. The co-ordinator will seek to protect itself against such eventualities, partly through an indemnity from the company.

- *Commercial risk.* The co-ordinator is likely to enjoy a widely-based commercial relationship with the various parties to the financial restructuring. This is particularly so between banks but may, for instance, also exist with the shareholders, suppliers or customers of the company being restructured. Any disagreements can strain relationships conducted in other arenas.

The steering committee

In the case of financial restructurings involving a large number of banks, the bank group almost invariably appoints a steering committee. This consists of a panel of representative banks drawn exclusively from the bank group. The committee's objective is to provide a manageable forum to discuss and resolve issues in which the entire bank group has an interest. The role of the steering committee is administrative not advisory. The co-ordinator will, in the first instance, provide regular reports to the steering committee.

The principal role of the steering committee is to represent the different interests that may exist within the bank group. In particular, its function includes:

- Reviewing progress at the various stages of a loan workout transaction.
- Offering guidance to the co-ordinator on negotiations with the company.

- Assessing information produced by the reporting accountants and other advisors.
- Evaluating the various restructuring options from the perspective of their different constituencies in the bank group.
- Helping formulate counter-proposals for negotiations with the company.

The steering committee is also responsible for agreeing and expressing support for (rather than recommending) various proposals to the wider bank group, including the restructuring agreement.

The steering committee tends to operate primarily during the period leading up to the signing of a financial restructuring agreement. In some instances, it can continue to have a role in the post-restructuring agreement stage, particularly if the banks' exit strategy essentially involves a winding down of the company by way of an asset disposal programme.

Ideally, the bank group will delegate certain decisions to the steering committee, and thereby enable the transaction to be implemented speedily. This will probably not occur during the preliminary stages of a transaction, but may come into operation once a moratorium is formally agreed.

Composition of the steering committee

The steering committee should ideally comprise only a small number of banks and other large creditors. This is in order to ensure that meetings can be convened readily and conducted efficiently. Experience tends to suggest that a steering committee comprising, say, between 10 and 20 per cent of banks by number and, say, 50 per cent by value will not normally involve more than seven banks. Hopefully, a smaller number will fulfil the criteria, which will provide a representative group. The committee will usually be appointed at the first meeting of all the company's bankers to inform them of a company's financial difficulties. It should subsequently be approved formally by the remainder of the bank group. In practice the co-ordinator will have given some consideration to appropriate candidates prior to the all-bank meeting and will make its own suggestions. Nevertheless, the offer of steering committee membership should strictly be extended to every member of the bank group. In any event, the committee members should broadly reflect the varying interests of the bank group. Suitable parameters for the composition of the steering committee may include:

- A combination of banks previously providing committed and uncommitted facilities.
- A mixture of domestic and overseas institutions.
- Agents or lead banks for existing syndicated facilities.
- Banks providing particular types of banking facilities, for example, hedging products.
- Other specialised institutions with large exposures, for example, leasing companies, or credit insurers.

It is common practice to choose an odd number of members to take part in the committee in order to facilitate voting procedures. Steering committees' decisions tend to be taken on a one member, one vote, basis. The co-ordinator tends to be the chairman and a member of the steering committee.

In some larger loan workout transactions, sub-committees of the steering committee may be established, either to represent conflicting or diverse interests amongst the bank group, or to take forward particular or complex aspects of a financial restructuring. For example, a loan workout involving a debt for equity swap may have a sub-committee focusing on equity-related matters.

Qualities required of steering committee members

Each steering committee member has three distinct mandates:

- To represent its constituency in the bank group in negotiations and decision-making.
- To support the co-ordinator in its negotiations with the company.
- To consider its own position as a banker to the company.

Hence the steering committee members need to manage a potential three-way conflict of interest. Strictly, however, the weight of a bank's responsibilities as a steering committee member should lie with the first two points above. As with the co-ordinator, the role should be approached by adopting and applying consistent principles so far as possible. Banks using their positions on the steering committee to protect their own interests tend to weaken the mandate of the committee. In particular, secret agreements with the company by steering committee members undermine confidence and can be open to legal challenge. It follows, therefore, that any bank wishing to accept a steering committee membership should be prepared to give due consideration to the wider interests of the bank group, even if sometimes they conflict with its own interests. In addition:

- Wherever possible, at least a majority of steering committee banks should be drawn from those organisations with previous experience in the role.

- Steering committee banks must have the resources to provide personnel of the right level of relevant experience to attend what may become frequent and time-consuming meetings.

- In the interests of efficiency, representatives from the steering committee banks should have sufficient authority to take decisions at meetings without a regular need to revert to their respective head offices or credit committees.

- The steering committee or co-ordinator may be the only practical source of temporary liquidity support to a company. Members of the committee should have the capacity to provide such support, provided any proposals are consistent with wider commercial principles.

Facility agents and security trustees

Where the existing financing arrangements of a company involve syndicated facilities and the provision of security, there will probably be one or more banks acting as facility agents or security trustees. These are formal roles, documented in the respective facility agreements, and entail fiduciary responsibilities that the relevant banks will need to continue to discharge, until it is agreed otherwise.

Normally, facility agents and security trustees continue to perform their roles during a moratorium, and even once the loan restructuring agreement is executed. The restructuring agreement may involve new facilities and new or additional security. Where this is the case, or it replaces entirely the previously existing agreements, a new facility agent and security trustee will need to be selected. Invariably this will be the co-ordinator, if it is a bank.

The role of the facility agent under a financial restructuring will involve the common operational agency functions under a syndicated credit, including monitoring compliance with the terms and conditions of the facility, administering roll-overs, and being responsible for serving a demand on the company if the bank group votes for such a course of action. Likewise the role of the security trustee will involve holding the security and agreeing to (partial) releases as required. In addition, the security trustee will be responsible for holding or distributing the proceeds of any security realisations, or enforcing security if so instructed by the bank group.

Position of individual banks

Most modern lending agreements contain cross-acceleration or similar event of default clauses. As a result, when a company defaults on payment or breaches certain other conditions contained in any of its loan agreements (which remain unremedied and are not waived), lenders under other facility agreements have the separate right to demand repayment. In the case of contingent indebtedness such banks may, they may demand cash collateral from the company for any contingent indebtedness outstanding.

Each bank needs to decide separately whether to pursue unilateral action against the company to try and recover all, or part, of its exposure. There is no obligation for an individual bank to participate in a loan workout, or to sign any of the documents which accompany a voluntary moratorium or restructuring.

Clearly peer group pressure and wider considerations involving the rest of the bank's portfolio will play a part in each bank's deliberations. If a bank intends to maintain good relations with its peers, and considers their support for other cases in the future important, it will take into account its wider, rather than transaction-specific, interests. Financial restructurings carried out under legislative frameworks have the advantage of preventing a minority of lenders frustrating the interests of the lender group as a whole.

Several banks within a bank group may have limited operations in the country involved and may not have specialist workout teams to represent them in the loan workout transaction. In this event a bank will usually be represented by the relationship manager or loan officer who normally manages the company's account. Banks with the appropriate capability will transfer the case to a central workout unit which will have staff who are experienced in handling the process.

Once a bank with a relatively small exposure does decide to participate in a loan workout, it is likely to play a limited direct role in the process. It will normally be confined to registering its views with the co-ordinator and steering committee. The principal objective for banks with relatively small exposures, or those who accept that they will be bound by the majority view, is to ensure that their preferred representatives have influential roles in, for example, the steering committee. They will then be concerned to ensure that they are kept informed of developments.

8

OTHER KEY PARTICIPANTS IN LOAN WORKOUTS

Introduction

In the majority of loan workouts, the only parties likely to be involved in negotiations will be the company, its bankers and their respective professional advisors. However, there are other stakeholders in the business who will have a direct interest in the outcome of the financial restructuring. Most of these will normally adopt a passive role unless circumstances require otherwise. In theory all the parties affected by a restructuring could become directly involved in the process.

Ultimately, the issue of which parties take an active role in the restructuring negotiations will depend on the circumstances of each case. In this chapter, the issues relating to the participation of selected non-bank financial creditors are highlighted. Often, holders of debt securities in a company can play an influential role in shaping a restructuring, particularly as their interests can conflict with those of banks. Similarly, providers of leasing or receivables financing arrangements may be in a unique position compared to other creditors. The recent proliferation of trading in distressed debt has also created an important need to take into account the interests of debt traders in a loan workout. Additionally, other parties such as suppliers and customers are considered.

The more technical issues relating to the inclusion of particular creditor groups in a moratorium and a debt workout agreement are explored further in Chapter 17.

Factors limiting participation in loan workouts

The direct participation of the majority of stakeholder groups in a restructuring transaction is limited by factors such as:

- Relatively modest individual exposures.
- Diversity of backgrounds.

- Ignorance of problems.
- Existing subordination to the secured interests of bank creditors.
- Weak negotiating position against more powerful interests.
- Inability or unwillingness to dedicate resources to the management of an intensive loan workout process.
- Desire to avoid the risk of being called on to support the provision of additional funding.
- Avoiding becoming a party to any moratorium and risking the stoppage of debt being serviced.

In the interests of practicality, it would be impossible to manage a loan workout if a large number of parties with wide and varying interests were to become involved. In some countries, the inclusion of a wide range of stakeholders is required by the prevailing bankruptcy or other legislation. However, even in such situations, the role in the restructuring process of many of the participants is usually passive.

Nevertheless, from time to time, cases may arise where a particular non-bank creditor, or another interested party has such a material stake in the affairs of a company, or its position is so similar to that of the lenders, that it chooses to be included in the negotiations in order to protect its interests.

Non-bank financial creditors

This group comprises specialist non-bank providers of finance. They can be significant creditors of a company and are therefore more likely to be involved in any loan workout negotiations than, say, trade and other creditors. There is a very wide range of parties that fall within this definition and this chapter is limited to highlighting a few of the more common participants. The attitude of non-bank financial creditors will be heavily influenced by their constitution, the terms of the finance provided to the company, and their objectives from the workout.

Holders of bonds and other capital markets instruments

It is increasingly likely that a company in a debt workout will have outstanding capital markets instruments such as bonds, private placements, long-term debentures, or certain types of preference shares. Holders of these instruments will frequently need to be included in the financial restructuring negotiations alongside the bank creditors, although they often adopt a distinct stance as a separate creditor class. One of the features with this creditor class is that it usually comprises numerous private or institutional investors represented by a trustee. This can create a number of specific difficulties during negotiations.

For example, frequently the financial instrument is in bearer form and so it is very difficult for the company to identify who the ultimate creditor is. This makes it difficult to enter into negotiations, or canvass support. Decision-making by such groups can be relatively laborious. It usually involves a complex and time-consuming process requiring the trustee to present any significant decisions to a full vote of holders of such instruments. Although the overall amount owing is usually material, it can be made up of numerous small holdings. The incentive for each bondholder to participate or vote on a restructuring proposal is small. Bondholders often see themselves as investors, rather than credit providers. Therefore their attitude is likely to be somewhat different to the banks and they will be more reluctant to become involved in a complex and time-consuming restructuring. Additionally, there are particular difficulties where bondholders hold subordinated instruments. In such situations they have the ability to wind-up the company, whilst a restructuring may see them with little residual value left in the company. There are considerable 'free rider' problems as a result.

In some countries, institutional bondholders approach loan workouts with a wider perspective. They take the longer-term interests of their portfolio and the company into account in their deliberations. In such situations, their strategy is likely to be more consistent with those of the company's bankers.

Generally, the terms of issue of bonds give their holders relatively little power to stop a restructuring, provided the bondholders themselves are not affected. If it is impossible to bind dissident bondholders to the terms of a restructuring, then if their consent is essential to a restructuring, formal proceedings will be inevitable.[1]

Leasing companies

Leasing companies can form another important financial creditor class. They are often part of larger bank groups and their attitude may be influenced by the approach of the parent bank, if it is also participating in the workout. Independent leasing companies are often more reluctant to participate in any formal debt workout proceedings. They see themselves as providing secured finance relating to specific operating assets, rather than meeting a company's general financing requirements.

The terms of the lease agreement will provide for ownership of the asset to remain with the leasing company. It will therefore consider that it has effective security and can protect itself by re-taking possession of the asset and selling or renting it elsewhere. Clearly, the nature of the asset and its residual value and marketability will be important considerations. In many cases where the amounts owing are relatively modest or the asset financed is not considered critical to the business, leasing obligations are treated in the same way as trade creditors and lessors are not invited to participate in the moratorium.

Particular problems may arise in the case of short leases that are financing wasting assets, and which require replacement over a relatively short cycle. In these situations, unless the leasing company agrees to write new leases, there will be a cash flow drain on the company as those assets require replacement. Nevertheless, in the context of the loan workout process this can be treated as more of a medium-term problem that is capable of being resolved by the restructuring. Solutions might include the provision of adequate new financing to replace the assets, or the restructuring itself might provide sufficient confidence to the leasing company about the financial viability of the business.

Receivables financing companies

The position of factoring, invoice discounting and forfeiting companies and securitisation programmes can become another important issue in loan workouts. As with leasing, financial arrangement can either be provided by the subsidiaries of major banks, or independent operations, and their philosophy will be influenced accordingly. The significance of this creditor class lies in the nature of the finance provided. Where they are involved, they tend to be important providers of short-term working capital finance to the company and can therefore play a critical role during a financial crisis. Nevertheless, it is difficult to compel them to join a moratorium or restructuring because they are not dependent on the company for repayment of their debt. In fact they often extend finance on a non-recourse basis. As a result, even if they take no steps to protect their position, they are likely to achieve full repayment in a very short period, usually less than 90 days.

Arguably, where non-recourse finance is being provided, participation in a workout should make little or no difference to the purchaser or discounter of the debts since its risk is against the standing and quality of the debtor rather than the company. For the same reason, there is very little motivation for them to commit to the on-going financing of the company, as would be required by a moratorium. In practice receivables financing providers rely on the company to provide regular information and debtor listings, or on the collection of debts. They will also rely on the effectiveness of agreed documentation and security between the company and its customers. Where there is a risk that the company could fail, resulting in additional work in collecting debts, exposure to documentation risks, and the potential for an increased level of disputes, claims, and counter-claims, the provider of such finance may decide to withdraw the facility from the company. This can quickly lead to a cash crisis and alternative sources of finance will need to be found.

Debt traders and investors in distressed debt

Debt traders are not usually a direct participant in a workout but are, nevertheless, a potentially important party that can have a significant effect on proceedings. Debt traders essentially fall into two basic categories:

- Brokers, whose role is limited to bringing a seller and a buyer together for a fee.
- Traders, who may carry a short-term portfolio as a result of buying debt in the expectation of finding a buyer to sell to at a profit.

Where a trader is unable or unwilling to close out a position it may find itself drawn into a workout as a principal party. More often, however, the traders' activities result in new third parties being introduced to the loan workout process. It is this aspect which is the most important from the perspective of the core participants in a workout, since it means that a potentially limitless new range of creditors can be introduced to a loan workout transaction whilst it is being negotiated.

Typically investors in the distressed debt market will be fund managers who buy for the funds that they manage, including so-called 'vulture funds', and end-investors who buy for their own account. Investors will have a range of different objectives when buying distressed debt. These objectives influence how they are likely to act in a debt workout. Investors can be broadly classified according to five different investment objectives:

- *Enhanced yield.* Generally this group consists of relatively low-risk takers and becomes involved towards the end of, or immediately after, a restructuring when most of the terms are known, or the banks involved are seeking an exit. The investors in this category aim to enhance an already attractive interest rate margin with the discount to par on purchase. Participants in this market often include banks seeking to augment their portfolios with a higher yield instrument and perhaps position themselves favourably ahead of a hoped-for refinancing on finer terms as a company returns to health.

- *Capital gain.* Investors with this objective typically seek a 'turn' between purchase and sale by buying a company's debt at a large discount in the expectation of a significant improvement in its prospects. Exit may well take place long before a restructuring is finally agreed. A material increase in the price at which the debt is traded, or the estimated liquidation value of the company, would allow this type of investor to achieve its required rate of return at sale prices well below the par value of the debt. This places such investors in a very different position from the banks and other creditors, who are carrying a par investment cost.

- *Equity play.* The criteria adopted by these investors will be based upon equity models which makes debt for equity swaps an acceptable, or even preferred, solution. The investment is seen as an inexpensive entry into a company's equity and their attitude will be influenced accordingly. As with the investors pursuing a capital gain, the interests of this group will very often conflict with the senior debt lenders involved in a workout.

- *Trade investment.* Such investors are relatively rare in more developed financial markets but may be seeking either to buy a competitor cheaply, or gain access to confidential and commercially sensitive information. In some transition countries, such as Poland, this can be a legitimate route to acquire control over companies, for instance by converting purchased debt into equity.

- *Greenmail tactics.* This is a relatively small group that looks to benefit from a particular set of circumstances during a crisis by 'selling' their co-operation for a disproportionate improvement in the value of their stake. This is most often achieved by securing a material blocking stake. Such tactics are more common in the United States than in other countries.

For a variety of reasons, therefore, debt traders can have a substantial bearing on the debt workout process, both positive and negative. The positive aspects stem from the increased liquidity created by debt traders and their ability to be part of the solution for banks and other creditors. They can remove blockages in negotiations by providing an exit route to lenders who do not wish to participate in a loan workout. However, debt traders can have a potentially destabilising effect on a transaction by introducing different attitudes to the problem, because of the timing and the cost at which they, or entities they have on-sold debt to, become involved.

Box 8.1 below summarises the advantages and disadvantages of allowing banks involved in loan workouts to assign or sell their loans.

Box 8.1

Advantages	Disadvantages
Seller	Additional administration and management distraction. Potential leakage of confidential information.
Exit from problem loan, potentially reducing current or future losses. Improve quality of loan portfolio. Improve capital adequacy ratios. Improve standing with rating agencies. Remove costs and management distractions.	Creates instability within the bank group: • Increasing and frequently changing number of lenders. • Different economic agenda in view of disparity of entry price. • Unknown motives—legal purchaser may not be acting on its own account.
Buyer	• Unilateral ability to block proposals: 'greenmail'. • Propensity to litigate if this offers a better return. • Can be driven by short-term financial considerations. • Purchase price reflects the stability created by other lenders' support.
Short-term opportunity to make a 'turn'. Long-term investment opportunity offering potentially high yields. Opportunity to 'influence' course of restructuring.	
Banking group and company	Adverse reaction from: • Market. • Public and customers. • Employees.
Offers a means of removing a 'problem' lender. Opportunity to attract 'new money' into the transaction.	

Suppliers and other creditors

Suppliers and trade creditors are rarely directly involved in a financial restructuring. Nevertheless, suppliers are a critical factor in the workout process. For the company, it is vital to retain the co-operation of key suppliers in order to maintain access to raw materials and essential services, particularly where alternative sources of supply are limited. Additionally, since most suppliers also provide extended trade credit, any change to these arrangements will have a serious effect on the liquidity of the company. Maintaining the confidence of these parties is crucial.

Trade and other creditors can be very difficult to control. They usually tend to be numerous, with relatively small exposures to the company, and are often willing automatically to resort to legal action against a company for non-payment of overdue debts. Although they are unlikely to gain anything in the event of the company's liquidation or bankruptcy, the threat of legal action can be a powerful weapon against, principally, the company's bankers who would suffer substantially greater losses. One of the prices of stability, therefore, is to keep trade creditors paid up to date, although subject to very strict control. Provided invoices are settled reasonably on time, suppliers are usually willing to continue trading with the company and may even extend trade credit.

The extent to which this issue will need to be managed will depend on the degree to which the company's problems are widely known. Where the position of the company is widely publicised, or is subject to rumours, it is important to identify the key creditors and customers and develop a strategy for dealing with them.

Preferential creditors

Preferential creditors are those with liabilities connected with taxation, sales tax and payroll. The standing and rights of this creditor class will vary between jurisdictions. However, they will often constitute a relatively significant sum, which in many cases either carries a legal priority ranking over other forms of unsecured debt. In the case of wages, the will also be an operational priority. They will usually be supportive of a company's rescue, particularly if a large company is involved.

Customers

A company's customers can also have a critical influence over the success of a financial restructuring transaction. As with suppliers, they are rarely directly involved in the workout process. Customers will want to be confident that they can rely on their supply chain and that they will not suffer interruptions or deterioration in the quality of supplies as a result of the company's problems. A company which holds a monopolistic position, or is in an industry where it is difficult or expensive for its customers to switch suppliers, will be protected to some degree in the short-term.

Customers also play an important role in the company's working capital considerations. A company which is known to be in difficulty may find that its debtors are even slower than normal in paying for goods and services, exploiting the former's weaker bargaining position. This can exacerbate a company's short-term liquidity problems. Alternatively, customers may seek better terms for continuing prompt payment arrangements.

Conversely, key customers can be a major source of support to a company in financial distress. For example, they can alleviate any liquidity problems by agreeing to pay their invoices promptly. Customers can extend their help further by providing working capital finance to a supplier undergoing a financial restructuring.

Governmental and other agencies

The attitude to debt workouts and the framework in which they are enacted, will be heavily influenced by the relevant regulatory authorities and governmental agencies in the jurisdictions involved. Regulatory or governmental agencies will usually include one or more of the Central Bank, the Banking Industry Supervisor, the State Treasury or the Ministry of Finance, and Trade Associations.

These bodies are primarily charged with creating the appropriate framework and conditions at the outset, for workouts to have the best chance of succeeding. Their on-going role is to influence and supervise the overall process rather than to become involved in individual transactions, unless these are of such importance that they affect the national interest. The regulatory authority may choose to encourage participants to work to resolve differences and may apply pressure with varying degrees of subtlety to achieve its aims. At times it will be called upon to act as mediator and, in the case of multinational transactions, may well discuss a position with its counterpart in another jurisdiction, if necessary.

In some countries, especially where the restructuring of a company will have major social repercussions, government agencies or the relevant line ministries can mobilise financial and other support for the company.

The exact role chosen by such regulatory or governmental bodies will vary from one jurisdiction to another.

[1] P. R. Wood, *Principles of International Insolvency*, Sweet and Maxwell, London, 1995, p. 308.

[2] INSOL Lenders Group, Report of the Debt Trading Sub-Committee.

[3] INSOL Lenders Group, Report of the Debt Trading Sub-Committee.

9

EXTERNAL ADVISORS

Introduction

External advisors make a significant contribution to loan workouts, by providing expert support and advice to the main participants. The principals in a workout are unlikely to be adequately resourced, or skilled, to fully address the wide-ranging specialist issues that will arise. This would be the case even if there were experienced workout teams involved. Accountants and lawyers generally form the core of the advisory teams supporting the principals. Both the company and its lenders engage separate teams of professional firms to assist them during the transaction.

The focus of this chapter is on the independent external advisors engaged to advise the bank group. The case for involving external advisors in general, and independent advisors in particular, is presented. The arguments often put forward against their appointment are also outlined. Reporting accountants play a key role in loan workout transactions. Issues relating to their selection, appointment and role are examined. The responsibilities of other major advisors are also considered.

Reasons for engaging external advisors

The need for external advisors will depend on the particular circumstances of a transaction. This section highlights some of the more common reasons for their involvement in loan workouts.

Figure 9.1 below summarises the key attributes of external advisors, many of which are explored in detail in this chapter.

Expertise

Companies and banks employ professional advisors as a matter of course when undertaking complex transactions such as mergers and acquisitions. The same principles apply to loan workouts. These transactions invariably require highly complex issues

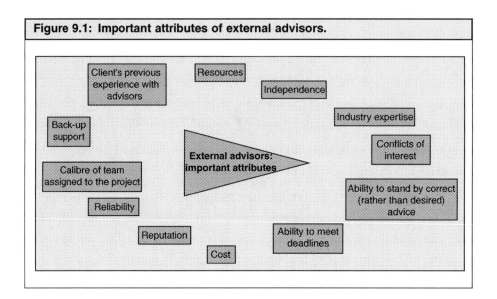

Figure 9.1: Important attributes of external advisors.

to be addressed across the full range of commercial, operational, financial and legal disciplines. In addition, they need to be managed under stressful conditions and time and resource constraints.

Legal documentation accompanying the moratorium and restructuring will often be lengthy and complicated, reflecting the complexity of any agreement reached. All participants will wish to ensure that the terms and conditions of any agreement are fully and accurately documented by experienced lawyers.

Resources

Negotiating a large loan workout is likely to be time-consuming. Participants will need to deal with considerable uncertainty, a substantial workload and many technical and specialist issues. In cases involving a group of companies with interests in more than one jurisdiction, the bank group and the company will need to have access to specialists with local knowledge.

The company is unlikely to have adequate staff to undertake the reviews that may be required of its strategy, markets, products, operations and financial position. Frequently, the company's reporting procedures and internal management and financial controls will be inadequate and will need a complete overhaul. It may need to produce a revised business plan and financial projections in a short time, as well as concurrently implement a restructuring of its operations. At the same time, its resources will be absorbed in fire-fighting.

For their part, the banks will have insufficient staff and depth of experience to conduct extensive due diligence reviews on the company's operations, its current financial condition and outlook. The staff in the credit function of a commercial bank are trained to assess loan proposals and risk generally. They are not equipped to judge areas such as marketing, organisational structures, product and industry considerations, accounting and law.

Relevant experience

It is unlikely that the company's management team will have much expertise managing companies experiencing serious operating and financial difficulties. The ability simultaneously to manage professional advisors, negotiate with the company's creditors, and trouble-shoot, whilst at the same time normalising the company's operations is only gained over time. Motivation may also become an issue since the process of implementing and delivering a turnaround can be slow and drawn-out. This will require very different cultural attitudes and skills to those needed to run a successful company. Also, the company will be vulnerable to failure for a relatively long period, whilst it negotiates a loan workout. Advisors to the company who bring in-depth experience of loan workouts can make a substantial contribution.

Objectivity

This is a particularly important consideration for the bank group, and is dealt with below in the context of independent advisors. However, the company can also benefit from objective advice during a loan workout.

The company's management may be too close to the problem and lose sight of the important underlying issues. It may not believe there is a serious problem at all. Constant fire-fighting may impair its ability to stand back and assess the company's wider position. The management's views may have become so entrenched that it is unable to consider any of the alternatives available. It can also be that the Board is unwilling to challenge the views of a particularly influential stakeholder. Advice from a third party can add considerably to the management's ability to approach the workout objectively.

Independent advisors

The main objective of engaging advisors independent of the company is to protect the interests of the external stakeholders. For banks, independent advice brings many advantages. Considerably greater confidence may be placed on such advice. In addition, in many areas connected with workouts, for example, the valuation of assets, judgement is an important factor. Banks are able to rely much more on the output of a professional who is clearly acting on their behalf.

Independent advice becomes even more important where there is more than one lender involved. Most lenders will not be inclined to rely on information or advice prepared by, or for, one of the other lenders. Equally, because of the potential liability involved, a lender would not normally wish to support a proposal, or invite other banks to make decisions based upon information it had prepared for itself.

Arguments against engaging independent advisors

Resistance to the appointment of external, and in particular independent advisors, centres around a number of arguments. Their relatively high cost is often the principal factor, particularly when a company is not in a very strong financial position. Alternatively, the company might argue that there is a risk of a deteriorating position becoming a self-fulfilling prophecy. The introduction of independent advisors too early will probably contribute to, and might even accelerate, the process by signalling a problem. At times, such resistance may be reinforced by the banks' relationship or account officers, who also perceive such an appointment as a sign of failure. There may well be risks here and the costs often appear relatively high at the outset, but these issues are capable of being managed.

Often the actual reason underlying the management's reluctance to accept the appointment of independent advisors relates to personal pride and a sense that it is an admission of failure. There is also an associated feeling of loss of control.

It is always probable, of course, that the management of a company experiencing difficulty will be able to identify the causes of the problem itself and take appropriate corrective action. It is also possible that what seems to be a minor difficulty, or even a potentially larger problem, will simply be solved by itself if left alone. Ultimately, a company's management must be able to convince its lenders that it understands the company's problems and has taken the necessary steps to address them.

The need for independent advisors is often triggered by a cash crisis in the company, or the company informing its bankers that it has, or is likely to, breach covenants in its borrowing agreement. The nature and extent of the problem, whether or not it had been foreseen, the perceived abilities of the management team, and its performance in arresting any decline, will also be key factors. Much will depend on the commercial realities which stem from the strength and value of the relationship between the company and its bankers.

The banks may well accept the position that no independent advisors should be appointed to begin with. However, if continued slippage in performance or other problems persist, then it is inevitable that at some point the bank group will require an independent review and assessment of the company's affairs. If this initial assessment is unfavourable then the remit of the advisors will be widened to allow for a more fundamental investigation into the company's affairs.

Reporting accountants

During loan workouts, separate firms of accountants (or in some countries, consultancy firms), will be employed by the bank group and the company respectively. The firm acting for the lenders in a workout is often referred to as the 'reporting accountant' or 'investigating accountant'. The company will usually continue to work with its own firm of auditors.

Basis of engagement

The reporting accountants will be appointed by the co-ordinator of the bank group. This will follow consultation, where appropriate, with the steering committee or the other banks. The firm will act for, be accountable to, and produce a report for, the entire bank group. It would be very unusual for different banks to employ separate reporting accountants in a multi-banked workout.

Although often acting exclusively for the banks, the reporting accountants' fees are usually charged to the company as part of the lenders' transaction costs. In the short-term, however, given the financial vulnerability of the company, the cost of employing reporting accountants is underwritten by the banks. This provides a communality of interests to maintain effective control over costs, which can easily escalate in workout situations.

The relationship between the banks and the reporting accountants will be evidenced in writing by way of a letter of appointment. The scope of the assignment and any specific requirements will be detailed within agreed terms of reference. It is important to establish a clear and unambiguous duty of care between the reporting accountants and the banks. Technically, the reporting accountants will be engaged jointly by the company and bankers, with the principal duty of care to the banks.

Box 9.1

The merits of employing independent reporting accountants are demonstrated convincingly in the figure below, relating to the restructuring of Daewoo Corporation, part of one of South Korea's largest conglomerates. The results of a due diligence exercise transformed the balance sheet net asset position to a substantial negative net worth.

Box Figure 9.1

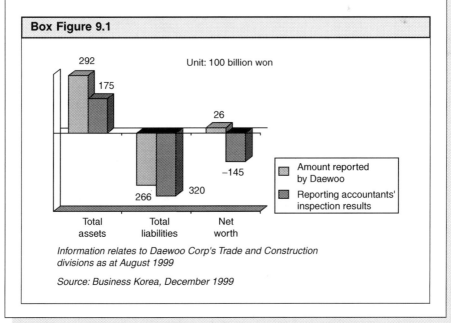

Unit: 100 billion won

292
175
26
−145
266   320

Total assets   Total liabilities   Net worth

Amount reported by Daewoo

Reporting accountants' inspection results

Information relates to Daewoo Corp's Trade and Construction divisions as at August 1999

Source: Business Korea, December 1999

Profile and qualities

It is important to instruct accountants with extensive direct experience of corporate recovery and insolvency to the role of reporting accountants. In practice bankers will tend to select the accountants on the basis of individual *partners* rather than the firm they work with. As a result, only a very small number of individuals within each financial centre tend to be instructed to lead teams on the largest high-profile financial restructurings. Nevertheless, such individuals must be able to draw on considerable resources from their firms to carry out the assignment.

Consultants (rather than accountants) are sometimes engaged to discharge the responsibilities of 'reporting accountants' in some countries, or in cases involving specialist industries. Increasingly, this is likely to be the exception, as the major firms of accountants extend their capabilities.

For larger transactions, the reporting accountants will be required to deploy significant resources at short notice. The assignments are often extremely intensive in terms of the volume of work, number of countries involved, and the time available to complete reviews. The reporting accountants may need to devote upwards of 25 staff and two or more partners, all with the necessary degree of experience, to the largest cases. Staff will be drawn predominantly from the corporate recovery or business turnaround units of the firms involved.

Another important factor in deciding which firm to employ is the need to avoid any actual or perceived conflict of interest. The company will frequently seek to influence the choice of the reporting accountants. A strong case is often made for the role to be fulfilled by its own audit firm. Ultimately the reporting accountants will report, and be responsible, to the banks. As such, their selection is essentially a matter for the banks and not the company. Ideally, the reporting accountants will have no other direct connection with the company or its directors. However, given the trends in consolidation among the large international accounting firms, finding an entirely independent firm of reporting accountants may not be straightforward. This is particularly the case where large multinational groups of companies are involved.

In those cases where it is decided that the banks will engage the audit firm to discharge the role of the reporting accountants, it is important for staff from that firm's corporate recovery unit to be employed to undertake the workout review, rather than the normal audit staff. In these cases it is usual for the firm to introduce internal arrangements to ensure that the reporting to the lenders and the company are kept separate. Nevertheless, in our experience engaging the company's audit firm to report on its own past work is generally highly ineffective and this practice should be avoided if at all possible.

The role of the reporting accountants

The activities of the reporting accountants will generally fall into one, or more, of the following three broad areas:

- A *preliminary assessment*. This comprises an initial review of a company's position with particular focus on the scale of its problems and, importantly, its short-term liquidity position.

- A *full review*. This involves a thorough and wide-ranging review of the various areas detailed within the terms of reference agreed with the banks and the company. One of the key functions of the reporting accountants is to test the reliability of information provided by the management and, if necessary, to make their own assessments and estimates. Their review should provide a comprehensive insight into of the group's financial and non-financial affairs and prospects. It will also recommend a solution and the way forward for the participants. The areas commonly covered by the reporting accountants are examined in more detail later in this book.

- *On-going monitoring*. In those cases where a restructuring is successfully agreed, the reporting accountants may continue to monitor the company's financial and operational performance on behalf of the lenders.

Nature of reporting

The reporting accountants will be expected to produce a written report of their findings with a copy made available to each of the banks. The report represents the independent findings of the reporting accountants, and is intended for the bank group, rather than the company. Frequently, they will follow up their written report with a brief presentation of the key findings. At this time, their findings and recommendations will be discussed and tested by the banks. Traditionally the report is reviewed by the directors of the company prior to such a presentation so that any objections or disagreements on matters of fact or opinions can be aired and corrected, or otherwise reconciled in good time. In some instances the reporting accountants' opinion of the management team and their recommendations to the bank group are excluded from the contents of the report made available to the directors.

The company's external auditors

Other than when they act as the reporting accountants, the company's external auditors are not usually required to fulfil any specific role in a loan workout. In practice, they may do so for a number of different reasons. These may include:

- *Audit sign-off*. Often the realisation that a problem exists is precipitated by a company's routine audit process and the need to sign-off the accounts on a 'going concern' basis. Amongst other measures, this requires a company to evidence to its audit firm that it has access to adequate lines of finance and that there is a reasonable certainty that these will continue to be extended by its lenders. In practice that means showing that the company has a sufficient level of committed facilities in place for a particular period in the future, varying from 12 to 18 months. A downturn in the company's financial performance may trigger a breach of covenants in its loan agreements. This can lead to a delay in signing-off the accounts, or a qualification in the company's audit report regarding its solvency.

- *Temporary assistance with resource.* Given the increased workload on the company's finance function during a workout, staff from the audit firm may be attached or seconded to the company. They would normally help with the company's business and financial review and the preparation of a revised business plan.
- *Preparation of information.* The audit firm may provide information to the reporting accountants to facilitate their review, or assist in the preparation of information memoranda in connection with the disposal of subsidiaries or individual assets.
- *Working capital statements.* In certain situations, particularly in the case of stock exchange listed companies, the audit firm may be required to make certain representations to the regulatory authorities in connection with the restructuring proposal. Adequacy of working capital is a vitally important area, which often causes difficulties in achieving consensus in loan workout negotiations.
- *Taxation advice.* The company's restructuring proposals may involve a complex corporate reorganisation and disposal programme. In such cases the audit firm will usually be commissioned to provide an opinion on the proposals and recommend the most tax-effective way to structure the transaction.

Legal advisors

In all complex debt workouts, the company and the bank group will employ their own firms of legal advisors. Unlike accountants in the same situation, a law firm cannot generally be expected to act for both sides in a workout transaction.

Usually a single law firm will act for and advise the whole bank group, and not just the co-ordinator and the steering committee. Despite this bilateral duty of care to each bank, it is not uncommon for some banks to employ separate legal firms to advise them independently. This is particularly the case where they are in a unique position, or, in the case of some banks, group policy requires it. Such separate legal advice would be obtained at the respective banks' own expense. More commonly, when more than one class of financial creditor is involved in a restructuring (for example, banks and bondholders), separate lawyers will frequently act for each class of creditor.

In the case of multi-jurisdictional transactions the main legal firm appointed will instruct other firms to advise on matters of local law, unless they have appropriately qualified in-house resources to meet such needs.

Role of legal advisors to the bank group

In most financial restructuring transactions, the legal advisors' activities will fall into six broad areas:

- Provision of general and on-going legal advice to the co-ordinator, the steering committee and the members of the bank group separately and as a whole.
- Review of the terms of existing loan agreements, other financing documents and any existing collateral arrangements.
- Review of the group legal structure and financial and other interconnections among the legal entities in the group.

- Review of the legal recourse situation and group entity priority positions (see Chapter 21 for an explanation of these concepts).
- Negotiation and drafting of a moratorium agreement.
- Negotiation and drafting of the debt restructuring documentation and any inter-creditor agreement.
- Preparation of new security documentation as well as filing and registration of papers post-execution.

Where the loan workout requires the banks to convert some of their debt into equity in the company, the legal advisors will also be involved in drafting and negotiating the terms of the share subscription agreements and any share marketing agreements.

Role of legal advisors to the company

The legal advisors to the company will have three principal roles:

- The provision of specific advice to the directors of the company on the duties and obligations imposed upon them by the laws prevailing in the relevant jurisdictions, particularly relating to insolvency legislation.
- Negotiation and review of the various documents and agreements which are normally drafted by the banks' legal advisors.
- General advice to the company on legal matters affecting its operations.

Investment banking advisors

The involvement of investment banking advisors will vary from case to case. In the case of workouts involving larger, publicly quoted companies, an investment banking team will usually be retained to advise the company's directors. The role of the investment bank will involve:

- Advising and guiding the directors through the restructuring process and negotiations.
- Assisting with, or undertaking with the support of accountants or consultants, a strategic review of one or more of the industry, core businesses, market positioning, product, marketing process, and cost structure of the company.
- Input in the development of an operational plan and financial structure of the company.
- Review of the company's business plan and forecasts.
- Undertaking business valuations of the whole or parts of the business by reference to peer group comparisons.
- Preparation of information memoranda and marketing of subsidiaries or individual assets for sale.
- Advice on stock exchange-related matters where relevant, such as the issue of announcements, or the temporary suspension of trading in the company's shares.
- Canvassing the views of institutional shareholders.

The co-ordinator will also need to consider whether or not to retain an investment bank to advise the bank group. The decision will depend primarily on the complexity of the transaction and the degree of specialist expertise required. For example, where the transaction involves a debt for equity swap, the banks will need professional advice from an investment bank. An independent evaluation of major corporate restructuring options, such as business disposals, spin-offs and demergers may also warrant specialist investment banking advice.

Other advisors and experts

Accountants, lawyers and, in larger cases, investment banks form the core of the advisory teams for the company and its lenders. From time to time, other specialist advice may be required. If it cannot be procured internally, the core advisory team will normally identify and engage such specialists on a sub-contract basis. The need for expertise will depend on the nature of the company and the type of solutions proposed as part of its restructuring.

Other specialists occasionally engaged in loan workout transactions include:

- Property valuers.
- Industry experts.
- Technology specialists.
- Public relations consultants.
- Providers of outplacement services.
- Environmental specialists.

Such experts are primarily engaged to advise the company. However, if a particular need is identified, the bank group may require independent expert advice as well. For example, a bank group will engage its own property valuers for loan workouts involving property companies.

---

[1] Uncertain future for Daewoo, *Business Korea (Seoul)*, December 1999, 14–16.

SECTION C

THE LOAN WORKOUT PROCESS

10

A FRAMEWORK FOR EXECUTING LOAN WORKOUTS

Introduction

A loan workout transaction involves a number of stages. Each of these stages is characterised by instability and lack of control, leading to the high execution risk of such transactions.

A methodical approach is required if a loan workout is to be completed successfully. The purpose of this chapter is to present a framework that enables such an approach to be adopted. The framework highlights the interdependence between the restructuring of a company's business and its financial restructuring. It then provides a series of steps that should be followed during a loan workout transaction.

The remainder of this section of the book examines the more important stages involved in the framework in more detail.

Loan workouts in context

Before considering the various stages in a loan workout transaction, it is important to identify its main constituents.

Typically, financial distress is likely to be a symptom of deeper business-related problems of a company. Conversely, if a company's financial problems arise from over-indebtedness (for example, as a result of making a highly leveraged acquisition), strains from the requirement to service such debt are likely to affect its business operations. As a result, a loan workout will involve the restructuring of the business as well as the finances of a company.

Figure 10.1 summarises the key elements of a loan workout.

A financial restructuring, which is the principal focus of banks in a loan workout, needs to be seen as a component of the wider restructuring of the operations of a business. Improving a company's operations and restructuring its finances are considerably

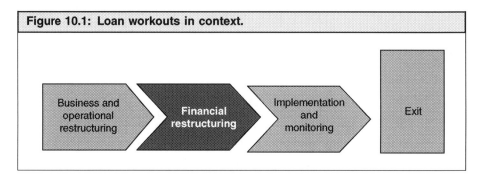

Figure 10.1: Loan workouts in context.

inter-linked. The success of a company's turnaround depends on how well a financial restructuring supports, and is tailored to, its business restructuring plan.

Moreover, the financial restructuring is very much the start of the process. Ultimately, the success of the loan workout depends on the company's ability to deliver the future financial outcomes envisaged in the restructuring plan. Lenders have a key role in monitoring the progress of the restructuring. The financial restructuring agreement can be key in designing a monitoring regime that provides lenders with access to appropriate information and sufficient powers to take corrective action where necessary.

Finally, a robust restructuring agreement must foresee how lenders will ultimately exit their position and get repaid. The term exit is used loosely in this context and may also include refinancing on commercial terms. Exit options need to be explored carefully at the time of the loan workout transaction. In particular, the feasibility of achieving the desired exit routes within target time scales must be assessed realistically.

Anatomy of a financial restructuring transaction

Restructuring companies is more of an art than a precise science. There is seldom one correct answer. Solutions have to be developed through a process involving a series of stages. Each of these stages builds on, or reinforces others. Considerable pressure exists during a financial crisis to arrive at and implement a solution quickly. If a methodical approach is not adopted, however, considerable risks remain that the restructuring will be fragile, susceptible to internal and external shocks, and will ultimately fail.

The stages in a typical loan workout transaction are highlighted in Figure 10.2 below and are overviewed in the remainder of this chapter. The figure presents a stylised structure of the loan workout process, with clear demarcation between the stages. In reality, there will be overlaps between them and it may be necessary to develop more than one stage in parallel. The critical issue, however, is that the further one's approach is removed from the highlighted order of activities, the greater are the risks to the transaction.

Stabilisation

Loan workouts tend to be triggered by crises. Such crises may arise suddenly, or may have been building up over a period and are crystallised by a certain event. The most tangible evidence of such a crisis is usually a liquidity crunch. Alternatively, other

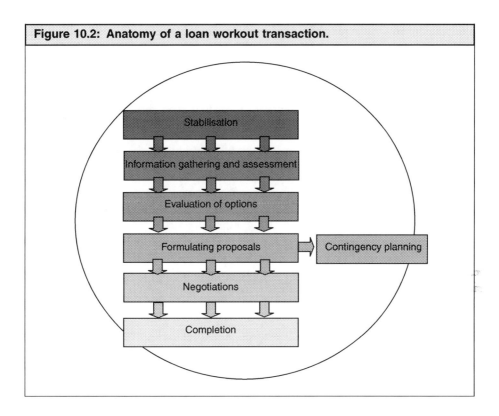

Figure 10.2: Anatomy of a loan workout transaction.

issues may lead to the company breaching its banking or other financial covenants. In turn, this triggers other events, such as the 'calling' of loans by other financial creditors, withdrawal of credit lines by the company's suppliers, or the loss of confidence by key customers. As a result, the company's management and other resources are diverted to continuous fire-fighting and addressing short-term problems, rather than addressing the core weaknesses of the organisation and developing a sustainable restructuring plan. The need to stabilise the business and, in particular, its cash position, is critical at this stage. Such stabilisation is typically achieved by way of a moratorium being agreed by the company's principal financial creditors, and the provision of short-term cash by lenders to alleviate liquidity-related problems.

Information gathering and assessment

Once stability is achieved, the immediate objective should be to start gathering information that will enable all the key participants in the process to identify the company's problems and, ultimately, form the basis of any negotiated solution. The information gathering phase can be broken down into various stages. The most important areas that need to be investigated are:

- The immediate cash needs of the company.
- Its current financial and accounting position.

- The company's medium- and long-term prospects.
- The sustainability of the company's existing financial structure.
- The relative recovery position of each of the company's major creditors, or creditor classes.

Any information gathered must be reliable and credible. To a large extent, this need can be addressed by appointing experienced reporting accountants or specialist consultants.

Evaluating options

Once a company's key problems have been investigated, the principal objectives of the loan workout need to be identified. For example, aims relating to the financial component of any restructuring might include the reduction of the level of debt in the company, an improvement in its working capital position, or an adjustment in the maturity profile of its financial obligations. Once these objectives have been identified, alternative strategies available to meet them are explored. Although there are usually a large number of theoretical possibilities, in practice a relatively small number tend to be feasible given the various financial, business and other constraints faced by a company in distress. The options need to be evaluated, generally with reference to their risk and reward trade-offs, and the preferred solution and contingencies identified. The implications of such an evaluation may differ between the participants, depending on their respective standpoints. Rigorous analysis and a well-structured negotiating strategy is the key to success in such circumstances.

Formulating proposals

In meeting the often competing needs of the participants in a financial restructuring, the final outcome tends to involve compromises, unless one party's negotiating position is overwhelmingly superior compared to the others, or the legal or regulatory regime grants advantages to a particular group of participants. Otherwise, the party that takes the initiative to explore options, develop solutions and formulate the proposals has considerable advantage over the others. Traditionally, this role rests with the company's management. However, to optimise their position, lenders need to ensure they have significant involvement in this exercise from an early stage. Where this is not feasible, it may be necessary to perform a parallel exercise to ensure that counter-proposals can be made on an informed basis. There is a critical need to be proactive at this stage.

From the lenders' point of view, a loan workout proposal needs to recognise their interests in protecting their position. It would need to meet the restructuring objectives identified earlier in the process. To be sustainable and, ultimately, gain the support of all the participants in the restructuring, it needs to be equitable. Finally, it needs to be technically feasible, and address all the relevant legal, regulatory, accounting and taxation issues.

Contingency planning should be an integral component of the proposal-formulating phase and back-up plans should be considered as a matter of course. The extent of resources devoted to developing contingency plans, and the detail they are considered in, will depend primarily on the perceived risk of failure of the preferred option. A well-developed and credible contingency plan can also be a valuable negotiating tool for lenders.

Negotiations

Negotiating loan workouts, especially where a number of stakeholders are involved, can be complex. Given different business, personal and financial interests, views on the preferred solution can vary greatly between the participants. However, voluntarily agreed loan workouts, by definition, require formal or informal acceptance by all the affected parties. Certain factors, such as a ready access to reliable information by all parties, a sense of involvement in the process and a perception that the proposed solution is equitable and at least attempts to recognise and balance the interests of all parties, considerably facilitates ownership and acceptance. For individual participants, or groups such as lenders, it is critical that the negotiations are approached on the basis of a credible negotiating strategy which is, in turn, grounded on analyses carried out earlier in the process.

Completion

Completion relates to technical issues such as drafting and agreeing the various legal documents relating to the restructuring and securing of formal approvals. The process can be particularly complex in certain types of transactions, such as those involving debt for equity swaps, or transactions involving bondholders. In certain regimes, approval from a court, or from a regulatory authority, may be required.

Box 10.1

A Framework for Corporate Debt Restructuring in Thailand (The 'Bangkok Approach')

Stage	Time
1. Call meeting of debtor, creditors and interested parties	Any time by debtor or creditor
2. First creditors' meeting, appointment of Creditors' Committee/Lead Bank (see Principles 6 and 7)	On seven days' notice after 1

Box 10.1 Continued

---

3. Creditors submit claims in writing to Creditors' Committee/Lead Bank	Within 15 days of 2
4. At any creditors' meeting a debtor representative with decision-making authority must appear and answer any questions	Continuous
5. Debtor's 'management' (i.e., directors or authorised officers) must submit at a minimum the following information: (a) assets, liabilities and obligations the debtor owes to third persons (b) property given by the debtor as security to creditors and the date given (c) property of other parties in the debtor's possession (d) the debtor's shareholdings in other companies or juristic persons (e) names, business and addresses of all creditors (f) names, business and addresses of the debtor's debtors (g) details of the property including payments which the debtor expects to receive in the future (h) all written consents for creditors to release to other creditors all information on the assets and liabilities of the debtor (see also Principle 8)	Within seven days of 2
6. The appointment of an independent accountant and/or other experts shall be carried out as requested by the creditors based on the agreed terms of reference	Within seven days of 2
7. Debtor submits all further information requested by creditors or independent accountant necessary to prepare plan (see also Principle 8)	Within two months of 2, extendable up to one month maximum
8. Plan submission by Creditors' Committee, debtor and independent accountant to all creditors	Within three months of 2, extendable up to two months maximum

Box 10.1 Continued

9. Creditor meeting on plan	10 days after 8
10. Creditors propose amendments to plan	Within seven days of 8
11. If plan consideration not completed, meeting adjourned to next business day	Next business day after 9
12. New creditors' meeting if valid request approved for adjournment of meeting to consider amendments to the plan	10 days after adjournment
13. Decision on whether to privately reorganise, formally reorganise under Bankruptcy Act, or liquidate	At creditors' meeting under 9 or 12 within three months from 2

Source: The Foreign Banker's Association, Thailand[1]

Although the various legal agreements conclude the loan workout transaction, they also define the framework and relationships between the participants in the ensuing period when the company needs to deliver on often very difficult objectives. The agreements, in particular, establish the monitoring regime for the lenders and also explicitly state their powers and authority in relation to the company, particularly if agreed targets are not met. In addition to focusing on financial and business considerations, these and other corporate governance issues should be taken into account when negotiating details of agreements.

Implementing the framework

The framework presented in this chapter outlines the overall approach and principles required for effective loan workout transactions. To implement it, however, these principles need to be translated into concrete steps. These steps are outlined below:

- The calling of a moratorium.
- Initial internal information review and the preparation of a preliminary action plan.
- Establishing the transaction framework with the company and the other parties.
- Appointing reporting accountants, lawyers and other advisors.
- Preparing a preliminary 'quick and dirty' report on the company and securing agreement on the way forward.
- Defining restructuring objectives.
- Preparing a full report and reviewing the options.
- Evaluating the major options.
- Structuring solutions.
- Negotiating and completing the transaction.

Box 10.1 illustrates how a framework for loan workouts similar to that presented in this chapter has been operationalised in Thailand, as rules to deal with the corporate

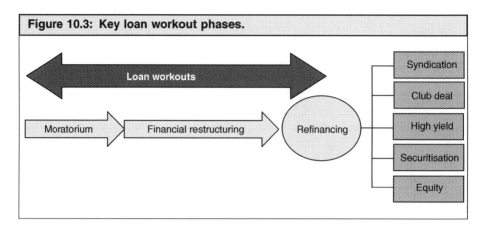

Figure 10.3: Key loan workout phases.

debt problems which arose from the Asian crisis. Of particular interest is the timetable envisaged for each of the stages.

The moratorium, restructuring and refinancing

The framework presented in this chapter stresses that a loan workout is a process, rather than an individual event. The operational steps required for its implementation can be broadly divided into three phases. Figure 10.3 above highlights these phases.

The steps outlined in this chapter principally relate to implementing a loan workout 'transaction'. The objective of these steps, which would be carried out during the moratorium 'phase', would be to agree a sustainable financial restructuring plan.

Once the company has completed its recovery phase and its financial health has been restored, it will probably look to refinance all its facilities on commercial terms. From the point of view of lenders, this would signal their 'exit' from the loan workout. Frequently, only a small group of core banks will participate in the refinancing.

Occasionally, the process may not extend beyond a moratorium. This might be because the company fails during that phase. Alternatively, the moratorium may have gained sufficient time to implement a short-term strategy to repay the banks. For example, this might involve a sale of assets, or of the business as a whole. On the other hand, the moratorium may have been sustained over an extended period during which the company's operations improve sufficiently to permit a direct shift to a commercially-based refinancing.

Part II of this book examines the various technical issues involved in the moratorium and financial restructuring phases in more detail. Chapter 11 highlights the major issues involved in restructuring the business of a company. Chapters 12 to 15 cover the various steps involved in implementing a loan workout transaction.

---

[1] The Foreign Banker's Association, *Framework for Corporate Debt Restructurings in Thailand*, 1998, Appendix I.

11

TURNING AROUND A BUSINESS

Introduction

Financial distress is a symptom of a company's wider difficulties, rather than a problem in itself. To resolve corporate financial crises therefore, it is important to identify and address the company's true underlying problems. Moreover, once the company's shortcomings have been identified, the business and financial restructuring process that is intended to resolve them, needs to be undertaken methodically to achieve the desired results.

The purpose of this chapter is to provide an overview of the business-related issues involved in a loan workout. The most common internal and external causes of financial distress are outlined. These are important because early identification of such factors enables problems to be addressed before they have a serious impact on the company. Moreover, once a company suffers a crisis, familiarisation with its most likely causes enables them to be addressed quickly. Related to this issue are various corporate failure prediction models and an introduction is provided to some of the most well known of these. The chapter then reviews the various components of business and corporate restructuring and how activities in this area are typically sequenced. Finally, the nature of the interaction between business and financial restructuring is explained.

Internal causes of corporate decline

Internal causes of corporate decline are those that are potentially controllable by a company's management. At the heart of such causes is often the failure of management to guide the company's activities appropriately. This can either be a result of inherent weaknesses in the management team itself, or their failure to develop appropriate structures and systems within the company that enable them to exercise control.

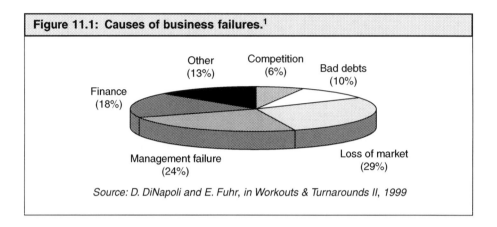

Figure 11.1: Causes of business failures.[1]

Other (13%)   Competition (6%)   Bad debts (10%)

Finance (18%)

Management failure (24%)

Loss of market (29%)

Source: D. DiNapoli and E. Fuhr, in Workouts & Turnarounds II, 1999

Figure 11.1 above, taken from a US survey, highlights management failure as the most common internal cause of business failure. Although the various internal and external reasons for corporate decline are dealt with separately in this chapter, in reality there is considerable interaction between them, with each exaggerating the impact of the others on a company's deteriorating performance. When the situation reaches a crisis, a number of these causes are likely to have played a role, albeit to a different degree.

Management weaknesses

Weaknesses in a company's management can arise from lack of experience or ability to discharge their responsibility. The problem becomes acute, however, when this is not recognised, or more usually, not acted upon even when the situation becomes apparent. Inability or lack of interest by the external stakeholders to exercise corporate governance, either directly or through their representatives in the Board of Directors is usually a reason for this. Such problems are particularly prevalent where a company is run by an autocratic Managing Director or Chief Executive Officer, without a team integrally involved in making important decisions. The larger and more complex a business's operations become the more impact management weaknesses have on its operations. Also, problems can persist longer with larger companies, with a greater crisis at the end.

Inadequate financial controls

Inadequate financial controls often tend to be a symptom of weak management. Access to reliable, timely and relevant information is a key raw material for management decision-making. Inadequate attention to this area risks incorrect decisions being taken. Access to information about the profitability of individual products or services, level and reasonableness of costs associated with a company's business processes, and the forecast financial position is essential if the company is to be managed effectively. The management of companies experiencing financial problems often does not have such information in a timely and useful format. Even when relevant information becomes available, no follow-up action is taken. Such problems are particularly acute when a company grows very quickly, either organically or through acquisitions.

Weaknesses in business operations

Companies experiencing weaknesses in their business operations often find themselves in crisis situations that are very difficult and time-consuming to address. A major problem in this area is a high cost structure compared to competitors. In the modern economic environment, this is likely to be as a result of a failure or inability to take advantage of technological advances and to reduce direct or indirect costs. Alternatively, competitors may be based in lower-cost locations, or have access to cheaper inputs. Low productivity, for example caused by an inefficient production process, or relatively high costs resulting from the nature of the company's supply chain, can also have an impact.

The other major weakness in this area that causes problems is ineffective marketing to customers. Very often companies, particularly those in traditional industries, tend to have a product or production bias, rather than a customer-focused business strategy. Given the rapid changes in market conditions today, constant development and redefining of products and services is required. Moreover, the company needs to ensure that it is meeting its customers' needs, making its customers aware of the benefits its products offer, and providing the range of supporting services that ensure they stay with the company. A company in crisis often finds that as its problems have increased, its marketing and sales functions have been the target of cost reductions, exacerbating the original weaknesses.

Weaknesses in corporate strategy

Failed corporate strategies are another major cause of company distress. There is considerable evidence that suggests that corporate acquisitions stand a high risk of failure. This is particularly the case for diversifications into unrelated business areas. Difficulties associated with post-acquisition integration are often underestimated. In addition, the complexity of controlling and managing the businesses is considerably enhanced as a company expands, both geographically and with respect to product and service markets. Overpaying for acquisitions, not unusual particularly in contested bidding situations, can cause severe financial strains.

Undertaking large capital investments can cause similar difficulties. Often capital requirements are underestimated, or cost overruns occur. Technical and other problems can cause start-up delays. Any new venture is risky, and matters such as inaccuracies in estimating the demand for new products and anticipating technology-related issues can cause companies difficulties. The failure of large, debt-financed projects is a very common cause of corporate distress.

Financial policy-related problems

Other business-related problems ultimately manifest themselves as weaknesses in a company's finances. These are often symptoms rather than causes.

The financial policy-related causes of a company's difficulties usually relate to excessive leverage, often resulting from the need to finance expansion by acquisitions. Companies may also have inappropriate financing strategies, for example with debt servicing obligations unmatched or unhedged against currency fluctuations.

Alternatively, the maturity profile of their financial obligations may be inconsistent with their cash generating ability. Also, the increasing world-wide trend in transactional banking causes complexities in financing arragements.

Other problems are caused by companies overtrading, with sales growing faster than can be financed from internally generated cash flow and working capital resources.

Operational control failures and fraud

Failures in a company's internal controls may occasionally have a significant impact on its survivability. Fraud is sometimes a major contributor to corporate distress. Its implications are particularly severe if it remains undetected for a long time. Inadequate attention to other major operational risks facing the company, such as exposure to environmental liability, or to regulatory risk, can also contribute to a company's problems.

External causes of corporate decline

The external causes of corporate decline tend to be market- or competition-related. Competition can be focused on price, normally in more mature markets or those with commoditised products. Alternatively, the emphasis of competition may be on the products or services, with participants in the market trying to meet customer needs more effectively. Companies falling behind in this process, for example through lack of market-focus, innovation or investment in technology, become vulnerable as competitors gain market share at their expense.

Also, the nature of a company's markets may change or, at an extreme, the market may completely disappear. An example of the former being the impact that the internet is having on the distribution channel of many products. Many companies in the distribution channels of various services, traditional travel agents being an example, will need to change their working methods completely to survive.

Sudden events, such as the failure of major suppliers or customers, can also trigger a crisis. Also, political, social and economic factors outside the control of the company can, at their most extreme, cause a company to fail. For example, an embargo on export of essential raw materials imposed by a supplier's government can potentially have a serious impact.

Although external events are, by our definition, beyond the control of a company's management, in practice a strong management team should be able to identify many of the external risks their company is exposed to, and make contingency plans, or take timely preventive action.

Symptoms of corporate decline

The causes of corporate problems manifest themselves in symptoms, many of which are discernible to outsiders. By themselves, each of these symptoms may not signal any major long-term problems in a company. However, any consistent trend showing the deterioration of a number of key indicators is usually a sign of an impending crisis.

Perhaps the most obvious indicator of a company's deteriorating competitiveness is a stalling or reversal in its volume of sales and profitability. These might indicate problems with the industry, or the company itself, depending on how a company's performance compares with its peers. For example, a declining market share is generally a signal of a company-specific difficulty. Also, vulnerabilities in productivity and margins are strong signals of business-related weaknesses. Problems in the business eventually impact on its finances. A worsening liquidity position, increasing debt levels, and general difficulties in meeting financial commitments are important indicators in this regard. Finally, these problems translate into wider governance and management difficulties, for example with increased turnover of staff and management (particularly in the finance function), adoption of less prudent accounting policies (often accompanied by a change in external auditors), and generally a more inward-looking management style.

Corporate failure prediction models

There are a number of models in use at present that seek to predict corporate distress. Most of them are quantitative in nature, aiming to identify signs of impending corporate failure from the trends and interaction between financial variables. Many of them, such as those used by the major international credit ratings agencies and international banks, tend to be proprietary models. They often build on other published academic work in this area.

One of the earliest such works was undertaken by Beaver in 1967.[2] His model is based on the notion that a firm's liquidity acts as a buffer against bankruptcy. After empirically testing a number of financial ratios, he found that a firm's cash flow to total debt ratio worked as a good predictor of corporate failure up to five years before the event.

Perhaps the best known bankruptcy failure model is that developed by Edward I. Altman in 1968.[3] He calculated 'Z-scores' for companies, based on adding the following ratios with different weightings:

$$Z = 1.2 \frac{\text{working capital}}{\text{total assets}} + 1.4 \frac{\text{retained earnings}}{\text{total assets}}$$

$$+ 3.3 \frac{\text{earnings before interest and tax}}{\text{total assets}} + 0.6 \frac{\text{market value of equity}}{\text{total liabilities}}$$

$$+ 1.0 \frac{\text{sales}}{\text{total assets}}$$

According to the model, Z-scores above 2.99 suggest that a company is healthy, whilst those below 1.81 indicate potential failure. Altman's model, however, suffers from a number of shortcomings. Its predictive ability decreases rapidly after about two years. Moreover, the appropriate weightings for the various ratios can change over time, between countries and for different industries.

In addition to those based on quantitative analysis, some corporate failure prediction models have also been developed that rely on qualitative data. One such example is that developed by Argenti in 1976.[4] His model looks at many of the underlying causes of corporate distress highlighted earlier in the chapter. It groups the indicators into:

- *Management defects*, such as autocratic Chief Executive, passive Board of Directors and lack of management depth.
- *Accounting defects*, for example, weaknesses in budgetary control and inadequate costing systems.
- *Mistakes*, such as excessive leverage, overtrading and large projects suffering problems.
- *Symptoms*, including Z-scores, creative accounting and high staff turnover.

Weighted scores are given to the various indicators, out of a total possible score of 100. Companies scoring below 25 are deemed likely to fail.

None of the corporate failure prediction models available at present are effective under all scenarios. They tend to be sensitive to the time horizon of data and various industrial, economic and other country-specific factors. As a result, their reliability is uncertain. Nevertheless, they can be very useful as part of a comprehensive early warning system for corporate distress, which also involves qualitative analysis in the other areas highlighted in the chapter.

Situation in developing and transition countries

State-owned enterprises in developing and transition countries suffer from a unique range of problems. Many years of government intervention to use such enterprises as tools for carrying out the government's economic policies have rendered their operations ill-equipped to operate in a market-based system. A lack of commercial orientation, combined with weaknesses in areas such as marketing, management information systems and quality control, contribute to their unprofitability. At the same time, these enterprises carry excessive debt, which has been taken on to fund losses, or uneconomic investments, over many years. More qualitative and market potential-oriented indicators are required to judge the future viability of such enterprises.

Achieving short-term operational stability

As highlighted elsewhere in this book, a company suffering financial distress usually finds itself engulfed in uncertainty. The priority in this situation is to gain a degree of stability in the company's operations so that its long-term potential can be ascertained, and an appropriate plan of action developed. The key to achieving stability is cash control. Cash needs to be conserved and a liquidity buffer created that enables the company to continue operating as normally as possible. Often this requires control over all cash payments, however small, to be centralised and only essential expenses to be approved. On a wider scale, a critical review of the company's expenditure plans needs to be undertaken to stop entering into any new non-essential commitments. If possible, existing commitments should be renegotiated.

There is often an associated need to improve the company's information systems to enable effective control over its liquid resources. As highlighted previously in this chapter, it is often weaknesses in such systems that lead to corporate crises. The initial focus should be on developing systems and processes that facilitate the monitoring and control of the cash position, ideally on a daily basis, throughout the entire group. Subsequently, the aim would be to establish information systems that enable accurate identification of matters such as product and business unit profitability, returns on capital and assets of various parts of the business, and trends in major financial indicators.

During this phase of a crisis, there is also a constant need to address urgent problems and emergencies. Resources need to be dedicated to handling these issues so that, for example, matters such as litigation are not left unaddressed and exacerbate the company's problems. Concurrently, the company's management should seek to establish communications with the major stakeholder groups to secure their support and develop a framework that will provide the basis for going forward.

Finally, it is clearly important that whilst the urgent issues relating to the crisis are being addressed, the business's day-to-day activities should continue. The crisis-related matters should be delegated to a specific team involving senior officers and, if necessary, operational responsibilities reassigned so that there are no gaps left in this area.

Components of enterprise restructuring

Assuming stability is achieved, a considered information gathering and assessment exercise can be carried out into the causes of the company's problems. The various options available to stakeholders to resolve the situation can then be identified. These matters are dealt with further in Chapter 13, but essentially, there are three broad strategies available:

- *Short-term exit*, involving action such as the liquidation, or the sale of the company or its business.
- *Medium-term holding strategies*, which are essentially short-term strategies carried out over a longer period, say of up to three years, involving some restructuring of the company to enhance its attractiveness or value.
- *Long-term strategies*, involving the restructuring of the businesses and assets of the company, complemented by a restructuring of its finances. In practice, this may also incorporate elements of the other two strategies.

Given the focus of this chapter on the long-term restructuring and turnaround of enterprises, this is dealt with below. As Figure 11.2 below illustrates, there are essentially three interdependent components of such strategies.

Organisational or project-related restructuring focuses on the efficiency and competitiveness of the individual business units of the company. A restructuring programme in this area would involve matters such as increasing the efficiency of the production process, reducing direct costs and overheads, strengthening the marketing function, and developing a more effective management information system. Corporate restructuring, on the other hand, will seek to realign the scope of the company's activities and businesses so that it is consistent with its financial and management capacity as well as the objectives of its key stakeholders. Activities such as business and asset disposals, mergers, joint ventures, and improvements in the group's organisational structure would be typical corporate restructuring activities.

Closely linked with a company's organisational and corporate restructuring is the need to restructure its finances. The financial restructuring would be agreed on the

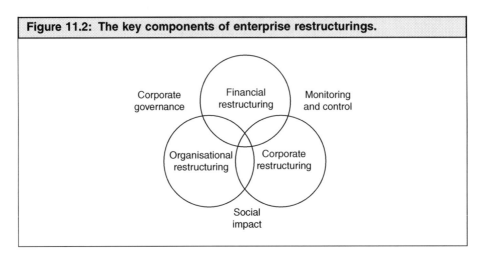

Figure 11.2: The key components of enterprise restructurings.

basis of the plans for a company's business and corporate restructuring; and its success will depend considerably on how effectively such plans are implemented. Elsewhere in this book, business restructuring has been used as a term intended to include both organisational and corporate restructuring.

Corporate governance and monitoring

From the lenders' perspective, the dependence of a company's financial restructuring on the success of its business restructuring requires a number of further issues to be addressed. Chief amongst these is a strengthening of the corporate governance of the organisation. In addition to implementing changes required in the composition and structure of the company's management team, this would involve improving the way such a team is incentivised and supervised. The strengthening of the non-executive membership of the company's Board of Directors, or the Supervisory Board where appropriate, is often required. In addition, lenders themselves may need to become more closely involved in the on-going governance of the company to ensure that the restructuring plan is delivered. For example, this could be through the lenders' steering committee or creditors' council where such structures exist, or as members of the company's Supervisory Board where this is permitted.

A key prerequisite for improved governance is the ability to monitor a company's performance during the turnaround period to ensure that it is meeting the objectives under its restructuring plan. In some countries, existing laws and regulations may not enable lenders to do so through more common governance structures. The financial restructuring agreement can be used to provide various powers to the lenders in this event.

Social and reputational consequences

A wider issue that might need to be considered by lenders, particularly in developing countries, is the social impact of any restructuring plan. There is usually considerable pressure to avoid, for example, employee lay-offs. This matter needs to be dealt with carefully as it can have wider repercussions on a bank's reputation and its business. Ultimately, unless an enterprise can be commercially viable, its prospects are likely to be limited, and failure to take timely action leads to a greater loss for the society as a whole. Nevertheless, the manner in which societal impact is dealt with needs to be considered in light of the cultural and political expectations in the country.

Sequencing restructuring activities

Typically in corporate distress situations, various restructuring options are considered after the stabilisation and information gathering phases. If appropriate, a business and financial restructuring plan is agreed after a period of negotiations. When implementing the terms of the agreement, the components of a typical restructuring highlighted earlier in the chapter are usually implemented in sequence. The objective of such sequencing is to take into account the financial, organisational and environmental constraints facing the company's stakeholders.

As Figure 11.3 below illustrates, the financial restructuring is typically the first step in the process. This has an immediate impact by providing for debt reduction, deferral of debt servicing obligations and any new financing made available as part of the agreement. In addition, the provisions of the financial restructuring may continue to have an on-going impact during the restructuring period through further variations in the financial structure of the company, for example by way of loan draw-downs, debt repayment, and changes in the interest rates charged.

Business restructuring is formally embarked upon as soon as the restructuring plan is agreed, although some activity in this area may be initiated earlier, as part of the stabilisation phase. Organisational and corporate restructuring are implemented in parallel, and both can be broadly divided into two sequential phases. The period required to complete each type of business restructuring, or the timing of the phases, may vary considerably depending on the situation, although organisational restructuring generally takes longer.

Short-term action

In the short-term, a key priority is to address any need to strengthen the company's management team, both at the head office and, where relevant, the business unit

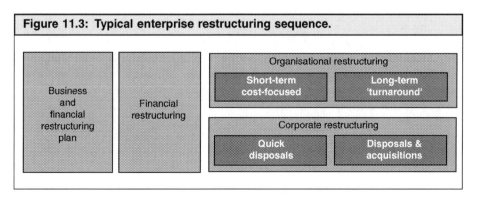

Figure 11.3: Typical enterprise restructuring sequence.

level. The focus of organisational restructuring during this phase is usually on cost reduction and efficiency enhancement. This includes matters such as the reduction of surplus staff and other overhead expenses, rationalisation of the company's product range to eliminate unprofitable lines, improving purchasing systems, strengthening the management information and control systems, and further improving working capital and cash flow management. The emphasis in corporate restructuring is on closing unprofitable subsidiaries and implementing planned disposals that are relatively easy to realise, such as standalone, profitable and non-core businesses that are attractive to buyers. The organisational and management structure of the business would also be redesigned to enhance effective management.

Long-term restructuring and turnaround

To the extent that the first phase of organisational restructuring lays the foundations for a turnaround in a company's performance, the next phase builds on it. After having increased the efficiency of the business's operations through a mostly reductive process, the focus of organisational restructuring now is on growth. Thus, emphasis is placed on increased marketing, the introduction of new products consistent with the new turnaround strategy, and investment in new plant or technology. The company may also start hiring staff with the new skills that it now requires. Corporate restructuring will see the more difficult disposals being carried out in this phase, if necessary after some action has been taken to improve their attractiveness to potential buyers. The company may also start making some 'bolt-on' acquisitions to strengthen parts of its operations. Ultimately, this period might see the sale or the merger of the company with a stronger partner. Also, new growth-oriented management skills may be required as the company leaves its 'workout' mode.

Interaction between business restructuring and loan workouts

As highlighted previously, there is considerable interdependence between a company's business and financial restructuring. The former is often heavily influenced by the needs of lenders. At the start of the restructuring process, there is pressure on a company to reduce its indebtedness and conserve cash to reduce its lenders' exposure. This is reflected in the need for quick disposals and elimination of cash draining activities, even though some of this action may be inconsistent with the long-term interests of the company's shareholders. Similarly, investment in new technology and substantive spending in areas such as marketing can only start at a later stage in the process once the company has generated cash either internally, or through disposals. Lenders are generally reluctant to provide new finance for these activities in such risky situations. Also, there is usually little incentive for shareholders to do so, as much of the benefit of such investments is likely to accrue to lenders.

[1] D. DiNapoli and E. Fuhr, Trouble spotting: Assessing the likelihood of a turnaround, in D. DiNapoli (ed.), *Workouts & Turnarounds II: Global Restructuring Strategies for the Next Century*, Wiley, New York, 1999, p. 7.

[2] W. Beaver, Financial ratios as predictors of failures, *Journal of Accounting Research 4* (suppl.), 1967, 71–111.

[3] E. I. Altman, Financial ratios, discriminant analysis and the prediction of corporate bankruptcy, *Journal of Finance 23*, 1968, 189–201.

[4] J. Argenti, *Corporate Collapse: The Causes and Symptoms*, McGraw-Hill, London, 1976.

12

THE INFORMATION GATHERING AND REVIEW PROCESS

Introduction

To resolve a company's problems successfully by undertaking business and financial restructuring, such problems must, by definition, be identified correctly. Problems should not be confused with symptoms. The key problems underlying the symptoms of financial crisis can only be identified after a thorough, diligent and methodical investigation has been conducted into the company's business and financial affairs. Of all the steps highlighted in our loan workouts framework, this is definitely the most critical. The information gathering exercise should also be extended from identifying problems to collating data that will be the basis of developing a solution.

The key objectives, steps and outputs of the information gathering and review process are highlighted in this chapter. The importance of first collating information available within the bank is stressed, which enables a more focused action plan to be produced for the subsequent stages. The wide range of business, accounting and financial information needed to formulate a financial restructuring proposal is outlined, along with how the information gathering process needs to be broken down into a number of stages to meet interim objectives. Finally, the legal and other specialist information needs are presented.

Initial internal appraisal

The information gathering process begins within the bank. The importance of separating a bank's loan workout activities from its client relationship and credit functions has been highlighted previously. However, for this separation to work effectively, it is critical that as much of the information and knowledge about the client held within the bank is transferred to the loan workout transaction team at the beginning of the process. Gathering information about the company and the history of the client's relationship with the bank in the first instance enables the workout team to:

- Minimise diverting the management's attention away from the company's affairs to providing information already available from internal bank resources.
- Access information and opinions from officers that are not necessarily formally recorded in the bank's files.
- Plan subsequent activities on a more focused basis.
- Approach the transaction and the client professionally and confidently on an informed basis.

Tapping the tacit knowledge of bank officers who have dealt with the company previously can be invaluable. Personal comments often provide more insight than official documents. Thus, the assimilation of information recorded in the client's files should be reinforced with interviews with relevant personnel, although at the initial stage it is important to reserve judgement about opinions that might be expressed in the course of such discussions.

At the end of this internal information review phase, the transaction team should have made all reasonable efforts to gather all the information and knowledge about the company available within the bank. This phase needs to be carried out relatively rapidly as there is considerable pressure on the team to start taking action. It is unlikely that the team will be able to gather all the information it needs, or that all the data gathered will be up to date. The important principle is to gather as much information as practically possible from within the organisation before looking outside.

Information gathered at this stage will include:

About the company

- The company's activities and the markets it serves, including its principal competitors.
- Recent corporate history and principal events affecting the company.
- Recent financial information and status reports.
- Management team profiles and, more importantly, the bank's relationship and credit officers' opinions of the members of the management team.
- Causes underlying the company's current difficulties.
- Group legal structure—this is particularly important for diversified companies with many subsidiaries.
- Details of loans and security and other actual and contingent liabilities, including those legal entities within a group which are formally liable.

About the company's relationship with the bank

- History of the bank's relationship with the company, including recent developments.
- Breakdown of the bank's actual and contingent exposure to the company, and the level of provisioning already made against the exposure.

- Opinions of the bank's relationship and credit officers on the client generally and their views on possible solutions.
- Likely attitude of other principal parties, such as major shareholders, other banks, major creditors, management and employees.
- Legal and other documentation relating to loans, guarantees and security from the client, including internal bank decisions and approvals.
- Other information which may be pertinent to the particular case.

One useful tool at this stage is a checklist for preliminary information that would provide a guide to ensure all possible areas have been covered. Checklists have certain drawbacks, for instance relevant items not included could be missed from reviews. On balance, however, they are usually helpful, particularly if some members of the transaction team are not very experienced. The team leader should in any event tailor the checklist to the individual case.

The transaction team should prepare a plan of action on the basis of the initial review of internal information. The preliminary action plan is mainly intended to assist in co-ordinating the team's administrative work during the 'set-up' phase of the transaction, and would cover activities such as:

- Requesting missing information or documents from other parts of the bank.
- Arranging meeting(s) with the company.
- Arranging separate or all-bank and creditor meeting(s).
- Preparing a shortlist of potential reporting accountants and other advisors.
- Commissioning legal reviews on matters affecting the bank in particular.
- Achieving short-term stability. This would involve setting a time frame for the initial phase and action required to ensure the company's survival during that period.

Action lists, with activities, deadlines and responsibilities are a particularly valuable tool in workout transactions. They help the team leader co-ordinate the team's activities. Each participant involved in the transaction knows what is expected of them and the deadlines they need to meet. They are also useful communication tools and they help inject urgency and momentum by focusing on deadlines. Perhaps more importantly, updating them periodically requires the team to step back and measure the achievements of the transaction, revisit the planned and new activities that are required, and identify new bottlenecks and constraints. Either the transaction team or its advisors should regularly circulate appropriate action lists to all relevant internal and external participants in the loan workout. The recipients, in turn, should promptly inform the bank transaction team of any developments, such as slippage in the timetable.

Obtaining information externally

Information available within the bank will not be complete or current. This will need to be supplemented by more up to date information about the company's business, its financial condition, and the position of the other financial stakeholders. Much of this information will come from the company.

The information necessary to develop a loan workout proposal can be broadly grouped under the following categories:

- That relating to the company's business operations, its markets and their prospects.
- Historic, current and prospective financial information.
- Information relating to legal matters.
- Information about the company's indebtedness.
- More specialised data, usually to support information gathered under the first four groupings. This might include the valuation of assets, or about the technology employed by the company.

A breakdown of the company's borrowings with respect to its various subsidiaries and the facility providers is a key input in developing a financial restructuring proposal. The nature of information required in this area is dealt with in Chapter 21.

For the purposes of this chapter it is assumed that independent reporting accountants perform the task of gathering business and financial information about the company, and independent legal advisors carry out a legal due diligence investigation. Of course, the nature of the information required will be similar, irrespective of whether independent advisors are engaged to carry out the task. However, allowances would need to be made for the reliability of information provided by the company that has not been independently verified.

The information gathering stage itself will most likely be broken down into a number of steps, where the focus gradually shifts from short-term to longer-term issues. The steps taken and the number of reports to be prepared by the advisors will depend upon the circumstances of the company and the magnitude of its problems. Reporting accountants are normally required to prepare a number of reports. On the other hand, legal advisors usually prepare only one.

Reports of reporting accountants

Reporting accountants' reports can be broadly categorised into one or more preliminary reports and a full report. In some large or time-critical transactions, the preliminary report can be sub-categorised into 'quick and dirty' reviews and preliminary status reports. Figure 12.1 highlights the sequence of reports typically produced by reporting accountants.

The nature and contents of the reporting accountants' reports will be governed by their terms of reference. This will be drafted by the co-ordinating bank's transaction team on the basis of the information gathered in the course of the initial internal information review, and after preliminary discussions with the company's management. The terms of reference are likely to be more focused the more confident the transaction team is of the nature of underlying problems, or the shorter the time is available. Hence, the advantages of breaking the information gathering stage down into smaller segments. This enables the necessary information to be gathered about whether to expand and extend the exercise to investigate the company's problems and possible solutions.

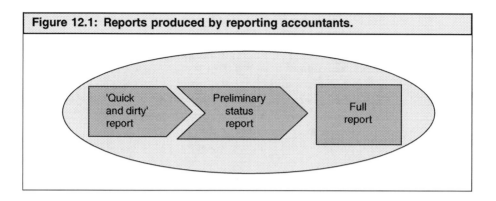

Figure 12.1: Reports produced by reporting accountants.

The 'quick and dirty' report

Often banks and companies react to a financial crisis only after the position becomes highly unstable. The company critically needs cash and, more importantly, needs to demonstrate some measure of financial support to the outside world. However, invariably in such situations, reliable financial information about the company is lacking. In such cases it would be imprudent for banks to advance further funds without adequate investigation.

The banks, and usually the co-ordinating bank if a group of banks is involved, must try and stabilise the company's position in the short-term so that an investigation can be carried out. At a minimum, this will involve continuing the existing exposures to the company. In cases where the position is absolutely critical, the bank and the company should consider calling a meeting of key financial creditors immediately with a view to agreeing a short-term moratorium.

The moratorium, or standstill, would be designed to allow time for the reporting accountants to undertake a very quick review (commonly referred to as a 'quick and dirty' report), which should take no more than a few days. This review will typically assess the extent and nature of the company's immediate problems and whether any value can be salvaged. If so, the extent of the company's immediate cash needs and availability of collateral to support an advance by one or more banks would be estimated.

The preliminary status report

If the company's position has not reached a critical stage, or its financial position has been stabilised temporarily, then the reporting accountant is instructed to prepare a report on the status of the company. This preliminary status report, also known as the 'due diligence report', is intended to cover items of fact. It will involve investigating, reviewing and commenting on the company's existing position and the circumstances leading to its current difficulties. It is effectively a financial, accounting and legal review of the firm. There is likely to be little value in commissioning advisors to prepare detailed reports on the prospects for the company and its markets before receiving the findings of the preliminary status report.

The focus of the reporting accountants at this stage will be on the current state of financial affairs of the company. This will involve carrying out a due diligence investigation on the company's financial records and preparing a full and accurate statement of its financial position as at the most recent accounting quarter end. It may also include a review of the latest year-end statutory accounts prepared by the company. One of the key areas of emphasis of the review is to ensure that all its liabilities, whether actual or contingent, are accurately accounted for. This will be reinforced by legal and other specialist audits, as necessary.

A preliminary estimate of the recoveries of the various creditors of the company in the event of its liquidation is an important requirement at this stage. Expected losses on liquidation are an important consideration for lenders when deciding whether to provide further support to the company.

Other areas covered in the preliminary report include a review of the company's current areas of activity, its operations, its organisational structure and the adequacy and reliability of its reporting systems. Also included is an assessment of the quality of the management team, and the extent to which management weakness may have contributed to the company's difficulties. The objective is to identify the company's principal operational weaknesses and the underlying business-related causes of its financial difficulties.

In groups involving a large number of subsidiaries, with relationships with a range of lenders, the scope of the reporting accountants' task will be considerably widened. The financial performance and balance sheet for each of the subsidiaries will require analysis. Additionally the recovery position of each lender, with respect to each borrowing entity, will be estimated.

The reporting accountants should also be able to provide a preliminary indication of the options open to the banks at this stage. It is generally in the management's interests to retain control over the company and pursue a restructuring, whereas it may become apparent at an early stage that a trade sale of the business is the best option for the company's creditors and, possibly, also its shareholders. An early identification of options will enable the banks to start proactively pursuing their preferred options without, at this stage, excluding other alternatives.

Following up on the preliminary status report

Once the preliminary status report has been issued, all the relevant parties need to reach agreement about its conclusions. Generally, the company's management should be given the opportunity to review and comment on its findings, but disagreements often remain about the nature and, more frequently, the extent of the company's problems. The more that differences are narrowed at this stage, the easier it will be to implement the subsequent stages of the restructuring.

The banks will next need to evaluate whether or not it is realistic to attempt a business and financial restructuring. Assuming that the company's management, shareholders and lenders agree to co-operate, they will need to agree the broad approach to tackle the problems, and the way forward. At this point the banks will need to make an important decision. Do they believe that the existing management is capable of implementing the required turnaround strategy? If not, then it is vital to explore alternative ways in which the necessary changes can be made.

The other key task at this stage is to agree between the company, the co-ordinating bank and other key financial creditors if appropriate, what the main objectives of any restructuring programme should be. Different creditors and other interest groups are likely to have different, often conflicting objectives. Although ideally detailed negotiations should not start at this stage, it is useful if the firm's business plan can be formulated with knowledge of such objectives.

The co-ordinator will usually assume responsibility for communicating the transaction strategy to the other banks and financial creditors and for securing their continued support. If a broad agreement has been reached to explore further the options for a financial restructuring, the moratorium would be extended to ensure that the exercise can take place in a stable environment.

The next stage requires the company's management team to prepare a detailed business plan to deliver a turnaround of the business. This needs to incorporate specific actions and a timetable to address the problems identified in the preliminary status report, and the restructuring objectives agreed between the participants. It is critical for the chosen company management, rather than a third party, to prepare the business plan. It is highly unlikely that a management team that does not have ownership of the business plan will be committed to implementing it. The co-ordinating bank will be closely involved in on-going discussions with the company's management as the business plan is developed.

The full report

The reporting accountants' full report typically has two key objectives.

Firstly, it is required to assess independently the company's industry and markets, as well as its prospects and its positioning within them. Based on this and on the strengths and weaknesses of the company identified at the preliminary status report stage, the report needs to present the range of possible options to meet the banks' objectives.

Secondly, it needs to include a review of the company's business plan and assess its achievability in light of the reporting accountants' knowledge of the financial and non-financial resources available to the company, the ability of its management team, and the prospects of the relevant markets. The critical input in this area is the advisors' ability to look at financial projections and identify the areas in which there are 'vulnerabilities'. Such vulnerabilities may be present where assumptions used by the management are optimistic (for instance, the growth rate of its markets) or where financial (a lack of working capital) or operational (inadequate distribution network) constraints have been underestimated. The key objectives of this part of the exercise are to present a 'worst case scenario' for the banks and to assess the likelihood of achieving the management's projected results.

The reporting accountants' full report will also incorporate the results of the work of other experts, for instance the banks' lawyers, property valuers and technical specialists. The contents of the report will include:

- Analysis of the principal problems facing the company.
- Comments on the business plan and its vulnerabilities.
- Review of the restructuring options available, including the strengths and drawbacks of each option.
- Financial outcome and risk:reward ratios associated with each option.
- Recommended course of action and arguments for pursuing it.
- Key information which they have taken into account in arriving at their views.

Where banks, or groups of banks have varying recovery positions and are likely to fare differently under different scenarios, such information must also be presented transparently in the final report. An independent 'dividend model' which simulates the distribution that would accrue to each creditor under different liquidation scenarios, would be prepared for this purpose.

Ultimately the decision on whether to pursue a restructuring or an alternative course of action usually rests with the company's bankers. An experienced reporting accountant should be able to identify the critical areas that are most relevant to forming a robust decision, and to bring all relevant information and independent expert opinion to the bankers' attention.

For a large company with many areas of operation, the final report may take some time to complete. There needs to be constant communication between the co-ordinating bank and the reporting accountant so that any relevant information is brought to the bank's attention immediately and prompt action taken. Weekly update meetings with all advisors are very valuable in this regard. There should be no material information in the final report which causes a surprise to either the co-ordinator or the company.

Other advisors' reports

The conclusions from other specialist advisors' work would normally be included as part of the reporting accountants' report. It is important therefore that the work of the various independent advisors is co-ordinated with that of the reporting accountants.

Of the other independent advisors involved in the information gathering phase, the lawyers play a particularly important role. They undertake a legal audit of the company's affairs, which includes reviews of:

- Legal titles of assets belonging to the company.
- Terms of major contracts.
- The group's legal corporate structure.
- Litigations in progress.
- Contingent liabilities, and the banks' security.

13

EXPLORING LOAN WORKOUT OPTIONS

Introduction

One of the most critical shortcomings of many loan workout transactions is their failure to explore alternative solutions adequately. Various pressures, predominantly those arising from the need to conclude the transaction quickly, or from a lack of preparatory information, contribute to a bias towards developing a quick solution. Additionally, a lack of preparatory work by the lenders often results in them simply reacting to proposals presented by the company.

It follows that it is critical that the transaction team working for the banks proactively explores the various business and financial restructuring options available to meet their preferred restructuring objectives. This will enable them to react constructively to the company's proposals, or present considered counter-proposals. This chapter groups the various restructuring options together, outlines their features, and explores issues relating to their implementation.

Review of debt workout options from the lenders' perspective

Financial restructuring options are numerous, ranging from basic debt reduction strategies involving, for instance, asset disposals, to more sophisticated tools such as debt for equity swaps. Such techniques can be broadly categorised into:

- *Short-term (immediate) solutions*, involving a quick exit for the banks, either through a sale of the business or its assets, or through other routes.
- *Medium-term solutions*, which are usually applied in situations where a short-term solution is desirable, but a more controlled exit is expected to maximise value.

- *Long-term solutions* involving reorganising a company's finances, accompanied by a restructuring of its underlying business.

Information from the reporting accountants' preliminary report should enable lenders to start exploring which of these options, or combination of options, should be pursued. With larger loan workouts, it is common to adopt a combination of short-, medium- and long-term options to develop a financial restructuring 'package'. For instance, the restructuring may involve the disposal of part of a business, raising cash from shareholders (both short-term solutions), earmarking property for disposal when the property market improves (medium-term), and rescheduling of the company's debt (long-term). The aim of the exercise is to meet the objectives agreed by the participants in the restructuring, given the internal and external constraints faced by the company.

In addition to the transaction-specific issues, a bank's choice of restructuring options may be influenced by its debt portfolio-related strategy. For example, a bank seeking to reduce its activities in a particular sector or country will have a bias toward short-term strategies for problem loans arising in these areas. Resources available within the bank to deal with problem loans will be another consideration.

Short-term 'exit' strategies

Short-term exit strategies are generally appropriate where:

- The returns achieved by the banks thereby are expected to be higher than those available through pursuing longer-term strategies. Or
- Although higher returns may potentially be achieved by implementing longer-term strategies, the marginal increase in return does not adequately compensate lenders for the accompanying increased risks and their cost of carry.

Figure 13.1 below highlights some of the more common short-term financial restructuring strategies.

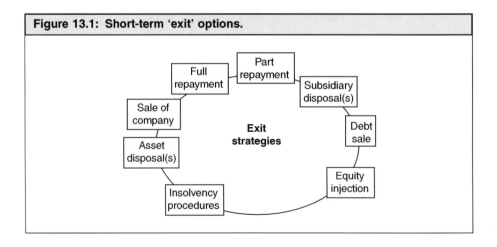

Figure 13.1: Short-term 'exit' options.

Repayment

Immediate repayment of loans, either fully or in part, is rare in loan workouts. However, it may be possible for the bank or the company to persuade another party, say an existing or new shareholder, or indeed another lender, to fund a loan repayment. A full repayment is likely in situations where a particular bank has a relatively small exposure to a company. It is more likely, however, that a part-repayment of a loan may be negotiated, either as a component of a wider restructuring solution, or because a bank simply wishes to exit and the proportion of loan thereby recovered is deemed to reflect the bank's estimate of likely recovery.

Sale of the company

One of the most effective routes of immediate exit is to persuade the company's management and shareholders to sell the entire business immediately. If the business is disposed of without any debt, the proceeds received can be used to repay the banks, fully or in part, depending on the value achieved. Alternatively, the business may be taken over by another party, including its debt. In such instances, the banks would need to be satisfied about the credit standing of the enlarged group after the takeover. Potential buyers may seak to negotiate concessions from the banks, either in the form of reschedulings or debt write-downs, at the time of such takeovers.

There is often a choice between selling an entire company, or parts of it, by way of asset sales or the sale of shares in the parent company or its subsidiaries. Various legal, tax and accounting considerations affect the ultimate decision, and these should be considered by the banks in the light of professional advice. One of the particular advantages of selling a business as a sale of its assets (including any trademarks owned by the company) is often that banks are not required to give warranties against the company's contingent liabilities, which is often the case for the sale of a business.

Debt sales

The sale of debt is another short-term option. In countries with liquid markets in corporate debt, this can be a relatively straightforward exercise. Nevertheless the market for distressed debt is often thin and narrow. In some countries, debt sales require preparing and publicising information about the company and very careful control of the disposal process. Debt sales also require various legal, regulatory and taxation provisions to be in place. Moreover, they are also dependent on the prevailing banking and relationship culture. They may not therefore be a practical option in all jurisdictions.

Insolvency

The commencement of insolvency procedures is another short-term option. Very often, liquidation or bankruptcy is perceived by workout departments as a sign of failure. This is not necessarily so, particularly for businesses without any commercial viability. In such situations, the commencement of legal recovery procedures is the only option consistent with the bank's objective of maximising returns. Insolvency procedures can, however, be susceptible to various shortcomings and may not be a practical solution in all countries, particularly for marginal cases.

There is usually strong resistance from the company's management or shareholders to the types of short-term strategies highlighted above, primarily because they usually have most to lose. Provided the banks' approach is formulated after the assessment of full and, so far as possible, accurate information, banks should move decisively. Short-term strategies are inherently risky as they may not be achievable within the required timescale, or realise the target values. The need for appropriate contingency plans is therefore critical. It is important to establish and impose strict deadlines for the preferred and fall-back options. In addition, the banks may have to take a proactive role in searching for buyers of assets or the business, given possible lack of management support for that option.

In pursuing short-term exit strategies, banks may occasionally be required to accept the consideration in the form of instalments. In other cases, they may need to continue extending credit, or even advance new credit to the buyer. Unless the buyer offers full recourse to his assets and he has a strong credit standing, any such arrangement is not an exit. It is essentially a deferral of the problem. In the absence of immediate cash payments, bank guarantees should be insisted on from the purchaser. As a last resort, a full charge on the assets being sold should be retained until the final payment is received.

Medium-term 'controlled exit' strategies

Medium-term loan workout strategies are essentially the same as the short-term exit strategies discussed previously, but implemented in a controlled manner over a period of time. Broadly, medium-term strategies are executed over a period of, say, one to three years. These are predominantly undertaken to overcome any anticipated difficulties in executing an exit strategy within a very short time. Occasionally, reschedulings or restructuring programmes may be implemented over the medium-term as the preferred option. This is particularly appropriate if a company's difficulties are not serious.

A controlled exit is appropriate where the advantages of deferring an exit outweigh the potential risks associated with continuing to support a company over an extended period.

Advantages

The principal advantage of a medium-term strategy is that it presents a better prospect of realising the optimum values of the assets or businesses of a company. The time available could be used to make the asset or business more attractive to potential purchasers. For instance, if it is proposed that an operating unit within a company is to be sold, legal and organisational changes can be implemented to make it more autonomous. Cost reduction strategies, such as reducing staff levels, can also be implemented over this period. Another situation where controlled disposal strategies could be pursued is where the prevailing market for such assets or businesses is depressed and an upturn in the market is anticipated. However, probably the most common reason for pursuing a medium-term strategy is that it enables the seller to avoid conducting a disposal on a 'fire sale' basis. This is particularly relevant where the selling company is in a weak negotiating position, which is often the case as a result of publicity of the company's difficulties.

Disadvantages

The principal drawback associated with controlled exit strategies is the risk that the banks' position may worsen over the holding period. This can result from a number of factors, including:

- The value of the assets earmarked for disposal may in fact fall over the holding period.
- The position of the business being sold may weaken; in any event, it may be incurring losses throughout the period.
- There is a risk of leakage of cash or other assets from the company.
- Banks may have to provide additional funds to ensure the company can survive and operate in the holding period.
- The costs of holding and administering a difficult credit, in terms of staff resources and cost of carry, can turn out to be higher than anticipated.

It is impossible to evaluate scientifically at the outset the magnitude of holding risks involved in a medium-term strategy. The importance of information about the company's industry and market prospects, and the bankers' confidence in the company's management to pursue an agreed strategy, are critical in these situations. The risks involved in controlled disposal strategies are often underestimated by banks. As a result, the advantages of better price achievability tend to be overstated.

The risks associated with holding strategies are particularly high in the case of trading businesses, where confidence needs to be maintained in the company, often at the cost of the banks funding losses. Debt for equity swaps are sometimes used in controlled disposals of trading companies as they enhance stability by improving their balance sheets. A medium-term strategy is usually more appropriate for asset-based businesses, such as property companies, provided the market for such investments is not expected to worsen over the holding period. In addition to holding risk, other risks more often associated with long-term restructurings may apply in these situations. Such risks are explored later in Chapter 14.

If a medium-term strategy is to be pursued, the banks must take steps to minimise the risk of loss at the outset. This will involve very close monitoring of the company's performance, cash flow and asset positions, which can sometimes be on a weekly or fortnightly basis. The banks should require frequent meetings with the company's management, as well as site visits, to ensure that the banks' position is safeguarded. The progress of, for instance, the preparation for planned disposals must be regularly compared with the pre-agreed timetable and appropriate action taken in the event of slippage. Contingency plans must also be prepared at the outset and implemented if the preferred strategy fails.

Long-term 'financial restructuring' strategies

Long-term restructurings usually have a horizon of between three and five years, although the term may be extended for exceptional cases. Short- and medium-term strategies principally rely on recovery through lump sum repayments from disposals of assets or businesses. These strategies are most appropriate where the banks believe that a company cannot service a substantial proportion of its debt. A prerequisite for a long-term strategy, on the other hand, is confidence that a company's debt is ultimately capable of being serviced in whole, or in part, on a sustainable basis from a company's business activities. Therefore, the crucial difference between a long-term strategy and short- and medium-term ones is that the company involved must be at least potentially commercially viable and creditworthy. Connected to this is the confidence that lenders can place in the company's management.

The principal objective of a long-term financial restructuring is to support a company's turnaround strategy by providing a capital structure which is sustainable, whilst meeting any immediate objectives of the company's stakeholders. A sustainable capital structure can be achieved by implementing a combination of financial and operating changes. These usually involve reorganising the profile of a company's debt servicing obligations, supported by actions to reduce the overall debt burden to sustainable levels. As Figure 13.2 shows, a wide range of long-term restructuring options are available.

Debt or interest reschedulings form the core of long-term financial restructurings. This is to be expected because it is usually a company's inability to support its immediate debt servicing obligations that necessitates the financial restructuring in the first instance. In addition, a company in financial distress inevitably suffers from liquidity problems and banks are normally required to lend new money as part of a restructuring agreement.

It is rare that simply restructuring a company's existing debt and providing new loans will solve a company's financial difficulties over the longer-term. Supporting action is often required, usually to reduce the company's debt level to a more sustainable level.

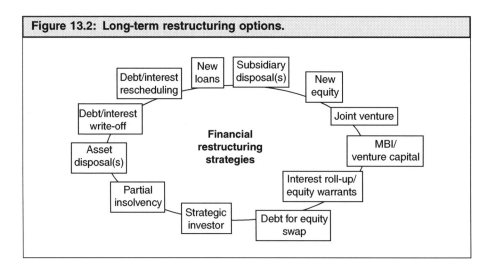

Figure 13.2: Long-term restructuring options.

Inevitably, these require action to raise cash in the short- to medium-term, requiring strategies that have been explored earlier in this chapter.

An important point in respect of implementing short- and medium-term strategies as part of a longer-term strategy is that in addition to raising cash, they must also be consistent with the company's long-term future. For instance, highly cash generative businesses or assets may not be appropriate for disposal as part of a long-term restructuring, as they could impair the company's ability to service debt. Also, activities that are perceived as key to a company's long-term business strategy may need to be retained, even if an attractive price were achievable immediately.

One of the other key techniques for reducing debt to sustainable levels is debt for equity swaps. Such transactions are considered in detail later in the book.

The risks associated with long-term restructurings are explored in detail in the next chapter.

14

EVALUATING
RESTRUCTURING
OPTIONS AND
DEVELOPING
PROPOSALS

Introduction

Potentially, a large number of options are available to restructure a company in financial distress. In practice, various constraints rapidly narrow down the range of feasible alternatives. Once the various options are packaged to develop alternative proposals that meet the restructuring objectives, two important questions arise:

- How do we know that the restructuring will improve the lenders' position, compared with, say, commencing insolvency procedures?
- When two or more different courses of action are possible, which should be preferred?

The process of developing restructuring objectives will have identified the financial and non-financial needs of the banks. Assuming this has been the case, the criteria for making choices can be narrowed down to the risk and return characteristics of the proposed restructurings. Evaluation in this context relates to estimating the potential returns from the transaction, assessing its risks, and considering whether the returns adequately compensate the banks for undertaking the risks.

Different types of financial restructuring-related risk are explored in this chapter. The principal components of returns are also highlighted, although this matter is treated in greater detail in Chapter 25, in the context of debt for equity swap transactions. Some tools for evaluating restructuring options are presented. Finally, issues relating to developing restructuring proposals are outlined.

Types of risk in a loan workout

Although significant advances have been made in assessing and modelling the various types of financial risk, the exercise remains relatively subjective. Assessing risk in a financial restructuring essentially involves three steps:

- Identifying the various sources of risk associated with the transaction.
- Estimating the level of risk associated with each of these sources.
- Judging the impact of the interaction of the different types of risk in the restructuring.

In a complex financial restructuring it is the first step: identifying the different sources of risk, which is the most important. It is also the least difficult component of the exercise. A thorough information gathering and review process, combined with the experience of a strong transaction team and its advisors, should enable at least all the principal risk areas to be identified.

For the purposes of this book, the principal sources of risk in a loan workout transaction are categorised into:

- Business risk.
- Financial risk.
- Structural risk.
- Reputational risk.

Apart from perhaps some elements of financial risk, many of the uncertainties associated with long-term restructurings are qualitative in nature. As a result, assessing the level of risk involved is essentially a judgemental exercise. A more accurate assessment of risk may be achieved by disaggregating each of the risk categories into sub-components, and seeking to identify the degree of vulnerability each is subject to. This exercise has the added benefit of encouraging a more analytical exploration of all the aspects of the transaction, and can often yield new ideas for possible solutions. Where risks are identified, the transaction will be structured to mitigate them so far as possible.

Each of the risk categories is explored in detail below.

Business risk

Business risk relates to the trading of the enterprise. It is essentially concerned with the uncertainty relating to the company being able to recover from its current operational problems. The key to identifying business risks is a detailed due diligence investigation that encompasses both the internal and external environments of the company.

When seeking to identify the business risks associated with a financial restructuring, banks will ask some of the following questions:

- Is there a strong core business?
- What are the current and forecast market and industry conditions going to be like?
- What is the uncertainty attached to future operating earnings and cash flow projections?

- Is a large turnaround in operating performance anticipated or required?
- How long is the turnaround expected to take? The longer the period, the more uncertainty is attached to the outcome.
- Are the products and technology of the company likely to be sustainable?
- Are there a large number of subsidiaries operating in different markets?
- What is the quality of the company's management, controls and information systems?
- Will (new) management deliver?
- How dependent is the company's turnaround on improvements in its markets and the general economy?
- What has been the period of difficulty to date and how serious has any associated adverse publicity been? Is there a risk that the damage caused by prolonged difficulties could be irreparable?
- Are there potential environmental liabilities involved?

Financial risk

Financial risk relates to the company's current and projected financial position. It essentially concerns the robustness of the company's post-restructuring financial structure, and the potential areas of financial vulnerability. For banks, this is usually the greatest area of concern. Assessing financial risk falls within the core expertise of most professionals involved in loan workouts; it is therefore often the main area of focus. There are two major associated drawbacks. Firstly, inadequate attention is devoted to the other categories of risk, which for some transactions can be considerable. Secondly, familiarity with assessing financial risks in normal credit evaluation processes can lead to a false sense of confidence. The difficulties and complexities involved in a loan workout can be underestimated. The exercise of assessing financial risk should therefore be conducted in the context of the diversity and greater magnitude of risk involved in a loan workout.

The following questions will help in targeting the key sources of financial risk in a loan workout transaction:

- What is the amount of new money likely to be needed over the workout period? The more this is, the greater is the potential additional loss arising from an unsuccessful restructuring.
- How stable are the group's financial arrangements?
- How high is the risk of cash leakages?
- What is the maturity profile of the restructured debt?
- What are the magnitude, frequency and probability of vulnerabilities identified in the projections by the reporting accountants?
- How much vulnerability do the post-restructuring gearing, projected facility headrooms and other financial indicators indicate?
- What is the extent to which the banks would be worse-off if liquidation occurred post-restructuring (rather than now)?

Structural risk

Structural risk is associated with the transaction and the non-financial terms agreed as part of the loan workout. These risks revolve around the possibilities of the restructuring agreement collapsing, and consequently the anticipated returns to the creditors not materialising.

Structural risks are associated with factors such as:

- How much time is available to complete the transaction? Complex transactions involving protracted negotiations and subject to numerous legal and regulatory formalities may take a considerable time to complete. In the interim, the company could run out of money.
- How achievable is the envisaged exit? Are the financial projections and the banks' exit dependent on interim asset or business disposals being achieved, within a restricted time scale?
- How long is the proposed workout period? A short one may not allow sufficient time for a full turnaround. Conversely, a very long workout period also indicates riskiness as uncertainties increase with time.
- What is the attitude of the bank group? Is it likely to continue to be supportive throughout the workout period, particularly if more finance is required?
- How supportive is the legal framework in the country?
- Does the financial restructuring need to comply with the requirements and formalities of a number of jurisdictions?
- How homogeneous is the lender group? The wider the divergence of interests, the greater the risk of the transaction collapsing.

Reputational risk

Reputational risk arises from being involved in a situation that may receive negative publicity or otherwise be detrimental to the banks' reputation. In fact, reputational risk may more frequently be associated with not pursuing a restructuring, and instead favouring insolvency procedures. This type of risk varies considerably between countries, and much depends on the commercial culture and society's expectations about the role of banks, or other groups of lenders.

Typical issues are:

- What is likely to be the impact of any publicity generated by the banks opting for insolvency, rather than a financial restructuring?
- What are the reputational considerations involved in the banks becoming major shareholders in the company pursuant to, say, a debt for equity swap transaction?
- What are the possibilities of legal or regulatory breaches from participating in the transaction?
- Could the company be exposed to environmental liabilities that will impact on the banks' reputation?
- What impact will participating in the transaction have on the banks' other business relationships?

Assessing the risk of a financial restructuring proposal

A typical credit department in a bank will measure the absolute risk of providing finance to a company. The lending decision will be based on whether the absolute risk is recompensed by the return on offer. In practice this traditionally translates into whether the transaction conforms with the institution's standardised policy parameters and criteria, rather than an evaluation of each transaction's risk:return profile.

In a loan workout situation, at least part of the risk will have crystallised. The focus will move to comparative (rather than absolute) risk. This will relate to the increase in risk from a financial restructuring proposal compared with the estimated risk of loss in the current event of default. The factors highlighted earlier in this chapter contribute to this increase of risk. These risks manifest themselves in the risk of greater loss for the bank from:

- A continued deterioration in the company's performance and erosion in the value of recoveries.
- The provision of additional finance.

Hence, lenders typically prefer loan workouts with shorter-term horizons. The longer the period involved, the greater the risk is of the company's position deteriorating. At the same time, the company is also more likely to need a higher level of new financing.

Although the risk assessment techniques in a loan workout are similar to those applied when evaluating normal credit proposals, the decision-making criteria differ greatly. Banks involved in a loan workout do not have the option to decide against lending to the company. The choice is whether to continue with any existing loans, and to provide any new finance. Otherwise the bank may face considerable losses. As a result, its focus moves on to how it can improve its position, or at least not allow it to get worse, rather than participate in a restructuring.

Consequently, in a loan workout all decisions must be compared with the alternatives available. A restructuring proposal may not be sustainable under strict conventional credit assessment criteria, but it may be a considerably superior solution compared with the alternatives. Conversely, the fact that the institution is already exposed should not imply that a restructuring must be agreed at all cost. The risk attached to each transaction needs to be assessed separately.

Generally, lenders will prefer options that provide greater certainty and which minimise, or eliminate, the need for additional finance.

Risk relating to new finance in a restructuring

Even if an individual bank does not provide additional finance during a loan workout, it will be sharing in the risk if it allows a priority in favour of those who do. Moreover, it will not benefit from the returns. In practice, banks are often willing to weaken their own position by giving priority to other, more willing lenders. Some of the reasons for this include:

- 'Credit fatigue'.
- A reluctance to seek the necessary internal approvals for new finance.
- Doubts about the realisation value of supporting assets.

Nevertheless, in loan workouts, it is particularly important to make decisions on the basis of the potential losses in the event of default, rather than the absolute levels of exposures.

Returns from loan workouts

Lenders earn returns from normal loans by a combination of fees and margins over various costs. *Prima facie*, these principles would also apply in restructurings where there is minimal risk of any loss to the lenders from a company's difficulties.

Calculating the return from a loan workout becomes a more complex exercise when there is a risk of potential losses involved. If the banks face any possibility of a loss from a company's difficulties, then the return from a restructuring must not only take into account any margins and fees earned from the restructured debt, it should also recognise the losses avoided by undertaking the restructuring. The following simplified example illustrates the point:

Margin and fees from restructured debt (assuming it will be repaid in one year)	4%
Losses avoided by undertaking the restructuring	10%
Total returns from the restructuring	**14%**

Thus, the relevant returns in this context are the marginal returns earned as a result of undertaking the transaction, not just the expected returns from the transaction itself.

This issue has important implications for evaluating and negotiating loan workouts. Firstly, it is important to identify not only the return from the restructuring proposal, but also that from the next best alternative. Secondly, as different banks or creditor classes may suffer different levels of losses if a restructuring is not pursued, their marginal returns from the restructuring will vary as well. At an extreme, the marginal returns of any new lenders, assuming they are offered the same terms as existing ones, can be considerably lower than the latter. Hence, it is easier to get existing lenders to advance new finance in restructurings than to attract new lenders.

Where the lenders are expecting to suffer losses, or there is uncertainty about whether ultimately all debt will be serviced on time, sensitivity analyses need to be carried out. A range of returns may be calculated, for instance on a likely, optimistic and pessimistic scenario basis, as inputs into the evaluation exercise.

In debt for equity swap transactions, calculating returns is more complicated, as the value of the instruments being offered in exchange for debt also needs to be estimated. This subject is dealt with in Chapter 25.

Structuring returns

The preceding section has assumed that the returns from a loan workout are pre-determined. In fact, negotiating returns from a restructuring can be a challenging exercise.

In a loan workout, the lenders typically carry *quasi*-equity risk. This is because the company's earnings and the workout value of its assets are inadequate to support the criteria required by conventional credit providers. A standard return on senior debt will not compensate lenders in this situation.

The risk being undertaken, and therefore the required return, can be reduced by taking additional security where this is available. In most workouts, this does not have a substantial effect however. A further option is to increase the present value of returns by, for example, negotiating the early disposal of assets. Provided this does not negatively impact on the value realised, it also has an added benefit of reducing risk.

Ultimately, the interest charged on any existing and new finance must be increased to meet the target rate of return for lenders. However, for a company that is experiencing problems in meeting its existing debt servicing requirements, an increase in its debt servicing burden is likely to exacerbate difficulties. Two broad approaches (or a combination of them) can be taken to address this situation:

- The cash flow impact of the company's (now increased) debt servicing obligations can be tailored to its capacity. This will generally require such obligations to be shifted back to a period when the company's earnings are expected to recover. This may involve, for example, rolling-up interest for a period, or agreeing a stepped-up interest profile.

- The returns could be accrued to lenders in an alternative form. For instance, they may receive warrants, or shares in the company, which compensate them for any gap between the required and actual rate of return.

Present values

The timing of transaction proceeds and other cash flows can have a considerable impact on the expected return. So it is important that returns are estimated on a present value basis. The basic cost of carrying funds can be used for this exercise for the sake of simplicity when the restructured debt is not considered to be materially more risky than normal loans. In many instances, however, the risk attached to such debt can be considerably higher, particularly if the different types of financial restructuring risk are taken into account. Estimated returns on mezzanine or equity instruments may be more appropriate as discount rates in those circumstances.

Liquidation value

The estimated liquidation value of the company's assets is perhaps the most critical item of information for bankers evaluating a loan workout. It essentially represents the worst-case, 'riskless' scenario for banks, and forms the benchmark against which all other options are evaluated. Although in reality, liquidation is not a riskless process, it can be approximated as being so in most countries with developed insolvency frameworks. In some countries however, considerable uncertainty can be attached to the liquidation process. In such cases, theoretical liquidation values may need to be appropriately discounted to arrive at a useful benchmark.

Liquidation values may be estimated on a number of bases. The most appropriate basis will depend on the most likely exit route for banks in the event of insolvency. The most common valuation methodologies in this area are:

- Break-up and forced sale, based on an assumption that the company will need to be liquidated and its assets sold off.
- Going concern in insolvency, which assumes that one or more buyers can be found for the business(es) of the enterprise.

The reporting accountants, usually with input from insolvency specialists, will advise the banks of the company's liquidation value relatively early in the transaction. The recovery position of different lenders may vary and each lender's recovery position would normally be estimated. In more complex transactions, a 'dividend model', representing dividends receivable from the liquidation pool of realised assets, will be created for this purpose. When recovery from liquidation is anticipated to take time, say more than a year, its net present value should be calculated.

Evaluation

Evaluating a transaction's expected returns in the light of its risks requires a methodology which is easily understandable and quantifiable. Quantification enables alternative options to be compared easily. Two relatively simple techniques that can be used to evaluate loan workout options are presented below. In both cases, the estimated recovery in liquidation is used as a benchmark 'risk-free' return, against which the potential returns from any restructuring are measured.

Internal rate of return

This is the more scientific method of the two that are proposed. It calculates the rate of return anticipated from the financial restructuring, when compared with the alternative of liquidation.

The financial restructuring is assumed to be a new 'project', and lenders are deemed to be investing an amount equalling to the opportunity cost of not undertaking the project (i.e., the expected recovery in liquidation). The net cash flows anticipated from the project are identified and the project's internal rate of return calculated.

The principal difficulty for this method lies in determining whether the internal rate of return offered by the financial restructuring adequately compensates for the risks being undertaken. The returns offered by similarly risky financial instruments might be used as benchmarks. In reality, given the difficulties in accurately estimating the different types of restructuring risk and the impact of their interaction, this is often challenging.

If the country has a relatively liquid distressed debt market, market discounts for similarly risky debt may be used. This is relatively rare, however. Alternatively, returns on a range of instruments carrying different degrees of risk (ranging from, say, start-up equity to low-risk mezzanine instruments) may be identified, and the transaction located within that range. The important point here is that given the various levels of approximations, it is impossible to estimate the required rate of return very accurately. The purpose of the exercise is to generate some confidence about the fact that the expected returns from the transaction are not substantially divergent from the risks involved. Information gathered from this exercise can also provide valuable support in negotiations.

The risk:reward ratio

The risk:reward ratio is a 'rule-of-thumb' measure that, although being less scientific than the internal rate of return method, is intuitively more easy to understand. This measure compares the returns available to the banks if the company were to be liquidated today, with that estimated:

- If the company fails after a restructuring is agreed.
- If the restructuring succeeds.

The estimated marginal loss in the event of failure is then compared with the estimated gain from a successful restructuring.

Thus, under the scenario illustrated in Figure 14.1, banks would be risking 10 per cent of their exposure for a potential upside of 30 per cent. The risk:reward ratio is 3:1. As with the internal rate of return method, the appropriate level of required return given the amount at risk is difficult to determine objectively.

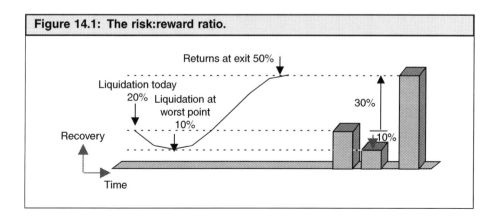

Figure 14.1: The risk:reward ratio.

The risk:reward ratio is very much a tool that requires input from more experienced workout specialists, who will be able to judge the probability of the restructuring failing. In the above example, if there is a better than one-in-three chance of the restructuring being successful, then this measure suggests that the restructuring should be accepted.

The risk:reward ratio is not a theoretically robust tool and should be used in conjunction with other evaluation methods, such as the internal rate of return.

Position of different creditors

The risk and return position of different banks and creditor classes will vary. Evaluation exercises will therefore be necessary for each bank or creditor class, in addition to the bank group as a whole. The results of this exercise are an important input for structuring inter-creditor arrangements in a loan workout, a subject which is covered later in the book.

Developing financial restructuring proposals

Once the various restructuring options have been evaluated, more detailed plans will be developed. The main responsibility for this rests with the company. However, if banks perceive that a company's proposals will not meet their requirements, they should prepare counter-proposals.

A key objective of any financial restructuring proposal should be simplicity. Complexity adds to the cost of the transaction, creates impediments in negotiations, and ultimately increases the structural risk of the transaction. This requires the critical parameters of the transaction to be isolated from the features that are desirable, but not essential.

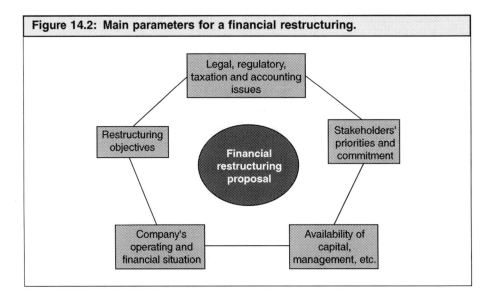

Figure 14.2: Main parameters for a financial restructuring.

Other potential constraints on the transaction need to be identified as well, so that any proposal is technically feasible. These include:

- *Legal and regulatory issues*—The need to ensure compliance with all prevailing laws and regulations.
- *Accounting and taxation*—Both in terms of their impact on the company as well as the banks.
- *Mechanics*—The required technical, legal and regulatory procedures that must be fulfilled.
- *Reputational issues*—The implications on the banks' reputation, both at the time of the restructuring and subsequently in their role as bankers, and in some cases as shareholders, of participating in the transaction.

Although technical issues should never be allowed to become the determining factors behind a loan workout, neglecting them can result in avoidable cost and uncertainty. Figure 14.2 summarises the key parameters that need to be considered when formulating loan workout proposals.

15

NEGOTIATING
AND COMPLETING
TRANSACTIONS

Introduction

Negotiation is a key step in any loan workout. In a typical transaction, this takes place at a number of levels, specifically:

- Between the company and its lenders.
- Among the lenders themselves.
- Between the company and its other stakeholders.

The company usually represents the interests of its other stakeholders, including shareholders, employees, customers and suppliers, in the negotiations with its lenders. The lenders may include a broad range of financial creditors, including bondholders. Figure 15.1 summarises the approach typically adopted in negotiating complex workouts.

The purpose of this chapter is to highlight some of the key prerequisites for successfully negotiating loan workouts. It also outlines some of the issues relating to the involvement of key groups of financial creditors in the process. Negotiations with shareholders is dealt with in more detail in Chapter 25, with reference to debt for equity swap transactions. Finally, matters relating to completing loan workout transactions are highlighted.

Ingredients of an effective negotiating process

As with other forms of negotiation, preparation is the key to a successful outcome. Such preparation, however, is often difficult where there is considerable uncertainty and instability associated with a company's financial problems. Nevertheless, steps can be taken to mitigate the effect of such shortcomings.

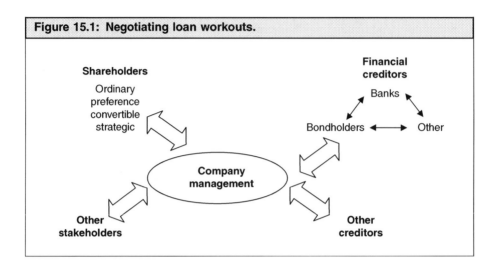

Figure 15.1: Negotiating loan workouts.

Information about the company and its finances

Information about the company's problems and prospects, and their financial impact on lenders, forms the foundation of a negotiating strategy. The more information that banks have at the start of the negotiating process, the stronger their negotiating position will be. Moreover, the task of negotiating the loan workout is made considerably easier if there is a broad agreement on the information about the company and the relative positions of the various creditors.

Two important factors greatly facilitate developing a strong information base. Firstly, information being used by participants needs to be, and must be seen to be, reliable. Secondly, so far as possible, all participants should develop their negotiating positions from a common platform of information. Independent reporting accountants can provide confidence to all participants on these issues.

It is important that at the commencement of negotiations the information base is as complete as possible. Often information emerges from the company only gradually, during the negotiating process itself. Such information usually tends to indicate a worsening position of the company. This is to an extent unavoidable, and may reflect an evolving situation. Nevertheless, many of the problems can be identified at the outset if that objective is adequately emphasised. Banks usually find themselves in a weaker negotiating position if they are constantly reacting to new information during negotiations.

Stability

The second key ingredient for conducting negotiations effectively is stability. This is achieved through a number of mechanisms, chief amongst which is a temporary moratorium. Stability enables time to be gained, so that discussions can progress calmly. At the same time, however, the temporary nature of the moratorium and other risks to stability should inject the appropriate degree of urgency to conclude negotiations rapidly. Moreover, stability also enables the participants to focus on exploring and debating longer-term issues, rather than be detracted by short-term fire-fighting.

Co-ordinating the negotiations

There are two broad approaches for structuring negotiations when a number of participants with divergent interests are involved. The first option is to let each participant in the lender group negotiate directly with the company. The alternative is to have one party, the co-ordinator, negotiate on behalf of the lender group. To represent the interests of the group as a whole, the co-ordinator, supported by the steering committee, would first need to arrive at a position that has been negotiated between the lenders. This route is usually more efficient and effective. It enables the lender group to adopt a more coherent, and therefore stronger, negotiating position.

Nevertheless, having a single co-ordinator representing the interests of all the financial creditors many not always be practical. This is sometimes the case where the interests of the participants are too divergent, for example, occasionally when bondholders, or providers of performance bonds are involved. In such cases, it may be more productive to have more than one party representing the interests of different classes of financial creditors at the negotiations.

Information dissemination

The issue of how much information to disseminate to all the participants and when to do so is clearly important. Lack of information creates uncertainty and undermines confidence. There is often a real concern among lenders that they are not being kept informed. This creates mistrust and can destabilise negotiations. At the same time, the co-ordinator will be expected to manage information flows so that the bank group's negotiating position is not jeopardised.

All communications between the lenders and the company should be channelled through one party, usually the co-ordinator. Otherwise there is considerable risk of the lenders' negotiating position as a whole being weakened as the company engages in bilateral negotiations.

The management of communications with the press and the public during the negotiation process is another critical area. The risk is that publicising temporary difficulties in negotiations will undermine confidence in the company or the restructuring. The company would be expected to take the lead in this process, but the lenders must be satisfied that their positions are not being undermined as a result. If necessary, lenders, or groups within them, may need to consider their own public relations strategy.

Negotiating strategy

Before entering into negotiations, it is important that the lenders develop a coherent strategy. In particular, they need to have considered and agreed a consistent position on matters such as:

- The *restructuring objectives*. These objectives underlie the restructuring options and loan workout proposals. A focus on objectives rather than specific targets provides the flexibility to explore alternative means of achieving them.

- Their *preferred and fall-back positions*. This is a basic requirement for all negotiations. There needs to be a good understanding of the degree of compromise possible on each of the negotiating points, and its impact on the position of each of the lenders. In particular, there needs to be a strong agreement on issues that are 'deal breakers'.

- A well-formulated *contingency plan* if an agreement cannot be reached on the restructuring. The resources devoted to developing contingency options would depend in part on the lenders' expectations of the loan workout negotiations failing.

- An assessment of the restructuring objectives and specific *needs of the other participants* in the negotiations. This helps to formulate a negotiating strategy that addresses these needs so far as possible. It also enables the negotiating team to prepare any counter-arguments.

Combining Voluntary and Statutory Procedures to Aid Loan Workout Negotiations

The need for unanimity causes particular difficulties in negotiating loan workouts. The 'hold out' problem associated with voluntary agreements is particularly acute in cases where a large number of creditors with relatively small exposures are involved. In some jurisdictions, this problem can be overcome by negotiating a debt restructuring with a company's major creditors, and then seeking recourse to statutory procedures which enable a transaction to be approved by a majority. Prepackaged bankruptcies, or 'prepacks' in the United States[1] and controlled receiverships in England are examples of such strategies. In the absence of a supportive statutory insolvency framework, however, such strategies can be risky and can lead to the company's liquidation prematurely.

Issues specific to the various groups directly participating in negotiations are considered below.

Bank lenders

The co-ordinating bank, supported by the steering committee and the team of independent advisors, plays a key role in negotiating loan workouts involving a number of banks. Together, their objective is to ensure that their own interests, as well as those of the lender group as a whole, are represented in the negotiations. In undertaking its role, the co-ordinating bank often has a fiduciary duty to ensure that the interests of all the banks are taken into account during negotiations.

Before entering into any negotiations, the co-ordinating bank will evaluate all options independently and formulate an appropriate negotiating strategy. The evaluation and decision-making process will usually have input from the banks' advisory team. The key aspects of this exercise should be agreed with the steering committee and the other banks before formal negotiations commence.

The co-ordinator needs to be firm but fair. Its prime objective is to minimise losses whilst ensuring it is being fair to the other stakeholders in the company. In most cases the main negotiations will be with the company's management. It is important to retain the management's co-operation and trust during negotiations as it is usually they who will be eventually responsible for implementing any restructuring.

A common danger is for banks to be drawn into separate, subsidiary negotiations at the time their advisors are gathering information. For instance, they may be pressured into an early repayment of a small creditor. There is a greater danger of becoming morally committed to a course of action by entering into premature discussions about solutions.

The negotiating strength of bank lenders will depend on factors such as:

- The relative negotiating strength of other interest groups.

- The gap between the value realisable immediately and that from the proposed loan workout. The smaller this gap is, the more indifferent the bank group will be between a negotiated restructuring and its alternative. Its negotiating position will therefore be stronger. A credible contingency plan is often a powerful negotiating tool in this regard.

- The strength and effectiveness of the insolvency framework in the country concerned. The banks' position is strengthened considerably if insolvency procedures are seen as a credible threat by the company and other stakeholders.

- The divergence of interests within the bank group. The more difficult it is for the bank group to be cohesive, the weaker its negotiating position will be.

Holders of bonds

Bondholders' impact on loan workout negotiations will principally depend on their background and investment objectives.

Long-term institutional holders of a company's bonds are likely to have invested some time ago, probably at the time the bonds were issued. Their risk:reward perspective will be similar to that of the banks. On the whole, they will be supportive of a loan workout and will adopt a negotiating stance similar to that of the lenders.

Traders in bonds, or non-institutional holders of, particularly, bearer bonds, often approach loan workout negotiations differently. They can be potentially a major source of instability. This is because:

- They are likely to be large in number but their identity is often unknown, causing difficulties in communications.
- Partly because of the above, it is difficult to influence them and their reaction is often unpredictable. This is especially so if they have no trustee to guide them.

- They are often located in a number of countries and are subject to different jurisdictions, thereby increasing transaction complexity.

- They may have very different financial objectives. For example, a bondholder who has invested at 50 per cent of face value will be happy to recover, say, 70 per cent. Such a bondholder will be more averse to a prolonged workout period than one who has acquired bonds at a much narrower discount. The latter's objectives will be more in line with that of the banks.

Negotiations with bondholders are greatly facilitated if the lead managers or agents to the issue become involved in co-ordinating the bond holders. They can operate independently, or as a representative in the steering committee.

Sharing detailed information with agents or lead managers during negotiations can often be a problem because as trustees, they may be obliged to share it with all the bondholders. This could result in sensitive information, such as the reporting accountants' reports, entering the public domain. Bondholders have an additional problem in receiving price-sensitive information about the company. Insider dealing regulations will inhibit their ability to trade. In such circumstances, the bondholders will often appoint their own financial advisors to verify information and facilitate decision-making, without becoming privy to all the facts themselves.

The banks' investment banking advisors can fulfil a crucial role in assisting with negotiations with the bondholders and advising on the relevant tactical and regulatory issues.

Shareholders

Shareholders may have very little or no value left in the company at the time a loan workout is being negotiated. Moreover, many of the operational restructuring activities associated with an accelerated reduction of debt, such as the disposal of assets or businesses, potentially act against their interests by reducing the long-term value of the company's equity capital. This conflict can be one of the most difficult elements of negotiating a financial restructuring. Shareholders' interests are more directly affected by debt for equity swaps, where they can suffer considerable dilution in their shareholdings. The issue of dealing with shareholders in loan workout negotiations is dealt with more fully in the context of such transactions, in Chapter 25.

Completing the transaction

Once a loan workout has been agreed by all the parties, the formalities surrounding the completion of the transaction need to be undertaken. These are primarily legal in nature and may include, for example, refinancing agreements, issuing of new share certificates and holding appropriate Board or shareholder meetings to approve the terms of the transaction. In addition, the transaction may be affected by regulatory matters that may require consents from the various authorities. New management may need to be formally appointed to the company's Board.

It is important that momentum is not lost after the terms of a restructuring have been agreed. One of the responsibilities of the co-ordinating bank is to ensure that it is properly advised by its legal advisors on the legal and regulatory formalities, both its own and of the company, so that a legally effective agreement can be enforced.

Any public announcements about the transaction will need to be co-ordinated between the company and its lenders. Also, matters such as the lifting of suspensions over dealings in the company's shares must be arranged, where relevant.

Documentation and agreements

The legal documents that are executed in a loan workout will vary between countries. Nevertheless, it is likely that they will address the following aspects of the transaction:

- *The moratorium.* A legal agreement relating to the moratorium is intended to be a stop-gap in the period between calling the moratorium and the presentation of the detailed review of the company's affairs by the reporting accountants. For the moratorium agreement to be effective, it will need to be drafted relatively quickly. A short-form moratorium agreement is commonly employed for this purpose. However, it is a matter of judgement whether or not to use such a document, since it often proves difficult to secure the formal agreement of all the parties to it during this period of uncertainty. Some banks prefer a '*de facto*' moratorium, without entering into a legal commitment. This is because various tax or provision-related issues can be triggered in their home countries if a commitment to a moratorium is made, an example being Japan.

Whilst a written moratorium agreement is preferable, unless this can be concluded successfully in a short period, the effort required to convince banks to sign it tends to be unproductive. As a result, it is not unusual for the co-ordinator to police a *de facto* standstill.

- *The restructuring.* The restructuring agreement will govern the terms and conditions of the transaction eventually negotiated between the bank group and the company. This will provide for the revised terms of the debt facilities available to the company and the conditions for any new financing advanced by the banks. It will also include various financial and non-financial agreements that will enable the lenders to monitor the company's progress in achieving agreed objectives.
- *Inter-creditor issues.* The provisions relating to inter-creditor issues are often incorporated within the principal restructuring agreement. These govern the relationship between the banks and incorporate the relevant agreed priorities as well as any loss-sharing provisions. Inter-creditor issues are dealt with in detail later in the book.
- *Collateral.* The various documents relating to the banks' security over the company's assets will also need to be signed and appropriate registration formalities completed.

Legal documentation relating to a loan workout agreement can either be structured as an override arrangement to existing agreements between the banks and the company, or as a replacement.

Loan workout information memorandum

In many instances, the co-ordinator may need to 'sell' the loan workout agreement to the wider lender group. This selling process will be facilitated if the decision-makers in such institutions are presented with all the relevant information in a clear and focused manner. Such information has added credibility if it is presented by, or on behalf of, the co-ordinator and the steering committee.

A memorandum that collates and summarises information from the various core documents of the restructuring can be very valuable in this respect, particularly if a large number of banks are involved.

Figure 15.2 outlines the major sources of data for the information memorandum.

The information memorandum will include:

- An introduction to the group, including the group's organisational structure, and the background to its difficulties.

- Historic and current financial information about the company, including any adjustments made as a result of the due diligence by the reporting accountants. A commentary on key trends would also be included.

- The proposed business strategy agreed under the restructuring plan, including disposals, overhead reduction, and management changes.

- Projected financial information consistent with the proposed business strategy, including sensitivities, contingencies and key underlying assumptions.

- The key elements of the loan workout proposal, including the restructuring terms for existing debt, collateral-related matters, the relative treatment of the various classes of lenders, new finance-related issues, and other key terms.

- A financial evaluation of the restructuring proposals, highlighting the returns on liquidation compared with those offered under the restructuring for the various classes of creditors, the sensitivities attached to such projected returns, and the key risks attached to the restructuring.

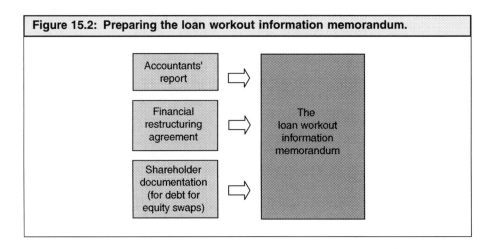

Figure 15.2: Preparing the loan workout information memorandum.

- A summary of the provisions of the main legal documents.
- Other matters, such as any outstanding legal and regulatory issues, key steps and the timetable going forward.
- A 'term sheet' summarising the proposals for restructuring the exposures of each separate bank.
- If appropriate, an expression of support for the proposal by the co-ordinator and the steering committee, including their own agreement in principle to the proposals.

---

[1] S. Chatterjee *et al.*, Resolution of financial distress: Debt restructurings via Chapter 11, prepackaged bankruptcies, and workouts, *Financial Management*, Tampa, Spring 1996, p. 5.

PART III

THE MORATORIUM AND FINANCIAL RESTRUCTURING

SECTION A

THE MORATORIUM

16

ESTABLISHING A
MORATORIUM

Introduction

A stable environment is necessary for a company's problems to be investigated thoroughly, and a considered loan workout solution agreed. The principal objective of a moratorium, which is also known as a standstill in the context of corporate workouts, is to provide such stability.

Moratoriums can take different forms. They also have various implications for the company and its lenders. The key issues relevant to calling and structuring a moratorium are covered in this section of the book. The focus of this chapter is on explaining what a moratorium is, its main benefits and shortcomings, the key principles involved in structuring them, and the scope of moratorium agreements.

The concept of moratorium discussed in this book differs from the term when applied in the context of sovereign debt. In such cases, a moratorium may refer to the act of a soverign borrower unilaterally announcing a temporary suspension of its debt servicing obligations.

Causes of a moratorium

The most common trigger for a moratorium is a liquidity crisis in a company, as a result of which it is unable to meet some or all of its borrowing commitments. Cross-default clauses quickly result in other loans becoming repayable immediately. The only alternative to court-led insolvency procedures under such circumstances is a voluntarily agreed solution between the company and its lenders. A moratorium is the first step in this process.

In particular, the most common precursors to a moratorium are:

- A default under a committed loan facility, particularly one involving the breach of a financial covenant.
- Failure to refinance a maturing facility.

- Withdrawal of loan facilities by the company's lenders.
- Failure to achieve some specific major disposal or other fund raising exercise.
- Adverse publicity.

Principal features of a moratorium

A moratorium is usually called by the company. This will follow a period of discussion with its main bankers, who will advise the company to convene a meeting of all its banks for that purpose.

A standstill calls for a general moratorium with effect from a specific date. This is usually the close of business on the day before the all-bank meeting. The moratorium will require each bank to subordinate some of its individual rights in favour of a majority decision of participating banks. During the period of the moratorium individual banks agree not to:

- Commence or continue any legal proceedings or other enforcement or recovery activity against the customer.
- Reduce, withdraw or amend any outstanding facilities.
- Demand any additional security or guarantees.
- Declare an event of default, make demand, or accelerate the facilities.
- Charge any default interest.

In addition, banks may collectively agree to:

- Extend new loan facilities.
- Call for additional security.
- Negotiate an increased pricing of their loans with the customer.

Consideration may also be given to imposing restrictions on assignments of distressed debt by banks during this initial standstill phase. For example, this could be achieved by requiring the prior consent of the banks' steering committee. However, such restrictions cannot be mandatory in some jurisdictions.

The banks' duty of confidentiality to their customers continues during a moratorium. This may be reinforced by express provisions in the moratorium documentation, or in separate confidentiality undertakings given to the company.

Legal forms

A moratorium can take a number of forms. It can range from an informal understanding between the debtor and its creditors, to a formal process governed by statute.

Often, lenders agree in principle to a '*de facto*' standstill, without actually executing a legal document, or entering into a formal commitment. Such *de facto* moratoriums are often easier to agree. Provided that the lenders are willing to co-operate and the co-ordinating bank polices the arrangement diligently, they can be enforced effectively. Nevertheless, *de facto* moratoriums can at times fail to stop opportunistic action by a minority of the bank group, which therefore risk the stability of the workout process.

Another alternative is for the participants to sign an initial abbreviated heads of terms that summarise the basic principles of a moratorium.

The key provisions of moratorium agreements are outlined later in this chapter.

Different types of moratorium agreements

It is the company's responsibility to call a moratorium and to invite its bankers to participate in it. Nevertheless, a moratorium is as much about the banks agreeing between themselves to abide by a code of conduct, as agreeing with the company to act in a certain way. A standstill can be a unilateral announcement by the company that it intends to suspend capital, and perhaps interest payments, whether or not the banks agree. In this scenario it is crucial for the company to police itself and ensure that all its creditor banks are treated equally. Alternatively, the banks as a group (or at least a majority of them) may agree with the company to comply with the particular terms of a moratorium. Thirdly, a moratorium may constitute an agreement between the banks themselves whereby they agree to subordinate their individual rights in favour of a majority decision of participating banks.

The choice between these alternatives will depend on the circumstances of the case. The overriding objective should be to keep the process simple. A moratorium is a means to an end (a restructuring), not an end in itself.

The factors influencing the choice between the options outlined above will be:

- *The degree of additional stability required.* Are all the major creditor banks supportive of the company, or is there a significant dissenting minority? Is it a small bank group or does it involve a very large number of banks with significantly differing positions?

- *The likely timescales involved in this first stage.* Is it a complex business with numerous activities, operating divisions and legal subsidiaries, perhaps based across a number of countries?

- *What is the moratorium seeking to achieve?* Is it designed to prevent banks from taking any action whilst urgent negotiations are taking place? Or is it designed to allow time for a full accountants' review? Is the moratorium intended to enable the company to dispose of assets, or even to permit an orderly wind down of the company altogether? A moratorium aimed at improving the lenders' position, for example, by raising new funds, is more likely to find greater support from them.

Length of the moratorium

It is important for the company to continue its day-to-day operations whilst a moratorium is in place. As a result, the banks risk a worsening in their position, as the company's situation and prospects might deteriorate during this period. For this reason, the length of the moratorium is kept relatively short, at least initially. A period of between one and three months is common, with extensions if necessary. The length of the moratorium will usually be determined by the time required to prepare the reporting accountants' reports, and for the banks to decide on the appropriate course of action in light of their findings. The period of the reporting accountants' investigations will be influenced by the scope of their work, balanced against how much new money is required by the company during that period. There may also be other commercial factors affecting the company, such as the need to sign a contract for new work that requires some form of performance bond.

Terminating a moratorium

Provisions for terminating a moratorium will be agreed at the time it is called. A moratorium can usually be terminated at any time by a decision of the 'majority banks'. Deciding on the number of banks required to make this decision and the proportion of the company's borrowings that they should represent is very much an art. For example, where there are only one or two banks with relatively large exposures, they will not want a large number of banks with a smaller aggregate exposure to gain significant influence over the process. Likewise the banks with smaller exposures will not wish to commit to a moratorium if only the bank with the largest exposures can terminate it. A balance needs to be achieved between the interests of these groups.

Unless a moratorium is extended at its expiry, each bank may be able to take unilateral action against the company without prior notice to the other banks in the group. Extending a moratorium requires the unanimous agreement of all of the banks. Sometimes, banks with outstanding grievances will delay extending the contractual moratorium period. In these situations the co-ordinating bank will seek verbal (and not legally binding) assurance from the dissident banks that they will not make any demand for repayment without giving the co-ordinator prior warning. A *'de facto'* moratorium will prevail.

Advantages and disadvantages of moratoriums

The key advantage of moratoriums is that they inject stability and provide a framework within which the participants can decide on, and progress, the appropriate course of action.

Other benefits of moratoriums include:

- The formalising of previously temporary arrangements between the company and its banks.
- The focusing of management's attention on the seriousness of the company's difficulties.
- The effective organisation of the bank group through representation on a steering committee, under the co-ordination of a lead bank.
- The establishment of a historic fixed reference point, i.e., the 'moratorium date' at the start of the process. The significance of this date is highlighted later in the book.

Nevertheless, the act of calling a moratorium can in itself create a number of problems.

- *Once a moratorium is called, the process becomes irreversible in practice.* This can lead to a lack of flexibility in the way that solutions can be formulated.
- *The duties involved in administering a moratorium can be onerous.* In particular, resolution of inter-bank issues and conflicts can often detract from the prime objective of achieving a sustainable financial structure for the company. This is particularly the case in the early stages of a loan workout.

- *The risk of a breach in confidentiality is significant.* News that a company is in formal discussions with its bankers may lead to instability, with a loss of confidence on the part of the company's suppliers, customers and employees. Delays in agreeing a refinancing exacerbate this problem.

- *The company's management's morale and effectiveness can often be adversely affected* by the workload, pressures and stigma associated with being part of a rescue operation, and key personnel may take the opportunity to leave. Most seriously, management's attention is diverted from the day-to-day running of the business, particularly once the reporting accountants start their investigations.

- *A moratorium tends to exacerbate the company's difficulties,* particularly in the early stages. This is because the task of addressing all the company's problems is concentrated into a short period, whereas many issues might have been manageable over a longer-term. For example, the very act of calling a moratorium may cause a breach in facilities which would otherwise have remained committed.

- From an individual bank's point of view, *calling a moratorium stops the clock.* As a result the bank loses the ability to independently pursue improvements in its own risk exposure.

Despite these problems, a moratorium is usually the 'least worst' option by default.

Underlying principles

A key prerequisite for a sustainable moratorium is fairness. Each participant in the moratorium needs confidence that no other will seek to take advantage, or that they will themselves be relatively worse-off as a result of agreeing the proposed course of action. This confidence can be maintained if certain principles are adhered to. They include:

- *The moratorium should provide for each of the creditors to be treated equally.* This is notwithstanding the relative importance of their previous relationships with the company or the size of their exposure. This applies to all aspects of the process, including the communication, the sharing of information, and the right to attend meetings.

- *No bank is permitted to improve its positions relative to any other bank.* This is distinct from the banks collectively seeking an improvement in their position, through a course of action that is acceptable from the bankers' perspective.

- *The on-going position of banks in relation to each other is measured against their relative positions at a particular point in time.* These 'day-one positions', commonly established as at the 'moratorium date', are the exposures that existed as at the close of business on the day before the moratorium is announced. The concept of 'notional liquidation' is applied in determining the participants' relative positions. This calculates the losses that each participant would have incurred if the company was liquidated on the moratorium date.

- *Any risks associated with providing on-going support should be borne as equally as possible* between the banks, in proportion to their 'moratorium date' positions.

■ *The principle of risk-sharing should also apply to the provision of additional liquidity* to allow the company to continue to trade during the moratorium.

Any costs associated with the moratorium (and the restructuring generally) are normally borne by the company. Costs incurred directly in connection with the moratorium, or in relation to the independent advisors acting for the bank group, should be shared equitably by the banks in the event that the company is unable to pay. This will normally be in proportion to their 'moratorium date' exposures.

Key provisions of moratorium agreements

Simplicity is the key to moratoriun agreements. There are usually considerable pressures to anticipate wide-ranging scenarios and accommodate separate needs. Ultimately, a focus on constructing a perfect moratorium agreement is likely to cause delays, divert resources, and may even contribute to the loan workout failing. In a multi-banked workout, the more comprehensive any proposed moratorium agreement is, the greater the likelihood is of one or more parties objecting to particular issues.

A moratorium agreement that focuses on a few key provisions, covers a relatively short period, and is flexible has a greater chance of being agreed and is likely to be the most effective. The parties accept that specific issues may arise over time which it will be necessary to 'agree to agree'.

Figure 16.1 summarises the key provisions that should be included in moratorium agreements.

The period of operation

The moratorium agreement will define the start date for the moratorium and set out the period over which it is to operate. The moratorium date is important as this will establish the relative positions of the banks. The moratorium start date normally remains fixed even if the agreement does not become valid from that point. For example, some banks may only agree to sign the agreement at a later date. In some

Figure 16.1: Key provisions of moratorium agreements.

Moratorium agreement

- Term
- Day-one positions
- Rights of acceleration
- Demand
- No reduction
- Interest
- Loss-sharing
- Delegated authority
- New finance

instances the agreement will contain provisions for a renewal of the moratorium. This can be designed to operate according to a number of provisions. Examples include a majority decision to extend or terminate, a steering committee decision, or an 'evergreen' arrangement subject to a notice period.

It is usual for a moratorium to be agreed for an initial period on the assumption that it will be subsequently extended. This enables the participants to maintain control over the loan workout. Often, interim milestones are agreed, which provide the basis of renewals. In extreme cases, moratoriums can be in place for a number of years.

Day-one positions

It is preferable to incorporate the 'moratorium date' exposures of each bank as a schedule to the moratorium agreement if at all possible. However, this is often not easy to establish and for the larger, more complex corporate groups this can take considerable time.

> The Berisford International plc workout in 1990 eventually involved some 60 banks with facilities well in excess of £1bn. At the outset it was thought there were perhaps less than 40 banks involved with facilities of around £600 m. It took four months to reconcile and agree the exposures of the various banks, and the exercise continued until the night before the signing of the restructuring agreement.

In some cases, therefore, the moratorium agreement may simply refer to the basis upon which the day-one exposures are to be calculated. The company and the co-ordinating bank remain responsible for resolving any disputes in this regard.

Postponement of rights of acceleration

Individual banks agree that they will not carry out any of the following, against the company, or any of its assets during the moratorium:

- Declare a default.
- Demand repayment.
- Commence or continue any legal proceedings.
- Exercise any security interests.
- Take any other form of enforcement or recovery action.

Repayment on demand

Although individual banks agree not to take action unilaterally against the company, it is likely that the moratorium agreement will confirm that all the bank facilities are repayable on demand subject to voting arrangements agreed between the banks.

No reductions

The banks agree that they will suspend previously documented loan amortisation arrangements. The banks will agree to allow revolving facilities to operate in the normal manner, with the company retaining any redrawing rights within the agreed limits. The limits will usually be based on the relative positions that existed at the moratorium date, although related complications may arise. These are dealt with in connection with 'loss-sharing' below.

Interest

The moratorium will either be documented to permit interest payments to continue on a normal basis, or provide for new arrangements. The moratorium agreement may also provide for all the banks to have their interest paid up to the 'moratorium date', so that they are all on an equal footing.

Loss-sharing

The moratorium agreement will provide for the banks to share in any shortfalls and costs in proportion to their relative positions as at the moratorium date. Where companies have complex group structures or borrowing arrangements, the loss-sharing arrangements can become very complicated. This can add considerably to the complexity of the moratorium agreement. Reaching a quick agreement to a moratorium becomes difficult in these situations.

Where the banks' exposures are complicated, the moratorium agreement may simply document the principle that any shortfalls in recovery by any bank will be shared *pro rata* to their 'moratorium date' positions. The agreement may also set out the broad procedural arrangements for resolving any disputes between banks in this area, perhaps by reference to binding independent arbitration. The reporting accountants may be candidates for this role.

The principles and issues involved in loss-sharing arrangements are covered in detail in Chapter 19.

Delegated authority

The agreement may provide for certain decisions to be delegated to a smaller group during the moratorium. This will ordinarily be a responsibility passed to the steering committee. The moratorium agreement might also document the appointment of a co-ordinator and steering committee, as well as the level of authority vested in them. It may also provide for a level of majority voting to operate in certain circumstances. However, although this level of detailed terms and formality makes for more efficient operation of the moratorium, it may make the agreement more difficult to achieve in the first place. Particularly in the early stages of the workout, banks may be reluctant to delegate important decisions to other banks.

Additional liquidity arrangements

Often, the calling of a moratorium results in all liquidity being removed from a company as undrawn lines are cancelled and the headroom in existing lines is withdrawn. As a result, unless the company is entering a particularly cash positive stage in its trading cycle, it will require access to additional finance. The moratorium agreement may provide for the sources and basis of such financing. Any proposed arrangement will be consistent with the broad principle that additional risks are to be shared equally between the banks during the moratorium. Sometimes, reference to provision of new loans is excluded from the moratorium agreement. Instead, a separate loan agreement is executed.

Other provisions typically included in a moratorium agreement address matters such as the remuneration for banks and the taking of security.

Documentation structure

An experienced legal firm will be employed to draft the moratorium agreement. In view of the potential difficulties of getting an agreement signed by all the parties, it should be drafted as flexibly as possible. This will avoid the need to vary it subsequently, as unexpected events occur.

The agreement can provide for a replacement facility. However, this is more cumbersome, time-consuming and does not provide the quick, temporary solution that is so central to an effective moratorium.

Accordingly, the moratorium agreement will usually be structured as a temporary amendment to the terms of the existing facility agreements of individual banks. This will involve most of the 'mechanical' aspects of the facilities continuing on the basis of the existing documentation. The new agreement will alter some of the provisions of each bank's facility document. The agreement will temporarily override the underlying facilities. Upon maturity, most aspects of this agreement will fall away, leaving each bank reverting to its existing, pre-moratorium contracts.

One of the disadvantages of a voluntary moratorium is that it can only bind those who agree to enter into the arrangement. For the moratorium to be totally effective, unanimous agreement is required. However, provided most of the key banks sign up to the moratorium, it is likely to be effective in practice. The small number of non-participating banks will usually not take any prejudicial action.

Where there are numerous different legal entities in a corporate group, the moratorium agreement may only be executed by the ultimate holding company, and perhaps a few of the main operating subsidiaries. The parent company then undertakes to procure that each of its subsidiaries will abide by the terms of the moratorium agreement. Often this is done in order to preserve confidentiality. It also has the benefit of simplifying the execution of the agreement.

In complex international support operations, where significant parts of a group operate largely independently, it may be more practical to execute separate moratorium agreements in each of the key jurisdictions. The lawyers and the co-ordinator will need to ensure that the various documents are harmonised and the stability of the main moratorium is not prejudiced by such a structure.

17

FINANCIAL CREDITORS AFFECTED BY A MORATORIUM

Introduction

Given that the principal objective of a moratorium is to provide stability during a loan workout transaction, the wider its scope is, the more successful it is likely to be in meeting this aim. *Prima facie*, if all the company's creditors agreed to a moratorium, instability would be minimised. In reality, however, there is a need to balance the need for stability against the complexities of involving a wide range of participants in a moratorium. Also, the involvement of some creditors in a moratorium may impair the company's ability to operate effectively during its currency.

Ultimately, judgement is required on the part of the company, the co-ordinator, and their respective advisors, on how to deal with these situations.

This chapter identifies the most common types of financial creditors that are affected by a moratorium and, ultimately, a loan workout. The nature of their involvement with the company, and the impact that might have on a moratorium, are also considered.

Determining who to include in a moratorium

Court-approved restructurings or formal insolvency procedures are binding on all creditors. In contrast, a bank-led loan workout is a voluntary process. The principal decisions revolve around whether the banks will continue to provide finance to the company, or extend new finance, and under what conditions. As a result, the only creditors involved in most loan workouts are:

- Banks.
- Other providers of debt.

- Financial institutions providing *quasi*-banking products, treasury management services, or other specialist financial instruments.

Creditor groups such as trade and other commercial creditors are usually excluded from the moratorium and the ensuing financial restructuring arrangements. In some cases, such creditors may nevertheless be included either because their continued support is fundamental, or because of special terms of trade offered by them, such as long-term credit. Trade creditors may also be included in a moratorium if they account for a significant proportion of the company's liabilities. This will be particularly true for many centrally-controlled economies, where inter-enterprise liabilities can be substantial. Similar considerations apply in deciding whether the government, acting as a creditor due to overdue tax and social security contributions, should be included in a moratorium.

Involvement of banks and other financial creditors

There are a number of reasons why banks and other financial institutions usually become involved in moratoriums and loan workouts, whereas other creditors do not. These include:

- *Expertise*—Banks are in the business of assessing risk, whereas commercial creditors generally are not. Banks are also better equipped to deal with the other technical issues that arise during a loan workout.
- *Additional credit*—Banks have the means to make available additional loans, which trade and other creditors are unlikely to be able to supply.
- *Resources*—In terms of systems and personnel, the banks have the time and resources to devote to loan workouts, which can be very time-consuming and costly affairs.
- *Motivation*—The exposures of individual banks are often such that they have a big interest in seeking to minimise losses. Other creditors may only have relatively modest exposures and may not consider it cost-effective to pursue repayment actively. They prefer to 'free ride' on the work of the banks.
- *Number*—A large company will probably have thousands of trade and other creditors. Involving these in the moratorium or workout would be administratively impossible.
- *Confidentiality*—This can be one of the key advantages of a voluntary moratorium involving a small number of parties. Confidence in the business can be preserved with respect to suppliers, customers, and employees.

Thus, the potential candidates for inclusion in a moratorium are principally the company's bankers and other financial creditors. To decide on which of them should be included, the first step is to identify exactly which banks, financial institutions, and other potential moratorium candidates are involved with the company. Once that has been established as far as possible, the second step is to decide on which specific parties qualify for inclusion. This judgement will be influenced by factors such as:

- The *nature* of their exposure.
- The *size* of the facility provided.
- The impact of the *jurisdiction* involved.

These decisions, which will be taken before the first all-bank meeting takes place by the company and its main relationship bank, will identify who is to be included in the moratorium and therefore be invited to the meeting. It will also influence which of the parties are involved in any financial restructuring that subsequently takes place as part of the loan workout. At the meeting, the parties will be advised of the extent of the company's difficulties. Also, confidential information will be made available. There will be considerable moral pressure on each party that attends the meeting to join the moratorium.

Even if a bank is not invited to the first all-bank meeting, it is still possible for it to be invited to join a moratorium at a later date. However, such a bank might feel aggrieved at not being informed of the company's problems until after the all-bank meeting. The bank may also have benefited from a reduction in its exposure since the moratorium date and will be reluctant to re-advance funds to re-establish the position at that date, as would be required under a moratorium. Alternatively, in some instances the banks that have joined the moratorium may only have agreed to do so in exchange for security over additional assets of the company. In this case, existing participants in the moratorium may object to any further parties being allowed to share in the collateral, thereby diluting their interests. It is therefore best to identify the potential participants in the moratorium as early as possible and avoid such problems.

The position of different financial creditors in a moratorium

The attitude and enthusiasm toward moratoriums of different classes of financial creditors will depend on the nature of their exposure to the company. This will affect their judgement of whether they will benefit from participating in a moratorium. At the same time, the impact on the company of their exclusion from a moratorium will need to be taken into account.

Figure 17.1 overviews the different financial creditor groups affected by a moratorium. Considerations relating to their participation in a moratorium are explored below.

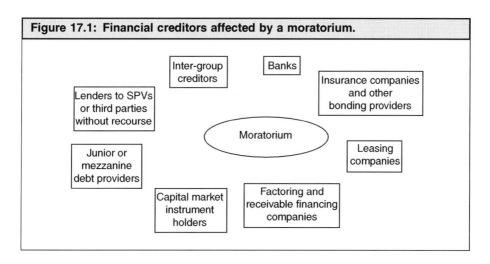

Figure 17.1: Financial creditors affected by a moratorium.

Banks

Banks will be the only participants in a moratorium in the majority of cases. In recent years banks have expanded their products and services, as well as the diversity of their distribution channels. Where a bank or any financial institution participates in a moratorium, it is preferable for it to do so in respect of all the facilities which it, or institutions related to it, make available to the company world-wide. This is in order to protect the company from the action by non-participants in the moratorium, for instance by reduction of facilities, on the basis of privileged information received from the bank and shared internally. However, there can also be strong reasons to exclude particular types of facility. The inclusion of the various parts of a diverse banking group depends in part on whether the company feels vulnerable to opportunistic action.

Insurance companies and other bonding providers

Performance bonds and guarantees are generally extended by banks, insurance companies and some specialist providers. Bonds provided by banks are nearly always included in a moratorium, usually because the bank also provides other facilities which will be included. However, insurance companies or other specialist providers will normally only be included where they are central to the company's ability to continue trading. For example, performance bonds and guarantees usually form a substantial part of the financing requirements of construction companies. These are required to support contract tenders, advance payments, and overall performance on contracts. The maintenance of such bonding arrangements is critical to the survival of such companies. Also, it is likely that as the group's financial problems become more public, its bonding requirement will increase. In such cases, providers of bonding services should be included in the moratorium.

Leasing companies

Unless leasing liabilities constitute a significant proportion of the company's overall debt, providers of these facilities are normally excluded from the moratorium, whether or not such services are furnished by a subsidiary of a participating bank. The main reasons for this are that:

- The indebtedness is effectively linked to an underlying asset.
- The lessor may repossess the asset relatively easily if the lease payments do not continue to be met (adversely affecting the day-to-day operations of the company).
- A leasing company is very unlikely to wish to participate in any new liquidity or debt restructuring arrangements.

As a result, the leasing obligations of a company are treated as part of its normal overheads and continue to be met as normally as possible. The leasing companies are unlikely to want to take any action if payment obligations continue to be met. Additional finance will have to be provided to the company if the leasing companies refuse to make additional replacement lines available in response to the company's financial problems. Provided significant sums are not involved, banks would prefer to risk having to meet such financing needs themselves, rather than increase the complexity of the moratorium by including another class of creditors.

Nevertheless, liabilities in respect of finance leases have occasionally been included in moratoriums. This is usually because the assets thereby financed were critical to the business (for example, ships, aircraft, containers, or printing presses). Other cases for their inclusion include a moratorium triggering cross-default provisions in such finance leases, or their significance in the context of the total liabilities of the company.

Factoring and receivables financing companies

The providers of factoring and receivables finance can rely on a third party to achieve repayment, without taking any action against the company. In most cases the finance is extended over a short period, with repayment often likely before the proposed end of the moratorium. Consequently, the mere passage of time will see such parties being repaid, in the absence of bad debts, independently of the company's fortunes. It is therefore unlikely that providers of this type of finance will agree to a moratorium unless they have a wider vested interest. A negative consequence of their non-participation is that this will increase the pressure on the company's cash flow and invariably lead to more finance being needed. On the positive side, additional assets will be released to provide security.

Holders of commercial paper, bonds, loan stock and other capital market instruments

Money and capital market instruments will often constitute a significant proportion of the company's total indebtedness where a company has access to these markets. This gives this class of creditor a powerful voice in any discussions that take place with the company and amongst the creditors.

The investors in capital market instruments are frequently different in character and objectives to banks. Furthermore, many of the capital markets products have features and structures which make them different from bank loans.

Typically, the holder of this type of instrument is an institutional or private investor. The investor is not interested in developing a commercial relationship with the company, and generally maintains a very passive role in relation to the company's affairs. Where the instrument is publicly traded, the investor is required not to breach the prevailing insider trading legislation. Also, where a secondary market exists, the investor can readily sell his exposure without becoming involved in a moratorium.

Motives and objectives will differ substantially between investors. Also, when bearer bonds are involved, the number of holders can be very large and their identity largely unknown. Ultimate ownership can also be difficult to establish even for registered bonds, because of the use of fronting organisations and nominee companies.

In the early stages of a moratorium, it is unlikely that any holder of these types of financial instruments will reveal their identity. Even if they do so, the negotiation process will probably take considerably longer than the term of the proposed moratorium. If a company's difficulties are kept confidential and no actual default situation exists under the terms of the instruments (which tend to be less restrictive than those for bank facilities), then holders of such instruments will normally not take part in the moratoriums. However their co-operation will probably be needed later in the moratorium and in the restructuring process itself.

Junior or mezzanine debt providers

These are institutions which provide subordinated debt. Frequently, this creditor class will be seen in companies that have been the subject of a management buy-out, or other highly leveraged transaction. Such companies tend to be more prone to financial difficulties. As a result it is not uncommon to find this creditor class in a loan workout. Furthermore, the providers of subordinated debt will often have an equity stake in the company, or have lent it senior debt.

The presence of a subordinated debt class introduces many complexities in a moratorium. Such creditors will have different starting points and conflicting objectives. Finding a solution which accommodates all their interests is extremely difficult.

The terms and conditions attaching to the subordinated debt will be a key determinant of a subordinated debt provider's involvement in a moratorium. Often the subordinated debt providers agree not to take action to accelerate payment for a given period after a default. This period might in some cases be up to three or six months. In such cases, the subordinated debt class has effectively pre-agreed to a moratorium. Their position after the expiry of the initial grace period will need to be considered.

Generally, subordinated debt providers are asked to participate in moratoriums. Their response depends on the commercial circumstances of the case. They are likely to participate in a moratorium if they consider that they can improve their negotiating position thereby. There will be an added incentive to do so if the banks are in a relatively weak position, for example if there is a large gap between the going concern and liquidation values of the company.

Because the starting point and the perspective of the subordinated debt providers are so different to those of banks, it is difficult to achieve a moratorium and eventual restructuring which fully meets each of the parties' objectives. Invariably, any agreement is a product of intense negotiations.

Lenders to special-purpose vehicles or third parties with recourse

Instances will arise where finance has been provided to ringfenced special-purpose companies, or third parties unaffected by the company's difficulties, but where the finance is guaranteed by the company suffering problems. The particular circumstances involved will determine how to treat such cases. Influencing factors will include whether or not the financial institution is a direct lender to the guarantor as well, or whether the banks participating in the moratorium propose to take additional security over the guarantor's assets. In the latter case, such a move would clearly disadvantage the lender to the third party or the special-purpose vehicle company. In some cases, a bank lending to the third party may hold a negative pledge undertaking from the guarantor company, requiring its consent to provide additional security.

Generally, provided the trading fortunes of the two businesses are genuinely separate and the indebtedness is supportable by the borrower without reliance on the guarantor, it is normal to exclude the underlying facility from the moratorium. However, the lender may be required to participate in the moratorium in respect of its rights under the guarantee by agreeing not to enforce it against the guarantor during the moratorium. Alternatively, if it does make a claim, it agrees to provide a replacement loan to meet any such claim. The replacement loan would then be subject to the terms of the moratorium. In return, the bank's contingent claim will share in the benefits of the moratorium, such as any security given.

Under such an arrangement a bank would be free to maintain a commercial relationship with the borrower, with the financing arrangements operating outside the constraints of the moratorium.

Inter-company creditors

This becomes an important consideration when dealing with a group involving a large number of subsidiaries. An efficient treasury operation will allocate surplus funds generated by cash positive subsidiaries to fund cash absorption in other parts of the group. This may take place directly between subsidiaries, or via a treasury company. Where inter-company debts arise due to funding decisions (as opposed to intra-group trading) then any change in these positions might advantage or disadvantage different financial creditors.

Consideration needs to be given to whether subsidiaries which are creditors of fellow subsidiaries of the same group are effectively asked to join in the moratorium. Frequently, as discussed in Section B, in the eventual restructuring agreement each of the companies in the group agrees not to make new loans, or to repay, or seek repayment of, existing inter-company obligations.

18

THE OPERATION
OF FACILITIES IN A
MORATORIUM

Introduction

Having decided who to include in a moratorium, the various parties need to agree the basis on which they are to participate. The key problem in this area revolves around determining the precise level of commitment that should be required from each party during the moratorium. Differences in operations of different types of facilities cause difficulties in comparison in this area. Moreover, many financing arrangements need to continue operating during the moratorium, and rules are required to ensure no single party is relatively better-off, or disadvantaged, as a result.

This chapter highlights the issues that can arise in determining the appropriate level of commitment for each creditor participating in the moratorium. Areas where alternative perspectives may lead to different results are also identified. The purpose is to stress the principles that need to be agreed in this area as part of the moratorium, with details agreed subsequently as part of the ensuing restructuring contract.

There is considerable scope for disagreement in this area and it is one of the main sources of contention between participants in a moratorium. In our view a universally agreed convention, or protocol, governing this element of the loan workout process would greatly facilitate the arrangement of moratoriums.

Determining commitment levels

Commitment levels at the start of a moratorium are important during its operation as these are often used to determine matters such as:

- The on-going commitment levels of the participants.
- Relative loss-sharing burdens.
- New money contributions.

- Fee sharing.
- Voting arrangements.

The commitment limit for each financial creditor is established by reference to the amount outstanding under the facility as at the 'moratorium date' (i.e., as at the close of business of the day prior to the all-bank meeting calling the moratorium). Therefore, the facility limit in a moratorium may not be the same as the original facility amount. Each financial creditor will find that the new commitment level in the moratorium for each of its facilities will be either the same, higher or lower than the commitment level under its original facility agreements. This will depend on whether each facility was fully drawn, in excess, or partially undrawn at the time.

An institution with a facility that is undrawn at the 'moratorium date' will not be required to participate in the moratorium, at least in respect of that particular facility. This applies whether or not the facility is a committed line or a revolving loan with many years unexpired. The reason for this is that the calling of a moratorium will constitute an event of default under most committed facility agreements. No financial institution will allow a facility to be drawn in such circumstances.

Issues relating to different types of facility

There are a number of features that can complicate the exercise of establishing the commitment level of lenders. Figure 18.1 below summarises the different issues that are dealt with in this context.

Gross and net exposure

The level of the facility outstanding is usually determined on the basis of the net position, i.e., after deducting the value of any credit balances over which the financial creditor can establish a legal right of set-off. The company will lose all available

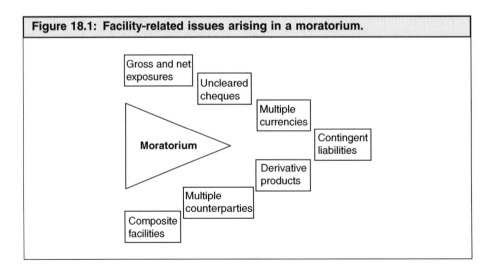

Figure 18.1: Facility-related issues arising in a moratorium.

headroom in the original facility agreements and some (or all) of the group's available cash balances. Unless the group is projecting to remain cash neutral or cash positive going forward, this will lead to a need for additional financing to be arranged.

Uncleared cheques in the course of presentation

The moratorium facility limit should be based on the balance after all cheques paid into the account in the days preceding the moratorium date have been paid by the drawee bank(s). In other words, the balance as at the moratorium date should be adjusted in the event that any cheques credited prior to that date are subsequently returned unpaid.

Multiple currencies

The moratorium limits can either continue to be denominated in the currency in which they are made available, or they can all be determined by reference to a currency equivalent limit based upon exchange rates prevailing as at the moratorium date. In practice, neither is perfect as the different circumstances of individual lenders and variations in types of facility can lead to distortions. For the purposes of this chapter it is sufficient to state that it is preferable for facility limits in a moratorium to be fixed in the currency of the outstanding exposure. Whilst this is valid for most situations, Chapter 20 examines in more detail the issues that can arise where facilities are provided in more than one currency.

Contingent liabilities

By definition, it is usually not possible to quantify an exact exposure in relation to contingent liabilities as at the moratorium date. The actual exposure cannot be determined until the liability is crystallised. The actual liability will lie somewhere between nil and the maximum amount stated in the relevant instrument.

The institution responsible for the contingent facility could simply be asked to continue on the existing basis up to the maximum amount outstanding as at the moratorium date. However, this ignores the fact that the probability and amount at which an existing contingent liability might crystallise almost certainly changes with time. Also, in practice it is not possible to replace one expiring contingent liability with another offering an identical profile. Issues relating to guarantees and other contingent liabilities are considered further later in this chapter.

Derivative products

Institutions may employ a system of notional limits for these facilities. However, such a system should not be used for the purpose of establishing a moratorium date position unless all banks agree to do so. Also, the same methodology must be applied to each exposure. In most cases, institutions are able to calculate the actual exposure on each of the outstanding contracts as at the moratorium date. Furthermore, financial institutions can employ a mark-to-market methodology to revalue contracts daily, and thus ensure that they continue to provide such facilities up to the level calculated as outstanding at the moratorium date. One difficulty, however, is that, market movements may result in an involuntary excess arising later. The banks will need to consider how to deal with this eventuality. This issue is often addressed alongside the new money provisions of any agreement.

Facility extended to multiple counterparties

This issue arises where an existing facility has traditionally been made available to more than one company in a group. For example, a situation may arise where a group over-draft arrangement is involved, but drawings at the moratorium date are outstanding in the name of some of the companies only. Other companies within the original facility arrangement may need to draw on the facility at a later date. This might improve or adversely affect the position of a particular bank participating in the moratorium. At the same time, it may not be compatible with any new ringfencing structure introduced as part of the moratorium. If the facility is available across a ringfence structure then it may have to be apportioned between the relevant companies in order to preserve the loss-sharing arrangements. Issues relating to loss-sharing and ringfencing are examined in further detail later in the book.

Composite facilities

Where a general facility limit is available to a company covering more than one type of facility, the loss-sharing provisions may be affected. Flexibility between loans, acceptance credits and overdrafts, or between non-debt facilities does not usually create a problem. Difficulties with loss-sharing arrangements can arise where a single limit is applied across both debt and non-debt facilities.

On-going operation of facilities

In this section we set out a standard approach for dealing with different types of on-going facilities in a moratorium. Although there may be instances where a different approach is appropriate, such exceptions should be justified by compelling circumstances.

Figure 18.2 summarises the different types of on-going facility that are considered in the rest of this chapter.

Term loans

The moratorium agreement should provide for each existing draw-down to be rolled-over at maturity. In each case, roll-overs should be subject to a minimum interest period of, say, three months to ease the related administrative burden. However, institutions are unlikely to roll-over their exposures beyond the moratorium. In addition, the roll-over dates of all the loans in the moratorium should be harmonised to ensure that no bank gains an advantage from the timing of interest payments.

Strictly, the banks should only be required to roll-over individual loan draw-downs where asked to do so by the company. The bank's commitment to the company is to make loan advances up to the amount outstanding at the moratorium date, when asked

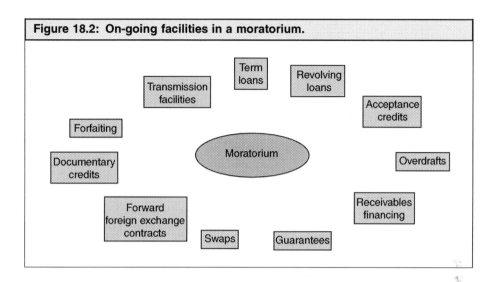

Figure 18.2: On-going facilities in a moratorium.

to do so. Their commitment to the other financial institutions participating in the moratorium is that if the company subsequently fails, the bank providing the loan will share the benefit of any improvement in its position (from a loan not being rolled-over) with the other institutions. If a moratorium agreement or loss-sharing arrangement cannot be relied upon, the co-ordinator should advise the company to keep its debt facilities as fully drawn as possible and not provide for any reductions. In some cases, this may require the company to alter its banking arrangements so that any credits paid in are handled through a reliable 'friendly' bank (perhaps the co-ordinator itself). This would ensure that these funds remain available to the company.

Revolving loans

Revolving loans are dealt with in the same way as term loans, except that the facility structure anticipates utilisation fluctuating in line with requirements. The facility should continue to operate normally within the level of utilisation outstanding as at the moratorium date, provided the issues highlighted in the context of term loans above are complied with by the parties.

Acceptance credits

This refers to facilities where funds are advanced by an institution against a bill of exchange or promissory note drawn upon the company itself. The treatment is almost identical to the position for loans. The moratorium will require the financial institution either to:

- Accept and discount a further bill of exchange. Or
- Provide the company with a replacement loan.

Each acceptance should be for a minimum interest period. This should preferably be the same minimum interest period agreed for the loans.

Overdrafts

Banks providing an overdraft facility will be asked to continue to permit the company to operate it up to the level of indebtedness outstanding as at the moratorium date. Banks that provide an overdraft are normally also amongst the company's core group of banks. They will usually have a close and long-standing relationship with the company, and have wider vested interests to consider. They will normally be institutions that can be relied upon to co-operate during a moratorium.

Usually, the overdraft facility applies to the bank account upon which the company draws cheques and into which it pays cheques and cash receipts. The overdraft balance may, therefore, represent a mixture of cleared and uncleared funds. The position will vary from country to country depending upon the relevant cheque and money transmission clearing cycles. For the purposes of the moratorium, the balance used is the position at the moratorium date after assuming that all cheques paid in are cleared. Any cheque paid in prior to the moratorium date that is subsequently returned unpaid is deducted from this balance.

As highlighted earlier in this chapter, gross and net overdraft facilities also require particular attention. Commonly, to facilitate a company's treasury management activities, banks extend overdraft facilities on the basis that some of a company's bank accounts may overdraw up to an agreed limit provided other accounts have credit balances to (partially) offset the position. In other words, an overdraft facility is extended on a 'net' basis. Normally this is only permitted where the bank has established a clear right to offset the balances in law.

Banks providing such arrangements will often cancel them in order to avoid any risk of such rights of set-off being challenged successfully by other creditors. In this case the new overdraft facility limit is based on the net position as at the moratorium date.

In some cases, a number of different subsidiaries within a group may share a common overdraft facility limit. In order to comply with the principles of a moratorium, this arrangement should cease. Individual overdraft facilities will be established for each subsidiary, based upon their positions as at the moratorium date. This is because any change in the overdraft positions of individual subsidiaries may affect the loss-sharing arrangement during the moratorium, and therefore potentially the position of financial creditors lending to the separate subsidiaries.

The position becomes particularly complicated where a group operates a single overdraft facility across various subsidiaries and also has a 'gross and net' arrangement in place. In this case both arrangements will have to be cancelled. At the same time, the basis of the distribution of any credit balances between the subsidiaries' overdrawn accounts will need to be agreed. Perhaps the fairest arrangement from the perspective of the other creditors is for the credit balances to be distributed *pro rata* to the overdrawn accounts. In practice, however, the bank affected will have the right to apportion the credit balances on whatever basis it considers appropriate (provided of course that this complies with its legal rights of set-off).

Due to their distortion to loss-sharing arrangements, any automatic, daily zero-balancing arrangements may also need to be cancelled.

Receivables financing facilities

This applies to all types of debtor financing lines such as factoring, invoice discounting, and discounting bills of exchange. Providers of such finance should agree to continue to provide their facilities up to the level outstanding as at the moratorium date.

In practice, inclusion of such facilities in a moratorium can be difficult because:

- The source of repayment stems from a third party. An institution providing such facilities may feel that the quality of the receivables it has financed is such that it will achieve repayment over a period of time without taking any action. Furthermore, the repayment profile is likely to be very short-term if no new advances are made. Full repayment can probably be achieved before the end of the proposed moratorium.
- The institution will need to be satisfied that it will be replacing existing receivables with new ones of at least the same quality.
- Debtors may be less inclined to pay up if they become aware that the company to which they owe money is in difficulty. The debt may be disputed if the payment due is part of a bigger contract on which the company is failing to deliver in any way.
- The receivables finance provider may be reliant upon the company for administrative matters, for example, in following-up slow payers and keeping records. If so, it may lose confidence in the company's ability to control these areas.

Guarantees

The following considerations apply to institutions providing any type of guarantee, bond, letter of credit (except a documentary credit), indemnity, or similar contingent liability.

Frequently, the provider of a guarantee retains the right to accelerate a demand against the company on behalf of which the guarantee has been issued, notwithstanding any claim actually being made under the guarantee. This takes the form of a right to demand cash cover. In such cases, the providers of the guarantees and bonds will be asked to join the moratorium.

In principle, the providers of guarantees will be asked to participate in a moratorium on one of the following two bases, or a combination of both:

- As guarantees expire, they agree to issue further guarantees when asked to do so, up to the nominal level of guarantees outstanding as at the moratorium date. Or
- They agree to provide loans to meet any claims under the guarantees issued.

However, because of the contingent nature of their liability, it can be difficult to:

- Quantify precisely their level of exposure as at the moratorium date.
- Ensure that the risk profile of the existing exposure is not altered where a bank is either required to join an extended moratorium, or to provide replacements upon expiry of guarantees.

Consequently, the potential remains for the parties to disagree about how these facilities should be treated. One solution is to categorise guarantees into two types:

- Those issued in support of large one-off specific projects, or contracts.
- Those issued in the normal course of trading, such as customs duty deferment bonds.

The issuer will be required to fund any claims and issue replacements within any headroom created by the expiry of existing guarantees in the latter case. Where the guarantee relates to a one-off project, then the issuer is still required to fund any claim under a guarantee outstanding at the moratorium date. However, it will not have to provide any replacements upon its expiry. In such cases the issuer's exposure is reduced without it having to share the benefit with other participants in the moratorium. This is simply because it is not possible to establish with certainty whether a liability existed at all as at the moratorium date. The issuer is, nevertheless, required to agree extensions to a guarantee relating to a specific project if such extensions are sought by the beneficiary or the company.

In some cases this distinction is not always clear. For example, when dealing with a construction company, each guarantee may need to be considered on its own merits.

A key objective is to ensure replacement guarantees are similar to the ones expiring during the moratorium. The moratorium agreement may require that the issue of further replacement guarantees is subject to the following conditions:

- That each further guarantee requested must be consistent with the usual practice of that issuer and the company. For example, in respect of type, currency, beneficiary, and geographic location of the beneficiaries.

- That the relevant issuers are not required to provide guarantees with a maturity beyond a certain period (say 12 months) after the expiry of the moratorium. The reason for such a margin is to allow the guarantee facility to be operative in practice during the last few months of a moratorium.

Swaps

The appropriate treatment of swaps under a moratorium can be extremely difficult to agree. The term 'swaps' can apply to a variety of derivative-based contracts. In the majority of cases, however, the contracts involve relatively straightforward interest rate or currency swaps.

When determining the inclusion of swaps counterparties in a moratorium, it is important to understand the nature of the underlying contracts and their importance to the company's hedging strategy. Swaps are likely to benefit the bank group as a whole, by providing a hedge against adverse currency and interest rate movements.

A swap involves a two-way contract between the company and the provider. It frequently confers identical rights and obligations on the two counterparties. Normally, a swap is a committed facility. It is subject only to limited termination rights, such as cross-default, cross-acceleration, or standard insolvency events. However, there may be other swap facilities that are capable of being terminated on demand by the bank, or which are subject to more standard loan covenants. It will be necessary to review the right of the counterparty bank to take action in the event of a moratorium being called. A bank that cannot take any action has effectively joined the moratorium on a *de facto* basis.

A swap can be 'in-the-money' if the bank owes money to the company, or 'out-of-the-money' where the company owes money to the bank. The liability as at the moratorium date can be established relatively easily, with the exposure normally calculated on a 'mark-to-market' basis. This is the amount owing by one party to the other assuming that the swap is closed-out. Where nothing is owing to the bank, the swap will not be included in the moratorium. Where the swap is in-the-money, there may be a preference for the swap to be continued, so that the benefits provided by the hedge can be retained. Equally, the swap could be terminated to release cash to support the company's liquidity position. The action agreed will reflect the circumstances of the company. Conversely, if a swap is 'out-of-the-money', the relevant bank will usually be invited to join the moratorium based upon its exposure as at the moratorium date.

Whilst it is relatively easy to calculate the exposure under a swap as at the moratorium, the actual exposure outstanding during the moratorium does not stay constant. The extent of any exposure under a swap contract is driven by third party events in the money markets. The calculated 'mark-to-market' position will alter daily according to the movement of interest rates and exchange rates. In theory, the exposure is potentially unlimited.

Upon joining a moratorium, a swap provider will allow its swaps to operate normally. This will involve both the bank and the company continuing to make the regular payments to each other as required under the swap contract. In the event that the two parties agree to close out a swap, then the swap provider is required to provide a loan to fund any amount owing to it by the company. Where the swap is 'in-the-money' the funds are either passed to the company as normal, or as otherwise directed by the terms of the moratorium. A moratorium agreement may also require a swap provider to extend or provide replacement swaps if any of the existing ones expire. This will depend on whether a swap was a one-off, or whether it formed part of the company's on-going treasury requirements.

The moratorium agreement will additionally need to provide for an increase in the company's swap-related exposure during the moratorium. Similarly, the loss-sharing provisions will need to consider how the benefit of any reductions in exposure is to be allocated. There are two broad options available in this regard:

- Swap providers take the risk of their swaps moving further 'out-of-the-money' during the moratorium. In such cases they do not have to share the benefit of any reduction in exposure. Or

- Any increase in exposure is treated as new finance and prioritised accordingly. In this case, any benefit arising from a reduction in exposure is shared amongst the banks in the moratorium through the loss-sharing provisions.

The amounts involved will influence the option chosen. The banks in the moratorium may not be willing to allow swap providers to be accorded priority status for movements in exposure which take a swap further 'out-of-the-money' if potentially large sums are involved. In practice, limits could be agreed beyond which the swap would be closed out.

The co-ordinator or the steering committee will be involved in all the decisions involving the continuation or close-out of swaps, in view of their wider implications to the company and the banks. Decisions in this area have impact on the company's interest rate and currency hedging policies, the value of collateral available, and the ranking of the creditors.

Forward foreign exchange contracts

Most banks are able to value foreign exchange contracts continuously on a 'mark-to-market' basis. The treatment of any unusually large, or one-off, contracts is generally considered on the same basis as for swaps. In other cases, the relevant bank is required to provide replacement or new foreign exchange contracts on existing terms, up to the level of its exposure as at the moratorium date. This is provided that:

- Requests for new foreign exchange transactions are in accordance with the historic and customary practice between the bank and the company.
- The maturity date of the foreign exchange contract is less than a number of months (often six) after the expiry of the moratorium. This is the same principle as for guarantees, and is designed to ensure that the facility remains operable during the final stages of a moratorium.

The moratorium agreement may require the relevant bank to provide a replacement loan for any foreign exchange contracts closed-out prior to maturity. This will depend on the relative size of the foreign exchange facilities compared to the total facilities extended by the bank group.

As explained in relation to swaps, the moratorium agreement will also legislate for how foreign exchange providers are treated if the underlying exposure exceeds or falls below their moratorium date positions.

Documentary credits

Providers of documentary credits will be required to continue issuing such facilities on existing terms up to the level of their utilisation as at the moratorium date, subject to the provisos on term and historic usage also applicable to bonds and foreign exchange contracts.

In the event that a company is unable to meet its indemnity obligation under the documentary credit, the relevant bank will be required to provide a replacement loan to fund the payment. This will commensurately reduce the level of its commitment for the issue of documentary credits. In these circumstances the bank would be entitled to exercise its right of lien over any underlying goods and apply the proceeds to reduce the replacement loan.

Forfaiting

Forfaiting is a source of medium-term finance for exporters and sellers. It is a form of supplier credit. A bill of exchange or promissory note is drawn on the importer or buyer and in many cases this is then guaranteed or 'avalised' by the importer's or buyer's bank. Forfaiting involves a financial institution purchasing this bill at a discount. The facility is made available to exporters but the risk is in fact against the importer. In those cases where the bill carries a bank guarantee or '*pour aval*' endorsement, the default risk is against the guarantor bank. Forfaiting can be relevant to a moratorium whether the company is an importer or an exporter, although it is usually the case where the company is an importer.

Where the company seeking a moratorium is the importer or the drawee of the bill, then those financial institutions that have discounted the bill will be approached to join the moratorium. If the bill has been guaranteed or avalised then the financial institution concerned may be reluctant to join the moratorium, prefering to rely upon the bank's guarantee. This judgement will be based on the quality and standing of the bank issuing the guarantee.

Where the company that is seeking a moratorium is the exporter or drawer of the bill, then there is normally no reason to involve the financial institutions to which it has sold bills of exchange. This is unless the bill has been purchased by an institution with recourse to the drawer as well as the drawee. Nevertheless, forfaiting may form a vital source of finance for the company, without which its liquidity position would worsen. In such a case it may be necessary to persuade the relevant financial institution to continue to discount bills of exchange drawn on third parties.

The moratorium agreement will require the relevant financial institution to continue to discount bills of exchange up to the level of exposure outstanding as at the moratorium date. In the event that a bill cannot be honoured, the financial institution will be required to fund the payment by providing a replacement loan.

Settlement and other transmission or funds transfer risks

Financial institutions provide a range of money transmission services and employ various methods of providing these services. Each institution has its own techniques of assessing and quantifying the risks involved with each product. Each case will need to be considered on its own merits, although frequently the overall values involved play a decisive role. In many instances, the risks involved in settlement and transmission services can be mitigated, or indeed eliminated, either by employing other methods of funds transfer, or by requiring payments to be received before funds are paid. Often the major settlement risks are incurred by the main relationship bank. Such banks are usually willing to continue providing facilities that carry only an intra-day risk, or perhaps one- or two-day risk at the most. This enables them to take corrective action if a company's failure is imminent. Where the service is vital to the company, the post-enforcement loss-sharing provisions in the moratorium agreement will be drafted to accommodate these types of facility if the issue cannot be otherwise resolved.

19

THE CONCEPT OF
LOSS-SHARING

Introduction

Loss-sharing is the generic term used to describe the provisions within a moratorium agreement that are concerned with ensuring its conformity with certain fundamental principles, which are that:

- All participants in a moratorium should be treated equally.
- No participant should be permitted to improve its position compared to any other whilst a review and turnaround are in progress.
- Any additional risks incurred after a moratorium is called should be borne by each participant *pro rata* to its exposure at the moratorium date.

Loss-sharing lies at the very heart of a moratorium, because it is concerned with treating all its participants fairly, and thereby engendering confidence in the process. Frequently, the loss-sharing arrangements agreed as part of a moratorium will be incorporated into any ensuing financial restructuring agreement.

The concept of loss-sharing is explained more fully in this chapter and its importance is highlighted. The various aspects of a moratorium's operations that demonstrate the need for loss-sharing arrangements are also outlined. Finally, relevant documentation-related issues are explored.

The importance of loss-sharing

In many moratorium and restructuring agreements, the greatest source of error and the potential for varying the participants' 'relative' moratorium date positions are found in the loss-sharing arrangements. Despite this, in practice it is one of the areas often given the least attention. The mechanical operation of specific loss-sharing provisions, and the potential impact of their interaction, is rarely fully understood. As a result, the relative impacts of different scenarios on the participants' exposures are not fully reflected in any agreements.

In many ways the expression 'loss-sharing' conveys a negative impression, since it implies failure. In fact, the majority of loss-sharing provisions are not aimed at directing the burden of losses. Their main objective is to equalise the position of the participants so that no participant gains an unfair advantage over another. In most cases, the 'loss-sharing' arrangements can provide a mechanism to share gains. For example, such gain might arise from the sale of assets, or other reductions in the exposure of participants during the moratorium.

However there is a subtle, if quite fundamental, difference between the 'loss'- and 'gain'-focused perspectives. A gain-oriented view assumes that, in the event of the company's insolvency during the moratorium, any eventual loss will be lower than the total exposure of participants at the beginning of the moratorium. A loss-oriented view focuses on the possibility that the total exposure of participants may increase after the moratorium is called. The implications of emphasising the potential for losses can be significant. Some lenders may agree to join a moratorium, even if reluctantly, as an acknowledgement of their wider responsibilities. At the same time, they may be opposed to an arrangement that might result in their exposure increasing. Therefore, the precise objectives and structures of the loss-sharing arrangements in a moratorium can be fundamental to lenders' decision-making. It is therefore important for each party to review the related provisions carefully.

Definition and framework

The loss-sharing provisions within a moratorium agreement can be defined as:

> The mechanism whereby, in the event of an overall shortfall being registered during a moratorium, such adjustments are made between its participants as are necessary to ensure that the collective loss or gain is shared between the participants *pro rata* to their relative exposures as at the start of the moratorium.

Under a loss-sharing arrangement, the relative positions of the participants are restored by making appropriate 'equalisation' payments between the participants at the appropriate time.

The loss-sharing arrangements are not catered for by a single provision within a moratorium agreement. Also, such arrangements do not operate in isolation from other aspects of the agreement, other than in the most straightforward cases. In practice the overall loss-sharing structure is the product of a number of provisions in an agreement that interact to produce the desired outcome.

A loss-sharing structure should be considered in two distinct stages. The first stage relates to those provisions that act to equalise the individual positions of banks and to recreate the relativity that existed at the start of the moratorium. The second stage relates to the sharing of any risks, costs, expenses and recoveries in proportion to the relative positions of the participants at the start of the moratorium.

Loss-sharing arrangements are often considered as being primarily a post-enforcement issue, which concerns only the lenders, and not the company. It could be argued that unless the company fails, there is no need to provide for how losses are to be shared.

However, in practice, many of the pre-enforcement provisions in a moratorium or restructuring are also part of the loss-sharing structure. As a result, and for reasons highlighted later in this chapter, loss-sharing principles should be followed as closely as possible in the pre-enforcement phase. In this case, some of the arrangements can have a material effect on the pre-enforcement position of the participants in a moratorium. As a result, these issues will be of interest to the company.

Loss-sharing and equalisation provisions contain crucial links between the pre-enforcement system of sharing the proceeds of any asset realisations and the post-enforcement system. In making that link it is essential that the sharing principles are preserved. For example, it is usual to permit holders of existing security to have priority for the proceeds of such security. Therefore it is important to ensure that such a benefit is not lost by a subsequent equalisation payment.

The level of detail required to implement loss-sharing arrangements will reflect the information available about the company, the complexity of the group's facilities, the stability of the loan workout process, and the time available to develop a comprehensive structure. The complexity of the governing documentation will reflect the strategic and commercial decisions made by the participants in this regard. If a simple agreement is preferred, the document will only present the broad principles relating to loss-sharing and equalisation. This is the minimum necessary in any moratorium agreement. Alternatively, the documentation may provide for a more comprehensive treatment of the mechanics of the related arrangements. The loss-sharing arrangements can become amongst the most complex aspects of the documentation in these cases.

Why is a loss-sharing arrangement necessary?

The basic principle in a moratorium is that all the participants should 'stand still', or freeze their exposures. In practice this is not possible. When lenders agree to join a moratorium, their commitment is in fact to continue to make available their respective facilities up to a predetermined level. Also, such facilities must be operated as normally as possible. The reference to a 'moratorium' relates to the postponement of any action against the company. It is therefore necessary to develop a structure that permits fluctuations in exposures, subject to an agreement that the relative positions of participants will be restored if events do not turn out as anticipated.

During a moratorium, changes to the lenders' relative positions can arise for a variety of reasons. The following are the most common:

- *The moratorium will usually include a variety of revolving credit facilities and overdrafts.* For the company to continue operating normally, these must remain operational. Banks provide a wide range of non-debt facilities which are similarly affected. If the company fails during the moratorium, the indebtedness under each of these facilities will most likely be different from that prevailing as at the start of the moratorium.

- *For certain types of facilities, it may not be possible to quantify the actual value of outstanding risk as at the moratorium date.* Guarantees are the most common example of this. In this case the exposure as at the moratorium date is assumed to be the maximum possible. The actual liability may of course transpire to be lower, or the guarantee may lapse.

- *For certain classes of facility, the exposure may simply expire with time.*

- *With the passage of time, certain subsidiary companies within a group may be sold as part of a turnaround strategy.* The actual or contingent indebtedness to the subsidiary may be assumed by the new owners. This will result in certain banks' exposure being taken over by a new counterparty, hopefully one which enjoys a better credit standing. This would be construed as effectively a repayment under the provisions of a moratorium agreement.

- *Facilities may be extended by different lenders in a variety of currencies.* Exchange rate movements during the moratorium may have a substantial impact upon the relative positions of the different lenders.

- *Some, or all, of the participants may agree to provide additional facilities* during the moratorium. Where this is extended on a basis other than *pro rata* to the exposures of all lenders as at the moratorium date, the relative exposures of lenders will change.

- *The proceeds of disposals may be used to prepay debt facilities* rather than to collateralise non-debt facilities, in order to reduce the company's interest burden. This will impact on the relative exposures of the participants.

Loss-sharing provisions and documentation

The loss-sharing provisions can be designed to operate in a number of ways across the company's overall facility structure in a moratorium agreement. The precise arrangement will depend on the complexity of the group's financing arrangements prior to the moratorium. The post-enforcement loss-sharing arrangements are normally contained within a separate inter-creditor agreement. Many of these concepts, which are subsequently incorporated in financial restructuring agreements, are discussed in more detail in Chapters 21 and 22.

The main components of a loss-sharing structure, some of which operate pre-enforcement whilst others operate post-enforcement, are as follows:

Equalisation

Equalisation is the mechanism by which the exposures of lenders are adjusted to restore their relative positions as at the moratorium date.

In most cases, changes will lead to a reduction in exposures, since the lenders are unlikely to agree to an increase in their exposure during a moratorium. In these cases, in the event of bankruptcy equalisation involves the affected banks sharing the benefit of such reductions with the other banks. This is usually done by a claw-back arrangement. The total amount of headroom under all the facilities as at the point of bankruptcy is calculated and collected from each bank. This is then divided amongst all the banks' facilities *pro rata* to their exposures as at the moratorium date.

Changes in utilisation levels arising from the impact of movements in exchange rates on currency facilities can also be dealt with by way of equalisation. These situations can be very complex. Issues relating to multi-currency facilities and loss-sharing are considered in Chapter 20.

For the most part, equalisation arrangements are effected post-enforcement. Nevertheless, it is possible to require pre-enforcement adjustments from time to time, for example, where the sums realised from asset disposals are significant, or individual positions have altered materially and permanently.

Priorities

Where additional facilities are required, ideally these would be provided by all the lenders *pro rata* to their moratorium date positions. This would enable the new risk to be shared equitably between all the participants. In practice this may not be possible. Banks that are not close to the company, or have a relatively small exposure, will not have the incentive to increase their exposures.

In practice, therefore, new facilities are often provided by the group's core bankers. In return, all the participants in a moratorium are required to approve a priority ranking for this new exposure. Where the value of the company's assets covers the new facility comfortably, all the lenders effectively share in the increased risk, by way of dilution in the potential recoveries amongst the existing facilities.

Ringfencing

This issue frequently arises in more complex corporate structures. Facilities may either be extended to different subsidiaries within the group, or be guaranteed by different subsidiaries. As a result, different banks may find that their exposures have a different risk profile to those of other participants in a moratorium. In such cases, the moratorium agreement provides for various businesses in the group to be grouped and 'ringfenced' for the benefit of specific financial creditors.

Distributions

All proceeds of asset realisations during a moratorium are distributed *pro rata* to the participants' relative positions as at the moratorium date, subject to any ringfencing considerations. In a pre-enforcement scenario, this would require any non-debt facilities to be cash-collateralised. This will be expensive for the company as the cash would be better employed in reducing debt. In such cases, it is preferable for the funds to be used to meet the company's funding requirements or to reduce debt, subject to a loss-sharing mechanism to restore the funds to the banks which have foregone a reduction in their exposures.

Indemnities

Inevitably there will be a number of costs incurred during a moratorium and the restructuring. The co-ordinator, in particular, will need to appoint reporting accountants and lawyers before any prospect of saving the company can be evaluated. If the company survives, these costs will be borne by it. However, in the event that the company fails to meet such costs, the moratorium agreement will provide for the lenders to indemnify the co-ordinator and other parties, on a *pro rata* basis, for costs incurred directly in relation to the moratorium.

Loss-sharing and different types of facilities

Different financial institutions will adopt different attitudes to a moratorium. Even amongst the participants, there will often be a number who will not wish to enter into at least some of its loss-sharing arrangements. This will be influenced by the types of facility they provide.

Those institutions providing secured or *quasi*-secured facilities will be reluctant to join the moratorium anyway, unless they are among the core bankers of the company. Leasing companies are frequently excluded from moratoriums. One of the reasons for this is that they are unlikely to participate in some of the loss-sharing mechanisms.

Some institutions may agree to a moratorium, but will not be willing to be bound by the main moratorium agreement. For example, bondholders may agree not to take action against the company, but will not be willing to advance additional finance, or to provide indemnities to other participants. Junior or subordinated debt providers, and those extending facilities to third parties subject to a guarantee from the company, will be similarly unwilling to accept some of the conditions in a moratorium agreement.

Financial institutions providing facilities for which the precise exposure at the start of the moratorium cannot be quantified will also find the impact of loss-sharing provisions on their own positions difficult to evaluate. This primarily affects those participants providing guarantees and letters of credit. They may agree to continue providing replacement bonds up to the nominal amount outstanding as at the moratorium date. However, an agreement to claw-back adjustments based upon the nominal value of bonds outstanding as at the moratorium date may be seen as unacceptably onerous.

There are a number of options available to address these problems. Firstly, it is possible to ascribe a notional exposure to each such facility. This may be based on the internationally recognised capital weighting for such instruments, being either 100 per cent, 50 per cent or 20 per cent. Secondly, each facility or guarantee could be valued by the reporting accountants as at the moratorium date. Alternatively, an independent arbitrator may be engaged for this purpose. Thirdly, it may be agreed that certain guarantee facilities will be subject to all the loss-sharing provisions, whilst others are excluded from certain aspects, such as the equalisation adjustments.

Sharing the reward as well as the risk

In theory at least, the moratorium agreement only needs to address loss-sharing provisions as a post-enforcement event. *Prima facie*, this would considerably simplify the ongoing day-to-day administration of the transaction and the associated documentation. The co-ordinator would not need to deal with any adjustments unless the support operation were to fail. However, in practice, confining loss-sharing to post-enforcement events causes many difficulties:

- It may become extremely difficult for an individual bank to quantify or monitor its true exposure during the moratorium, since it will not be possible for it to take into account all the adjustments provided for by the various documented loss-sharing clauses.

- A loss-sharing system that only becomes effective post-enforcement gives rise to a series of inter-bank indemnities at the pre-enforcement stage. This is because banks will effectively be assuming notional obligations to make equalisation payments to each other.

The participants in a moratorium will assume unquantifiable risks against counterparties in a system which is only designed to be operative post-enforcement. Banks normally operate comprehensive and strict exposure guidelines and policies against such risks.

Where a bank's exposure is indemnified by another participant in a moratorium, it may not attribute the correct risk weighting to the asset, and may allocate capital to it unnecessarily. Equally, where it has a notional liability under an 'indemnity', the bank is probably not reporting this risk to the regulatory authorities, and may not be receiving any reward for the risk. These implications of entering into loss-sharing arrangements should be addressed by the participants.

Inevitably, providing for some aspects of loss-sharing as a post-enforcement event is unavoidable. However, the provisions of the moratorium agreement can be structured so that the larger loss-sharing adjustments are either avoided, or effectively occur pre-enforcement. In this way, the value of final adjustments required in the event of a company's collapse is kept to a minimum and the scale of post-enforcement indemnities is minimised. This issue is addressed in more detail in Chapter 22.

Loss-sharing provisions in a restructuring agreement

Many of the issues relating to loss-sharing during a moratorium apply equally to the period covered by any subsequent restructuring agreement. Such agreements therefore need to incorporate mechanisms to maintain the participants' relative positions during their currency. As indicated earlier, loss-sharing provisions contained in moratorium agreements are often carried over into restructuring agreements for this purpose.

20

MULTI-CURRENCY CONSIDERATIONS

Introduction

The last three decades have seen significant growth in multinationals. Corporate treasury functions have become more sophisticated, actively looking to hedge the value of assets and cash flows in international markets. Banks and capital markets have also expanded world-wide and developed more complex products and service offerings. As a result, loan workouts increasingly have an international dimension. Frequently, the facilities involved in such transactions are extended by a variety of international banks, in different currencies, against the assets and earnings of different subsidiaries located in different jurisdictions.

Moratoriums seek to preserve stability during a loan workout by maintaining the relative positions of its participants. However, fluctuations in currencies during this period add to difficulties in meeting this objective, in addition to the other factors highlighted in the earlier chapters of this section. This chapter examines the problems created by currency movements in loan workouts and presents various approaches for dealing with them.

Causes of currency-related complications

As Figure 20.1 below illustrates, potential distortions from different currencies and movements in exchange rates can arise in a number of ways during a moratorium. Banking facilities in different currencies represent perhaps the most obvious and immediate area for attention. Currency-related complexities also stem from the geographic concentrations of value within the group, represented by collateral or earnings. In addition, distortions can arise where all the company's finances and its assets and earnings are denominated in the same currency, but the domestic or reporting currency of the lenders themselves vary.

Alternative approaches are available to deal with currency-related issues during a moratorium. This can cause disagreements between the participants as each will

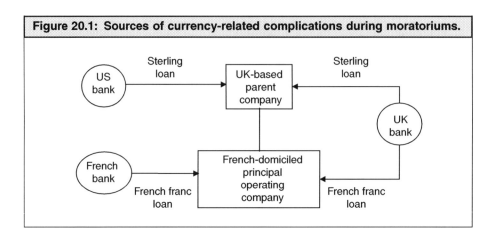

Figure 20.1: Sources of currency-related complications during moratoriums.

be affected differently, depending on the methodology adopted. In the absence of an established international convention in this area, the co-ordinator will need to judge the extent to which it is possible to address all the relevant issues in the initial moratorium agreement. It may be preferable to rely on a general statement of intent to ensure a moratorium can be established quickly. Irrespective of the approach adopted, it is important to be aware of the relevant issues at the outset. The aim should be to implement the preferred arrangements immediately following the announcement of a moratorium in order to avoid problems at a later stage.

Limits and utilisation

Multi-currency facilities are a source for the potential breach of a fundamental principle of a moratorium. Central to the philosophy of a moratorium is the principle that each lender should commit to continue extending to the company its existing facilities, with the limit adjusted to reflect the outstanding exposure as at the moratorium date. Even if the lenders do not take steps to alter their exposures during a moratorium, the movements in exchange rates alone affect the size of facility limits in relation to a base currency. The impact of such variations in limits caused by currency movements on the relative position of lenders needs to be addressed in a moratorium agreement.

When a moratorium is called, the participants need to agree how facilities denom-inated in a foreign currency are to be treated with respect to the applicable limits and the on-going operation of facilities. It is important to avoid 'currency equivalent' limits being applied to facilities, whereby the limit is quoted as the domestic currency equivalent of a foreign currency. There are two immediate reasons for this. The first is that such an arrangement leads to the need for the utilisation to be continuously re-valued in order to monitor compliance with the limit. This is administratively cumbersome. Even more importantly, if currency equivalent limits are employed, it may be necessary for the company to make payments from time to time, to keep the utilisation of a facility within its limit. Conversely, a bank may be required to permit further drawings within any headroom created by exchange rate movements. The facility limits at the moratorium date should, therefore, be established in the same currency as their utilisation as at the start of the moratorium. This methodology should be applied notwithstanding the currency in which a limit is specified in the original facility agreement.

Exceptions to this approach will be necessary where the company's facilities are intended to operate in a number of currencies. For example, a multi-currency overdraft facility may be involved, which is drawn in a number of currencies, in line with the company's requirements. Similarly, a forward foreign exchange facility will, by definition, involve two currencies and is probably available to hedge a larger number of currency pairs. In these limited cases, the practice is to permit utilisation to continue in the various currencies, with utilisation being maintained against a 'currency equivalent' limit. The provider of the facility is permitted to choose the currency of the 'currency equivalent' limit. Generally, where such exceptions are required, the facilities tend to be revolving. The level of utilisation fluctuates more through usage, than the impact of exchange rate movements. In any event, the relative importance of such facilities in a moratorium is likely to be relatively modest. The mechanisms for dealing with excesses or headrooms created by the movements of exchange rates are outlined later in this chapter.

For those facilities which operate in a single currency against a limit denominated in the same currency as its utilisation, the on-going operation will be straightforward. Utilisation can be measured directly against the agreed moratorium facility limit. In cases where multi-currency facilities and 'currency equivalent' limits are applied, the moratorium agreement will require the bank to permit the company to draw or utilise the facility. This will be so provided the aggregate equivalent value of all existing and proposed utilisations converted at the prevailing exchange rates does not exceed the relevant currency equivalent limit.

A 'currency equivalent' limit system may operate either because of the nature of the facility, or because all participants prefer to adopt the approach in relation to all the currency-denominated facilities included in the moratorium. A mechanism to preserve the relative positions of participants will need to be agreed in such situations. This will involve a combination of the following:

- Periodic adjustments to reduce utilisation back within the currency equivalent facility limit, or conversely to increase utilisation back to the limit. This will be particularly appropriate in the case of non-revolving facilities, such as term loans.

- Automatic priority status for the element of any utilisation which, at the point of insolvency, exceeds the equivalent facility limit as a result of exchange rate movements.

- Claw-back provisions in relation to any headroom in the facility at the point of insolvency.

For reasons mentioned previously, however, 'currency equivalent' limits should only be adopted in situations where facility limits cannot be practically denominated in the currency of their utilisation.

Distributions and loss-sharing

Movements in exchange rates will impact on the relative positions of lenders involved in a moratorium. To preserve their relative positions during the operation of the moratorium, it is necessary to consider:

- How the relative position of the participants can be established.
- How any gains or losses accruing to the participants as a result of exchange rate movements can be assessed.
- How these gains and losses can be shared between the participants so that their relative positions are maintained.

We suggested that, wherever possible, limits should be denoted in the same currency as the utilisation of a facility. Nevertheless, employing such a system will still result in changes to the relative position of lenders due to movements in exchange rates during a moratorium. In order to correct such distortions the loss-sharing arrangements in a moratorium need to allow for:

- Equalisation arrangements for each distribution to participants during a moratorium, or in the event of the company's insolvency.

- A system of priorities for involuntary excesses, or claw-backs in respect of headroom, as a result of exchange rate movements for those few facilities where 'currency equivalent' limits operate.

The mechanism used to establish how losses and gains are shared between participants can have a significant influence on the position of individual lenders. The following scenario, where one bank has provided a loan in US dollars and the other in UK sterling, illustrates the point:

	Moratorium date		Distribution date	
	(US$2 : £1)		(US$1 : £1)	
Exchange rate	*Loan amount*	*£ equiv.*	*Loan amount*	*£ equiv.*
UK Bank A loan	$20.0m	£10.0m	$20.0m	£20.0m
UK Bank B loan	£10.0*m*	£10.0*m*	£10.0*m*	£10.0*m*
Total £ equiv.		£20.0m		£30.0m

The movement in exchange rates between the two dates has been deliberately exaggerated for illustrative purposes. Now consider how the distribution of proceeds from the sale of £12 million of assets could be allocated between the two UK banks, consistent with the principles of equitable treatment in a moratorium. There are three basic systems that could be employed:

System 1

Principle: The distribution is allocated on the basis of the relative positions of the banks as at the moratorium date. Therefore each bank receives £6 million.

	Distribution date					
	Opening balance		Distribution amount		Net balance	
Exchange rate	(US$1 : £1)		(US$1 : £1)		(US$1 : £1)	
	Loan amount	£ equiv.	£ amount	$ equiv.	Loan amount	£ equiv.
UK Bank A	$20.0m	£20.0m	£6.0m	$6.0m	$14.0m	£14.0m
UK Bank B	£10.0m	£10.0m	£6.0m	$6.0m	£4.0m	£4.0m
Total £ equiv.		£30.0m	£12.0m			£18.0m

Effect: Bank A recovers 30 per cent, whilst Bank B recovers 60 per cent of its exposure (in currency terms) as at the distribution date. This will not be seen as equitable. Furthermore, in sterling equivalent terms, whilst Bank B has still achieved a 60 per cent recovery, Bank A has now suffered a £4 million increase in its exposure over the position at the start of the moratorium, notwithstanding the distribution. Not only is the relative distribution between the banks not equitable, but as a bank based in the UK, Bank A will feel disadvantaged in its position deteriorating in absolute sterling equivalent terms over the moratorium.

System 2

Principle: Each bank should share in any losses or shortfalls *pro rata* to their relative positions as at the moratorium date. In this case that means that after the distribution, their exposures should remain in the same proportions (in UK sterling terms) as at the moratorium date. As their sterling equivalent exposures at the start of the moratorium were the same (at 10 million each), their respective exposures after the distribution should also be the same. The shortfall between the amount of the distribution and the exposure outstanding as at the distribution date is £18 million. Hence each bank should retain an exposure of £9 million after the distribution.

Distribution date

	Opening balance		Distribution amount		Net balance	
Exchange rate	(US$1 : £1)		(US$1 : £1)		(US$1 : £1)	
	Loan amount	£ equiv.	£ amount	$ equiv.	Loan amount	£ equiv.
UK Bank A	$20.0m	£20.0m	£11.0m	$11.0m	$9.0m	£9.0m
UK Bank B	£10.0m	£10.0m	£1.0m	$1.0m	£9.0m	£9.0m
Total £ equiv.		£30.0m	£12.0m			£18.0m

Effect: After the distribution, in sterling equivalent terms, each bank has a shortfall of 90 per cent of its 'moratorium date' exposure. (The poor level of recovery in sterling terms is because the adverse movement in rates has increased the indebtedness by £10 million). On the face of it the banks have been treated equally. However, in currency terms, whilst Bank B is seen to have recovered only 10 per cent, Bank A has recovered 45 per cent of its currency exposure as at the moratorium date.

It is worth also noting that, provided the total value of realisations is sufficiently large, the outcome would be the same if Bank A had been granted a £10 million priority for the increase in its sterling equivalent exposure between the moratorium date and the distribution date.

System 3

Principle: Each bank should achieve the same percentage recovery of its underlying facility in currency or currency equivalent terms. This requires distributions to be made in currency based upon the exchange rates prevailing at the time of the distribution.

	Opening balance		Distribution amount		Net balance	
	Distribution date					
Exchange rate	(US$1 : £1)		(US$1 : £1)		(US$1 : £1)	
	Loan amount	£ equiv.	£ amount	$ equiv.	Loan amount	£ equiv.
UK Bank A	$20.0m	£20.0m	£8.0m	$8.0m	$12.0m	£12.0m
UK Bank B	£10.0m	£10.0m	£4.0m	$4.0m	£6.0m	£6.0m
Total £ equiv.		£30.0m	£12.0m			£18.0m

Effect: The overall recovery rate from asset realisations is 40 per cent of the distribution date currency equivalent exposures. Bank A receives a distribution equivalent to £8 million and Bank B receives £4 million. In both currency and sterling equivalent terms, each bank recovers 40 per cent and still faces a shortfall of 60 per cent going forward. However, in absolute sterling values, whilst Bank B has recovered 40 per cent, Bank A has seen its exposure increase since the moratorium date and may well feel unfairly treated.

Although it could be argued that each of these methods conforms to the principles of maintaining fairness, they clearly result in different outcomes for the banks involved:

- The first method shares the proceeds *pro rata* to the bank's moratorium date positions. However, the movement in exchange rates causes the relative exposures remaining to look inequitable. This appears to be the most flawed system, because the shortfall is not shared equitably either in currency or sterling equivalent terms. The principle should be that any shortfall or losses, rather than recoveries, should be borne in an equitable manner.

- The second method is often put forward as being the most appropriate. In this case the shortfall or losses appear to be shared equitably. This is achieved by altering the proportion in which recoveries are apportioned. However the system can lead to a bank either gaining a benefit, or being disadvantaged, purely on the basis of its domicile and currency of reporting. In the example above, the shortfall, but not the impact of exchange rate movements, has been borne equally between the banks. Losses have been shared based upon their relative positions as at the moratorium date. However, the effect of the adverse exchange rate movement has been borne substantially by Bank B, even though it was lending in the same currency as the domicile of the asset. The effect of using the system outlined in System 2 is to compensate Bank A for an appreciation in the US dollar exchange rate. However, where Bank A is a US bank it clearly will not have suffered any impact on its balance sheet, and it effectively receives an *ex gratia* reduction. This distortion can be exaggerated if a bank is given priority status for an element of a currency loan where the only change has arisen from exchange rate movements.

- In our opinion the third method is the fairest. The percentage amount of recovery and shortfall (or loss) is shared equitably whether measured in currency or currency equivalent terms. The only distortion arises where a bank has provided a loan in a currency different from its domicile or reporting currency. In this case, the amount of its balance sheet loss may be higher or lower relative to others, depending on the circumstances. In the example above where Bank A is a UK bank, it carries a higher (sterling) balance sheet exposure relative to its moratorium date position than Bank B. In fact, in this example, the exaggerated exchange rate movement has also led to its absolute sterling denominated exposure rising above its position as at the moratorium date. However, had Bank A been a US bank, then its balance sheet exposure relative to that of other banks would have been unaffected.

The fact that banks risk suffering different levels of balance sheet loss due to the provision of currency facilities is a matter for each bank to consider at the time it agrees to provide a facility. It is impossible for a moratorium agreement potentially involving numerous international banks to address all the implications of the treasury and balance sheet funding operations of each institution. In any event, other participants in a moratorium should not have to compensate a bank for the additional losses suffered due to the provision of foreign currency facilities. There may be opportunities to address specific concerns, for example by agreeing to convert the currency of facilities at the outset of a moratorium, or in the period thereafter. However, as discussed below, this is a matter for the bank group to consider in the context of the company's overall hedging strategy.

The scenarios set out earlier in this chapter also highlight the problems and inequities which can arise from a system based exclusively on 'currency equivalent' limits. In the example, Bank A could have operated a sterling equivalent limit. On this basis it would be necessary to employ one of the following methods:

- Use £10 million to pay down Bank A's exposure in order for the outstanding US dollar balance to remain within a £10 million equivalent limit.
- Agree a priority for the element of the exposure outstanding above a sterling equivalent of £10 million.

If Bank A were a US-based institution, this would clearly be to its advantage. Conversely, had the dollar depreciated against sterling, Bank A would be obligated to advance more dollars to maintain its sterling equivalent exposure level.

The basis described above under System 3 for sharing any shortfall or losses should be adopted when calculating all distributions, whether pre- or post-enforcement. The magnitude of any inter-bank adjustments required in the event that the company fails are kept to a minimum under this approach.

Accordingly, at the time of each distribution, all the banks' facilities should be notionally converted into the base currency using the prevailing spot rates of exchange and the proceeds allocated *pro rata*. The physical distribution should then be made in each appropriate currency using the same spot rates of exchange. The remaining limits should then be reduced accordingly. If the distribution is to be held as cash cover, this will ensure that the deposit matches the currency of the exposure.

Hedging

The overall hedging position of the company with respect to both assets and earnings should also be considered when addressing the impact of currency movements during a moratorium. This is in the interests of all the participants in a moratorium. In addition, as highlighted above, the banks should consider their own balance sheet positions.

The optimum wishes of the company and the banks should be catered for. Any changes in the currency of utilisation should be permitted that strengthen the company's overall hedging strategy, whilst improving the position of individual lenders with respect to their balance sheets.

Equally, in order to protect any established hedging strategies, banks should only be permitted to alter the currency of a facility with the joint agreement of the company and other banks. Any such conversions should be undertaken at the prevailing spot rates of exchange. Upon the conversion of a borrowing to a different currency, the relevant limit will need to be converted to the new currency using the same rate of exchange. Any cash cover held for that exposure should also be converted on the same terms.

SECTION B

FINANCIAL RESTRUCTURING

21

FINANCIAL RESTRUCTURING

Introduction

The financial restructuring is at the heart of a loan workout. By reorganising a company's finances, it provides a foundation for the company to turnaround its business. It essentially involves the company's lenders committing to revised terms for their financing over an extended period.

Many of the principles involved in a moratorium are extended into the financial restructuring. The key objective is to ensure that the participants' relative positions at the start of the loan workout process are preserved until the company completes a turnaround. As a result, a financial restructuring agreement often takes the form of a comprehensive extension of a moratorium agreement. Many of the mechanics and techniques described in this section of the book would have been initiated during a preceding moratorium. Of course, depending on the circumstances, a financial restructuring may in some cases involve a completely new refinancing of the company's previous position on new, entirely commercial terms.

The key elements of a typical financial restructuring agreement are highlighted in Figure 21.1 below.

The various objectives and principles involved in designing financial restructurings are addressed in this chapter. The focus is on the issues relating to revising the terms of lending agreements between a company and its lenders. In particular, the techniques involved in reorganising the financial arrangements of multi-subsidiary groups are highlighted. Chapter 22 deals with matters relating to the restructuring of financial arrangements between the lenders. The following chapter provides an outline of other key matters that need to be addressed in this area, including issues relating to the future monitoring and control of the company.

Objectives of a financial restructuring

A financial restructuring needs to provide an appropriate foundation for a company's operations during its turnaround. In addition, it needs to address various technical and

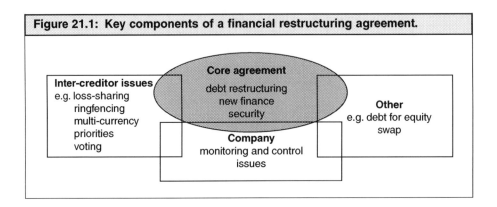

Figure 21.1: Key components of a financial restructuring agreement.

commercial issues for the lenders. The principal objectives of a financial restructuring are to:

- *Provide greater stability.* The moratorium agreement will have been arranged as an emergency exercise designed to provide short-term stability. The arrangement may even have been operating on a *de facto* basis, and may not even be documented. The financial restructuring is intended to place the company's financial affairs on a more stable, longer-term footing.

- *Formalise the basis upon which finances are provided.* Any moratorium-related documentation that does exist is likely to focus upon a small number of key concepts, rather than detailed terms and conditions. The financial restructuring provides an opportunity to introduce a more comprehensive financing agreement. This will aim to formalise the detailed arrangements which govern the operation of the company's facilities in keeping with the principles of a moratorium. The agreement will most likely also contain a more accurate breakdown of the company's borrowings than was previously available.

- *Provide a framework of facilities which meets the company's needs.* The basic concept of a moratorium requires all participants to maintain their relative positions during its currency. Although a good starting point, this is likely to be relatively inflexible. If carried through into the financial restructuring phase of the loan workout, this may not meet the company's requirements and is likely to be unwieldy. The financial restructuring provides the opportunity to simplify the arrangements whilst keeping as closely as possible to the principles of a moratorium.

- *Complete collateral arrangements and establish inter-creditor provisions.* Limited or no collateral may have been available to the lenders during the moratorium phase. The financial restructuring is usually the first point at which detailed arrangements can be made in this regard since the financial institutions will be committing to medium-term support for the company at this stage.

Developing financial restructuring proposals

The lenders in general, and the co-ordinator in particular, have considerable influence over the terms of any financial restructuring. Nevertheless, in a voluntary loan workout the interests of the lenders will need to be balanced against those of the company. Failure to secure the company's agreement will probably lead to insolvency procedures being instigated, with the associated disadvantages to the parties involved.

In addition to the company, the unanimous agreement of all the other participants involved in the workout needs to be secured. This requires that the restructuring proposals are fair to all the creditors. To address this issue, any moratorium that precedes the restructuring will have been based around the concept of 'notional liquidation'. This provides that the relative positions of each institution should be fixed to that which would have existed if the company were liquidated at the start of the moratorium. Inevitably, the financial restructuring will also adhere to this principle.

In the most straightforward cases, a company may only have one syndicated loan facility. In these cases the financial restructuring might simply require a rescheduling of the commitments by way of a full re-syndication. The relevant terms and conditions, including any financial covenants, are re-stated on terms acceptable to all participants in the restructuring. At this point, the banks may also demand formal security in return for agreeing to the restructuring, if this has not been granted already.

The most complex cases invariably involve large multinational groups of companies with numerous subsidiaries in various countries. These groups will have access to a wide range of banking facilities from a number of providers. In such cases, the financial restructuring will still centre on a fundamental rescheduling of the company's obligations, a re-statement of the related terms and conditions and, where required, the provision of additional facilities. However, the financial restructuring will also need to bring together all the different providers of finance and all the group's subsidiary companies into one single restructuring agreement. This is important because each bank will want the assurance that the other financial institutions have also committed to the on-going provision of finance. Also, they will want to ensure that they are being treated equitably in relation to the other financial creditors. In these cases the restructuring can become very complicated, incorporating a complex matrix of different interests. Where possible, the restructuring will be based around the grouping of individual subsidiaries which have common financing arrangements. This will result in a series of individual facility pools. The terms for each facility pool will be linked by a framework which imposes common terms, conditions and obligations on each of the parties.

Key information needs

Given the time constraints involved, the initial moratorium will almost certainly have been based on inaccurate or incomplete data about the company's obligations to each of its lenders at the start of the moratorium. This information gathering exercise will need to be completed so far as possible before a financial restructuring can be formulated. This database will assist in determining the company's financial requirements and the natural groupings of facilities and facility providers. The facility providers will probably be grouped according to the borrowing counterparty and extent of any guarantee support from other group companies. A key issue will be the identification of those facilities, or facility providers, that do not readily fit into any broad groupings. The frequency of these instances and the amount of finance involved have a major impact on the complexity of the financial restructuring.

Figure 21.2 below provides a summary of the information needed to develop a financial restructuring plan for a complex group of companies.

The co-ordinator will oversee the collection of this information. The company, the banks and the reporting accountants will supply or verify the details as appropriate.

It is critical that the process of assembling this information starts at the outset of a workout. Experience suggests that it takes a long time to assemble accurate information in this regard, particularly if large, multinational companies are involved.

The review prepared by the reporting accountants will also provide detailed information on the financial position of separate subsidiaries. When considering the financial restructuring options, it will be important to be aware of:

- *The range and value of assets.* The reporting accountants will have prepared a liquidation analysis of each principal subsidiary for this purpose. This will help identify where the financial creditors are likely to be protective (i.e., they are already in relatively strong positions, with large exposures) or, conversely, where the values involved are immaterial and the parties will adopt a more flexible attitude.

- *The operating performance of each subsidiary.* This will also help determine which subsidiaries are capable of supporting a given level of indebtedness. This information will be fundamental to determining the attitude of the banks within a restructuring.

- *The cash flow position of individual subsidiaries.* This will pinpoint where the major additional debt requirements are likely to arise.

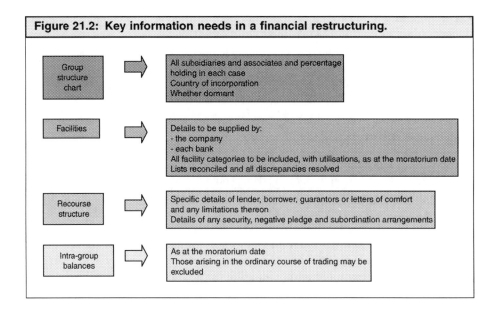

Figure 21.2: Key information needs in a financial restructuring.

The remaining information required is the company's turnaround plan and its financial implications. Financial projections based on the plan will determine the overall financing requirement and its timing.

Once the various items of information have been assembled, the company and the co-ordinator will be in a position to develop a financial restructuring proposal. At this point, some critical choices about the company's future financial structure need to be made. The decisions will need to take into account:

- The nature of the company's existing facilities.
- The need for ringfencing structures.
- New money requirements and priority rankings.
- Distribution provisions.

Ultimately, a balance needs to be achieved between a technically correct structure and one which is simple to understand and operate. The issues highlighted above will have a significant impact on the operation of such facilities, both individually and collectively. These issues are discussed in the remainder of this and the next chapter, with the latter dealing with inter-creditor provisions.

Entity priority and ringfence structures

In order to preserve the relative positions of the banks it may be necessary to 'ringfence' individual subsidiaries and associated companies, or groups of such subsidiaries and associated companies. A ringfence is a series of covenants intended to prevent leakage of assets from the debtor companies to subsidiaries or companies who are not involved in the security package, or who are not involved in a restructuring.[1] Two broad strategies are available for this purpose.

The first option involves excluding certain companies from the financial restructuring altogether. In certain instances it may be desirable, or necessary, to exclude some subsidiaries and associated companies in order to simplify the negotiations. Such an exclusion may be designed to avoid disturbing existing stable standalone banking arrangements, or to restrict the financial restructuring to the problem areas of a group. Conversely it can be employed to protect profitable parts of the group. Such exclusions typically apply to:

- Overseas subsidiaries with finances arranged locally.
- Joint venture companies.
- Companies that have a significant element of borrowings from non-bank institutions, who may be unwilling to co-operate.

In some cases, banks have agreed to release guarantees from a particular subsidiary in order to persuade key creditors that the relevant company would remain unaffected by a collapse of other parts of the group.

The alternative is to insulate the companies from each other within the framework of a restructuring agreement. This will apply where it is necessary to protect the interests of individual banks with exposure or recourse to specific parts of the group. This may involve the creation of a limited number of 'pools', where the value of several subsidiaries is grouped to support facilities provided directly to, or with recourse to, companies within the pool. This system will be appropriate where the banks can readily be divided into groups with each providing similar facilities.

A ringfence will always be required for each instance where a valuable subsidiary exists but not all the banks involved in a workout enjoy recourse to it as at the moratorium date. A ringfence pool may also be proposed for a group of subsidiary companies where various lenders have recourse to different companies within the proposed grouping. This is provided that the economic benefits to each institution are perceived to be similar or the values involved are relatively small. At an extreme, the range of businesses involved and diversity of creditor interests may be such that it will be necessary to ringfence every company in the group separately. Such an arrangement is commonly referred to as an 'entity priority' structure.

A ringfence can be created in two ways.

Firstly, it may be through the use of restrictive clauses in the restructuring agreement, covering asset and cash movements in and out of ringfenced subsidiaries, or pools. Cash movements fall into various categories, and the designer of the financial restructuring should consider whether to restrict some, or all, of the following:

- New intra-group funding.
- Repayments of existing intra-group balances.
- Interest on intra-group loans.
- Movements in intra-group trading balances (this is normally permitted).
- Management fees.
- Dividends.

Secondly, a ringfence can be implemented through the structure of the recourse and security arrangements in the financial restructuring. For example, a ringfenced subsidiary might be required to only support and collateralise its indebtedness to certain creditors. Alternatively, the subsidiary might grant security to support all the financing available to the group, but the position of individual creditors will be governed by a system of priorities.

Wherever possible, a full 'entity priority' structure should be avoided. A structure involving a limited number of 'pools' has significant advantages. In particular:

- It minimises the number of restrictions that the group's treasury and finance function will need to comply with.
- An entity priority structure will usually result in a significantly larger new facility requirement, since cash positive businesses will be prevented from passing funds to those experiencing a deficit.
- It will simplify the administration of the restructuring. This is particularly important in relation to arrangements for sharing disposal proceeds and other distributions in a pre-enforcement scenario.

New financing

Invariably, a loan workout will involve the need for new financing as the company is most likely to have been experiencing severe liquidity shortage. As highlighted

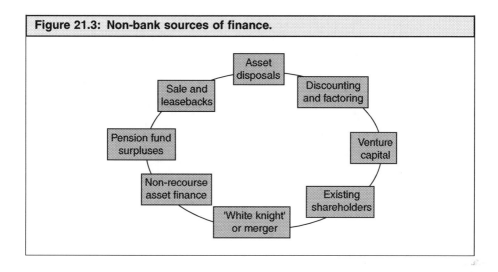

Figure 21.3: Non-bank sources of finance.

previously, this problem will be exacerbated by the moratorium, whereby all headroom is removed, and by the constraints imposed by any ringfence structures.

Additional finance increases the risk of the transaction for the lenders and its need should be kept to a minimum. Alternative sources of finance should be investigated before requiring lenders to provide new funding. Figure 21.3 provides a summary of the most common non-bank sources of finance during a loan workout.

In the event that the options set out in the figure above are not feasible, the banks participating in the restructuring will need to meet the company's additional financing needs. Wherever possible, each bank should be required to participate in the provision of any new facilities *pro rata* to its exposure at the moratorium date. However, this may not be practical for a number of reasons, including:

- A need for the facility to be arranged quickly.
- The benefits of keeping the administration of the facility to a minimum where a large number of banks are involved, and the financing requirement is relatively modest.
- Some banks will simply be unwilling to participate directly in the provision of additional facilities.

In situations where the risks attaching to new facilities are not shared by all the banks, a system of priorities will need to be developed.

There are a number of options for banks to provide new finance to a company during a loan workout. Some of these are outlined below.

Headroom

Banks involved in a workout may be asked to continue providing their existing loans up to the facility limit previously extended. The company will have needed finance at this level prior to its problems and, in the short-term, this represents the most straightforward means of accommodating the company's total financing requirements.

In practice, the amount of headroom available for release tends to be limited as the company is likely to have drawn heavily under its banking facilities in the period leading up to the moratorium.

Release of disposal proceeds

The banks will generally find it easier to agree to release the proceeds from disposals of assets than provide a new facility. For this reason it is wise to ensure that a balance is maintained in a disposals account rather than distribute the proceeds of disposals in full.

Increased or additional facilities

Where no other options are available the bank group will need to consider the provision of an emergency liquidity facility.

Interest roll-up

The banks can agree to roll-up interest after the start of a moratorium, this is normally accorded a priority status over the exposures as at the moratorium date. This might rank alongside other new financing, or behind it but ahead of the company's historic borrowings. A difficulty arises where different classes of creditors are asked to roll-up interest. For example, senior, junior, mezzanine and subordinated debt. Arguably, if the junior debt holders agree to roll-up interest, then they are effectively contributing to the new facilities and should be accorded some form of priority status. This is a particularly strong case if the senior debt will continue to have its interest payments kept current. On the other hand, it could be argued that all indebtedness to junior debt providers should always rank behind those to the senior lenders. This is a difficult area to determine equitably; the solution will often lie in the terms and conditions relating to the junior debt, and the relative bargaining strengths of each party. As discussed in the following chapter, the headroom, interest roll-up and increased facilities options are likely to be accorded some form of priority ranking. Priority ranking may also be agreed for the following circumstances.

Market movements

This will apply to banks that continue to provide loans subject to 'currency equivalent' limits of interest rate management products such as swaps and foreign exchange facilities. In these instances movements in exchange rates can lead to an involuntary increase in exposure above the level outstanding as at the moratorium date due only to movements in interest and currency exchange rates.

Preferential creditors

Different jurisdictions provide for some classes of creditor to have an automatic priority in certain circumstances, and against specific types of asset. Where the banks are the providers of facilities that attract preferred creditor status, there is a case for these to be granted a priority in a pre-enforcement scenario as well.

Transmission facilities

Funds transfer products will frequently involve funds being paid away before the bank is assured that the position will be covered by incoming funds from elsewhere. To enable the company to continue to manage its finances efficiently, such exposures may be permitted preferential treatment up to a pre-agreed limit.

Security-related issues

In negotiating a financial restructuring, one of the primary objectives for the lenders will be to obtain or upgrade security from the company. There are two distinct reasons for this:

- To rank ahead of other creditors and improve the level of recovery in the event of an insolvency of the company.
- To provide a measure of control over the way forward.

There are various constraints to this however, and the process of taking security during a loan workout needs to address them. The major considerations are outlined below.

Legal obligations and constraints

In many jurisdictions the directors of the company will have to comply with statutory obligations relating to the granting of security. In addition, there may be restrictions within the statutes of the company that need to be resolved. This is an area where suitable legal advice will be essential, especially if overseas jurisdictions are involved.

Consideration

The company will also be concerned to ensure that it receives value in return for granting security. This will address any 'preference'-related issues.

Timing

The point at which security is executed will be primarily an issue for the company and its advisors. This is one of the company's last strong negotiating cards and needs to be deployed effectively. A company will often decline to provide security until its financial status is clarified and any additional financing requirements established. Alternatively, the company might agree to provide only limited security initially, keeping items of real value in reserve.

Security is also a strategically important area for the co-ordinator and the steering committee to consider. In general the banks will wish to obtain security as soon as possible after the start of the moratorium, pending the review by the reporting accountants. This is in order to protect the banks during a period of high instability. However, the timing of the provision of security can also be a key tactical issue within the bank group. If the reporting accountants conclude that the company's prospects for viability are marginal, any security could be a valuable inducement to reluctant banks to participate in the financial restructuring. On the other hand, if the business collapses in the interim, the opportunity to improve the banks' position will have been lost. Careful judgement is required.

Scope

The co-ordinator will review what security is to be taken based on the information provided by the reporting accountants about each of the companies in the group. Ideally, each subsidiary in a group of companies would grant security over all its assets in favour of the banks. This would be in respect of both its own indebtedness and, as a guarantor, of every other subsidiaries' indebtedness. However, this may not be practical or achievable, particularly where overseas jurisdictions are involved. In these cases the banks might agree to restrict their security to a pledge over the share capital of the subsidiary. This provides a degree of control and captures the equity value of the business.

Consents

The banks' legal advisors will undertake a review of all existing security documentation and the various financing agreements. This review will confirm any existing security interests as well as identify the needs for any consents for additional security. In particular, any holders of negative pledge undertakings will be approached to consent to the provision of new security.

Format

The security will usually be granted in favour of one bank (often the co-ordinator) or, if non-bank institutions are involved, an independent specialist institution. The organisation will hold the security as a trustee for all the participants in the financial restructuring. In multinational workouts, different security trustees may be required for each jurisdiction. An agreement is needed to regulate the relationship between the beneficiaries of the security interests granted. This agreement will establish both the security trust, any related decision-making process, and how any proceeds arising from the disposal of underlying assets should be distributed. There are arguments for this agreement to be kept separate from any formal financing agreements between the lenders and the companies. Frequently the sharing arrangements are contained within an inter-creditor agreement. This enables the security-sharing arrangements to be kept confidential and any changes to be made without the involvement of the company.

Structural restrictions

For reasons discussed in the section on ringfencing, it may be desirable to exclude certain subsidiaries altogether from the security structure.

Costs

Taking and perfecting security across a number of jurisdictions is expensive and time-consuming. The company will be extremely cost-conscious. Whilst the banks would like to embrace as many assets as possible within the security structure, it is important to evaluate the overall costs and benefits of the exercise. The costs include the expense of taking the security, as well as enforcement if such action is eventually required.

[1] P.R. Wood, *Principles of International Insolvency*, Sweet and Maxwell, London, 1995, pp. 320–321.

22

INTER-CREDITOR PROVISIONS IN A FINANCIAL RESTRUCTURING

Introduction

Most financial restructurings focus on their impact on the company. Where a number of creditors are involved in lending to a company, however, addressing their respective requirements whilst meeting the overall objectives of a loan workout can be particularly challenging. Resolving inter-creditor issues can often take considerably longer than negotiating a financial restructuring with the company. This problem is particularly exacerbated if different classes of creditors with different objectives are involved in the transaction. The co-ordinator plays a critical role in this aspect of a loan workout, seeking to objectively balance the needs of the participants.

The inter-creditor agreement co-ordinates the relationship between the lenders over the term of a financial restructuring. The key provisions of the inter-creditor agreement are considered in this chapter.

Priority rankings

A key principle of a moratorium is that priority status should be accorded to any additional financing provided during its currency. Detailed implementation of such priority arrangements can be complicated. Moreover, there is no certainty that a priority arrangement will be acceptable to the participants in a financial restructuring. Nevertheless, some form of priority for additional financing should be aimed for. If the arrangement has been agreed in the moratorium phase of the workout, then it is reasonable to assume that it will be acceptable for the financial restructuring agreement.

Agreed priorities can be accommodated by way of rankings against security. Alternatively, the priority mechanism can be constructed by a system of indemnities and loss-sharing adjustments. The choice will depend on whether security is to be taken at all, or whether the banks are agreeable to loss-sharing arrangements and indemnities. From the perspective of an individual bank, a formal indemnity offers the best form of collateral. It may be the only viable way forward if the quality and value of the assets available is weak. Conversely, during a *de facto* moratorium, security may be the only route available if there is no documentation incorporating the necessary indemnity and loss-sharing clauses.

The providers of new facilities are likely to be the company's main relationship banks, which usually include those on the steering committee. Alternatively, they may be banks that have an interest in seeing a specific subsidiary of a company continue to trade. The main difficulty in structuring an appropriate priority arrangement lies not in finding banks willing to provide the necessary facilities, but in determining which companies and assets the priority should extend over. A commercial solution can be reached quickly where no ringfences exist between the main companies in a group, or only a very few such ringfences are present. The issue can become complex and unwieldy if a system of multiple ringfence pools, or an entity priority structure is introduced.

One solution to the problem is for any new financing to command an absolute priority over all the group's assets. However, there are a number of potential difficulties with such an arrangement:

- Banks benefiting from recourse to a valuable part of the group may object, particularly if they are involved with companies that do not require any additional facilities.
- A bank may already hold security over some of the company's assets and will probably not be willing to allow any priority to others in relation to those assets.
- Even if all the banks involved agree to grant an absolute priority, the proportions in which any new financing is supported by the assets of each ringfence pool has to be established.
- Finally, assuming such an arrangement can be agreed and documented, it needs to be capable of being understood and operated in practice. Considerable problems arise in this regard. The assets of the group are usually not realised equally across the different pools. When the assets of one pool are realised, the methodology for physically distributing the proceeds needs to be agreed.

The alternative is for new financing requirements to be established for each ringfence pool. Under this system, the priority ranking for the new financing within each pool is limited to the assets available from that pool. This is a more equitable solution, but also suffers from a number of drawbacks:

- This can easily become very complicated. It may be relatively difficult to establish the financial requirements for each ringfence pool accurately. Also, the system will inevitably result in a larger new financing requirement for the group than would otherwise be the case.
- It may not be easy to isolate the increased financing requirement for individual pools. This is particularly so if the group is vertically integrated and there is substantial intra-group trading.

- Even if it is possible to identify which parts of a group require the additional facilities, it can be argued that all financial institutions will benefit from the group remaining solvent and continuing to trade. This would be particularly true for institutions financing the ultimate holding company, but with no direct recourse to the assets of any of the subsidiaries.

The security may be structured to provide for several tiers of priority. Under a ringfence structure, different tiers may exist in each separate security pool. However, there are usually three fundamental levels of priority applicable to any security pool. These are highlighted in Figure 22.1 below.

It will be necessary for material intra-group balances outstanding as at the moratorium date to be recognised in order to preserve the relative position of bank lenders. This is particularly important where there is a ringfence around a subsidiary that owes an inter-company debt and it will be required to give security to its bankers. Detailed legal and accounting advice may be necessary to determine the most effective way of structuring such a transaction.

New financing which may qualify for priority ranking can arise in a number of ways. In particular, the new financing tier of priorities will include the undrawn headroom of existing facilities as at the moratorium date, if this continues to be made available. The second tier of priorities, which comprises the existing facilities, relates to their level of utilisation as at the moratorium date, and excludes any headroom included as part of the new financing provided to the company. To the extent that any value remains after the first two tiers of priority have been satisfied, the third tier is a 'catch-all' layer. The realised shortfall on any facilities from other ringfence pools, and excesses which have not been authorised by the rest of the bank group, would be included in this category.

There are infinite scenarios that could require a more complex arrangement than provided for by the basic layers of priority rankings outlined in Figure 22.1. For the

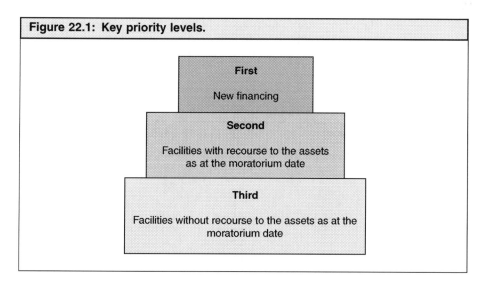

Figure 22.1: Key priority levels.

First

New financing

Second

Facilities with recourse to the assets as at the moratorium date

Third

Facilities without recourse to the assets as at the moratorium date

complex groups, each case needs to be assessed on its own merits and a practical, commercial approach adopted. The solution will ultimately be a product of discussion and negotiation.

Pre-enforcement distributions

There are two basic philosophies involved in providing for distributions of cash realised during the period of the financial restructuring. The first focuses on keeping the system simple by agreeing fixed percentages of allocation to each lender at the outset, based upon their broad positions at the start of the loan workout. This matrix is then applied to all distributions, at which time facility limits are reduced by the amount of the distribution. In the case of non-debt facilities, cash cover is set aside. The second approach assumes that it will not be possible to reach agreement between lenders to proceed on this basis. In this case, a system will be developed that attempts to mechanically reflect the consequences of a notional liquidation of the company as at the moratorium date. It should also be capable of accommodating subsequent variations in the participants' relative positions. In this scenario, the basis of allocations is recalculated for each distribution.

The first system is easier to operate, but it may be harder to agree. The second approach is still relatively straightforward. Once a reasonable sum of cash has been accumulated from disposals or cash generative trading, it is distributed to the banks according to the agreed priorities. After settling all the priority obligations, proceeds are distributed *pro rata* to the relative positions of the banks as at the moratorium date. The distribution will be simple to operate provided the structure of the company's finances is relatively uncomplicated. Table 22.1 below illustrates the concept.

In practice, companies will often have elaborate legal and financial structures, with a variety of banking relationships. The day-to-day operation of the company's facilities and other factors will also impact on its financial position. This significantly complicates the allocation of distribution proceeds. It may also be necessary to include in the distribution any inter-company creditors lending to entities in different ringfence pools, provided such loans were outstanding at the moratorium date and ranked *pari-passu* with bank facilities. Foreign exchange rate fluctuations may also impact on distributions. Table 22.2 opposite illustrates the concept.

Table 22.1: Illustration of a Simple Series of Loan Distributions.

	Facility type	Standstill date limits and outstandings	New £8 facility extended	£10 Distribution 1 New	£10 Distribution 1 Old	£20 Distribution 2 Old
Bank A	Loan	£12.00	£2.40	£2.40	£0.60	£6.00
Bank B	Loan	£6.00	£1.20	£1.20	£0.30	£3.00
Bank C	Bond	£4.00	£0.80	£0.80	£0.20	£2.00
Bank D	Loan	£18.00	£3.60	£3.60	£0.90	£9.00
		£40.00	£8.00	£8.00	£2.00	£20

Table 22.2: Illustration of a Complex Distribution.					
	Facility type		Moratorium date		
		Exchange rate	Limit	Utilisation	Headroom
Bank A	Loan	DEM 3:£1	DEM 15	DEM 15	DEM 0
Bank B	Loan	US$1.5:£1	US$20	US$20	US$0
Bank C	Overdraft	–	£10	£6	£4
Bank D	Bond	–	£8	£4	£4
		New £7 facility extended	£15 Distribution		
			Exchange rate	New money	Old money
Bank A	Loan	£2	DEM 2.5:£1	2	?
Bank B	Loan	£2	US$1.7:£1	2	?
Bank C	Overdraft	£3	–	3	?
Bank D	Bond	£0	–	0	?

Where the participants agree to strictly adhere to their relative positions provided by the notional liquidation principle, a number of possibilities will need to be provided for in the inter-creditor agreement. The circumstances in which the relative positions of banks as at the moratorium date can subsequently change, together with the appropriate distribution procedures required to accommodate this, are outlined below. Chapters 19 and 20 explore these issues in greater detail.

Revolving facilities

This applies to any facility where the level of utilisation fluctuates from time to time. Distributions should always be made based upon the level of commitment contained in the restructuring agreement, and not the level of utilisation from time to time.

Contingent liabilities

The standard practice is to assume that the maximum liability under the agreement will crystallise and to provide cash cover on this basis. The provisions relating to revolving facilities apply where the bank is committed to provide similar facilities up to a limit. Depending on the nature of the liability, sometimes the parties may agree to allocate cash cover based upon a system of weightings. This arrangement will normally be protected by loss-sharing provisions based on the actual liability experienced post-enforcement. In some cases, the liability may subsequently expire, or crystallise at a lower level, and is not required to be replaced. In such circumstances, the over-collateralisation under any distributions to date is subject to a 'tip-in' provision and redistribution, in accordance with the agreed priorities and pre-enforcement distribution mechanics.

Currency facilities

Where more than one currency is involved, the distribution should be calculated on the basis of converting all the exposures to a common denominator at the relevant spot rates of exchange at the date of distribution. The physical distribution also needs to be made in the currency of the utilisation under the relevant facilities, using the same rate of exchange to convert the appropriate amount of distribution proceeds. In this way, where the distribution is to be held as cash cover, there will be no exchange rate risk involved.

New or increased financing

These facilities carry priority status and benefit first from any distributions. This may need to include the cost of employing advisors involved in the loan workout if these cannot be met by the company. Alternatively, these matters can be addressed by the provision of indemnities.

Distributions on an unequal basis

Banks are required to apportion distributions *pro rata* across their facilities. This is in order to avoid creating distortions that might arise upon facilities being cancelled or crystallising at lower levels. However, the financial restructuring and inter-creditor agreements may provide for distributions which are intended as cash cover to temporarily reduce debt facilities and thereby reduce interest costs. These will be released against appropriate indemnities.

Cancellation of facilities

Occasionally, some of the company's facilities may need to be cancelled. A number of circumstances can cause this, including:

- *Repayment and voluntary cancellation of a facility.* In this case the bank is normally required to 'tip-in' the value of the facility by drawing a replacement loan. The proceeds of this are distributed in accordance with the agreed priorities and mechanics of pre-enforcement distribution. There are some situations where the bank is instead allowed to retain the benefit of such events. In such cases, the bank will be required to return any proceeds it had previously received for redistribution.
- *Expiry of the underlying liability as a result of the passage of time.* The procedures for voluntary cancellation apply to these cases as well.
- *Sale of a subsidiary and novation of banking facilities to a third party.* It may be necessary to provide for complex sharing arrangements where it is likely that the shares in one or more subsidiaries will be sold. Share sales can be structured in a number of ways and Box 22.1 highlights the key issues involved in this process.

Box 22.1

Impact of the Sale of a Subsidiary from Within a Security Ringfence Pool

Box Figure 22.1

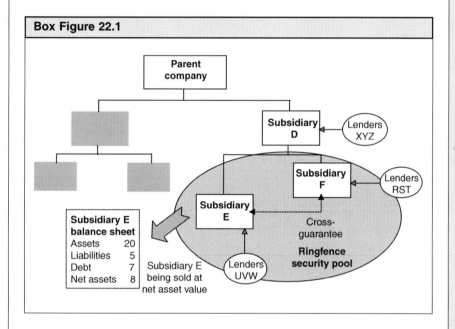

The shares in Subsidiary E are to be sold for £8 million. In addition, the purchaser will assume responsibility for £7 million of debt. The total benefit of the transaction to the group is therefore £15 million. A number of parties have an interest in these total proceeds.

The vendor of the shares is Subsidiary D. Accordingly, lenders XYZ will be entitled to share the £8 million in net proceeds amongst themselves. Lenders UVW provide the £7 million of loans to Subsidiary E. They will claim repayment of their loans from the purchaser, or agree to roll-over the facilities under new ownership. Equally, lenders RST also have a claim because they are the beneficiaries of a guarantee from Subsidiary E. Also, under the financial restructuring agreement, lenders RST and UVW have been placed in the same security pool.

From the perspective of the lenders, the total benefit of £15 million accruing from the transaction should be shared between RST and UVW. No benefit would flow to lenders XYZ until all the direct claims within the ringfence pool have been satisfied.

There will be cases where the assets of a group of subsidiaries are pooled for the benefit of various lenders, and a subsidiary is sold on terms which require the purchaser either to repay or assume responsibility for the loans provided by one of the banks. In such situations, the inter-creditor agreement needs to stipulate whether or not the relevant lender must still share the benefit of such repayment with the other banks within the ringfence pool. Alternatively, the issue can be left until it arises in practice and the particular facts can be established. With larger disposals requiring bank approval, a decision can be reached about how to treat the transaction as part of the consent process.

Where the benefit arising from a sale is to be shared, the adjustment can be made by requiring the bank to draw a loan in the name of another company in the same security pool and placing the proceeds in the relevant disposals account. This requirement would apply irrespective of whether the lender agreed to continue providing financing to the company being sold.

The same considerations apply in the case of non-debt facilities. In practice, however, it is frequently agreed that the banks involved can retain for themselves any benefit from the facility being continued under new ownership.

The terms of a share purchase will require existing guarantee arrangements to be released. In these cases it will also be necessary to consider how the proceeds are to be shared between those banks with recourse to the company which owned the shares, and the banks which had recourse to the company being sold.

It is apparent that even a moderately complicated combination of facility types, ringfences and priorities can very significantly increase the complexity of a financial restructuring. Against this background, banks often elect to keep matters as simple as possible in a pre-enforcement scenario, and necessary adjustments are deferred to a post-enforcement system of loss-sharing. This approach is easier to manage and, if the company survives, all the difficult calculations are avoided completely. However, often banks do not fully take into consideration the fact that under such an approach, they need to account for:

- The level of contingent indebtedness being carried by individual banks.
- The undisclosed level of individual inter-bank exposures.
- The additional cost of capital from assets weighted at 100 per cent which could legitimately have been assessed at 20 per cent.

Adjustments to equalise the positions of banks cannot be made on a 'real time' basis. In practice there will always be some inter-bank liability outstanding when a loss-sharing arrangement exists. However, a balance should be strived for that takes account of the practicalities involved. In our opinion, the rule should be:

- If the company's facility structure is complex, the pre-enforcement distribution arrangement should be kept as simple as possible. The banks will have to accept a potentially larger level of inter-bank indemnities that will not adjust until the facilities are either refinanced or enforced, and the loss-sharing arrangements are applied.

- If the facility structure is relatively simple, then the distribution provisions can be more sophisticated in the pre-enforcement scenario. This has the advantage of keeping the relative position of banks closer to that of a notional liquidation as at the moratorium date. In this way the level of inter-bank indemnities and post-enforcement loss-sharing adjustments are minimised.

Post-enforcement loss-sharing and indemnities

The concept behind loss-sharing was explained in detail in Chapter 19. Upon the enforcement of security a number of statutory provisions apply and these will vary between jurisdictions. The post-enforcement loss-sharing provisions are essentially a private contract regulating the manner in which the banks agree to share their aggregate losses once all the actions and requirements of the insolvency process have been satisfied.

The inter-creditor agreement will provide for any losses to be shared in the manner the banks agree at the outset. The most common arrangement is based upon recreating the relative positions that would have existed had the company gone into insolvency at the moratorium date. At the detail level this can require numerous eventualities to be catered for.

Ultimately, however, the loss-sharing provisions deal with a hypothetical situation and it is simply not feasible to predict how matters will transpire in every detail. For this reason, it is preferable to make the principles and concepts clear and then provide for the parties to submit to independent expert opinion or binding arbitration in the event of a dispute. Frequently the independent expert named will be the firm of reporting accountants, who will have accompanied events as they unfolded.

The co-ordinator will usually be indemnified by all the banks on a *pro rata* basis in respect of costs and expenses that the company fails to meet. The steering committee and co-ordinator will also expect to be indemnified by all the banks from all liabilities arising in connection with their roles, unless incurred as a result of gross negligence or wilful misconduct.

Decision-making and voting

The financial restructuring agreement will provide for the voting arrangements to make decisions during its operation. The various decisions that need to be made will be classified according to their importance. The key objectives in this area are:

- *To provide stability.* For instance, it would be inappropriate for decisions concerning acceleration or enforcement of security to rest with individual banks. Equally, each bank must be able to refuse an increase in facilities or extension of the maturity date.

- *To simplify the administrative burden.* This is particularly important where a large number of banks are involved and there is a need to react promptly to day-to-day issues.

Both the moratorium and the restructuring agreement will provide for up to four levels of decision-making:

- *Unanimous*. This will include any decisions to increase the banks' exposure, extend the term, amend the priorities and the sharing provisions, or change the voting arrangements.
- *Majority*. This level will deal with other major decisions, including those relating to larger disposals, major breaches of undertakings, or covenants and enforcement.
- *Steering committee*. Waiving minor breaches of the terms of the documentation, the majority of administrative decisions, and approval of smaller disposals are decided at this level.
- *Co-ordinator*. The powers in these situations will be as delegated by the steering committee or other banks.

A 'majority' of banks is established by reference to the value of outstandings as at the moratorium date and will be set at between 50 and 75 per cent. The circumstances will differ from case to case. Where exposures are concentrated across a small group of banks, it is common to add a minimum quorum by number of banks. New facilities may be excluded from the calculation to establish the voting percentages. This is most likely to occur where the new facilities are considered reasonably safe, or where contributions to the new facilities are calculated *pro rata* to the moratorium date positions. Voting arrangements should reflect the risks to the parties. It is an often-overlooked point that majority voting arrangements should also be considered from the perspective of the numbers required to block a decision.

It will also be necessary to consider whether non-debt facilities should be weighted for voting purposes to reflect the fact that the risk to the provider may be lower than the nominal amount of the facility.

In some cases, the voting arrangements may need to be more complex. For example, where a ringfence structure provides for several different bank interest groups, or where provision is made for percentage voting rights to be adjusted following the reduction of the exposure of an individual bank.

23

OTHER TERMS AND CONDITIONS

Introduction

The principal aim of all the participants involved in a loan workout is to resolve a company's financial difficulties. The company's lenders take a leading role in this process, principally because they are amongst the most adversely affected. Moreover, the lender's position continues to be vulnerable for a period after the financial restructuring, until the company's business has turned around.

During the turnaround, lenders need to closely monitor the company's progress. The restructuring agreement plays a key role in establishing the framework for this monitoring regime. The company commits to provide the necessary information to enable this to take place. Also, triggers are agreed that allow lenders to take action to protect their position if the company shows signs of failing to achieve agreed business and financial targets.

This chapter presents the most common commitments undertaken by companies as part of a loan workout. Also, typical financial convenants and the principles involved in establishing them are covered. Finally, other common provisions included in financial restructuring agreements are highlighted. All of these provisions are normally the subject of intense negotiation between the company and the banks, and between the banks themselves. The co-ordinator plays a key role in ensuring that an appropriate balance is maintained between the participants' interests.

Undertakings

As with all major syndicated facility agreements, financial restructuring agreements will usually include a section whereby the company undertakes to comply with a number of conditions. These conditions are divided into positive and negative undertakings. For groups with a large number of subsidiaries, it is common for just the main companies in the group to provide such undertakings. These entities then undertake to ensure that all the other subsidiaries in the group will also comply with the agreed terms and conditions.

Generally, undertakings are only required where committed facilities are extended. Breach of any of the undertakings by the company constitutes an event of default and allows the lenders to withdraw their commitment and, if they so choose, demand repayment. However, even if the facility is to be provided without any commitment it is still a good practice to agree the 'dos' and 'don'ts' in the restructuring agreement. This explicitly sets out the company's obligations over the term of the restructuring agreement.

The undertakings are at the centre of the mechanisms used by the lenders to control the loan workout. These clauses will be wider-ranging and more restrictive than those found in a standard syndicated facility agreement. Nevertheless, an excessively restrictive agreement is unhelpful. It either results in frequent breaches, or requires the lenders to be involved in a number of consent or waiver requests. Ultimately, it is preferable to adopt a reasonably commercial stance that allows the company to operate as normally as possible.

Clauses relating to undertakings will reflect the circumstances underlying each transaction. A list of the principal areas typically addressed is provided below:

- *Provision of regular financial information*—This will set out the nature of the financial information to be provided by the company. In addition to audited annual accounts, quarterly or monthly management accounts will normally be required. The banks may prescribe the exact format and scope of the information that the company needs to present to them. Where the situation warrants, management accounts may be independently reviewed or audited. This function is often carried out by the reporting accountants.

- *Notification of certain events*—These clauses will require the company to notify the banks of any material litigation, arbitration or insolvency proceedings commenced against any of the companies in the group, or any other 'event of default' specified elsewhere in the restructuring agreement.

- *Compliance with important operating provisions*—Under these clauses, the company will undertake to maintain all the appropriate licences, authorities and consents required to carry on its business. In addition, the company will commit to maintain insurance cover over its assets and businesses.

- *Change of business*—The company undertakes not to alter materially its main business activities.

- *Announcements*—The company agrees not to make any public announcements or issue any press releases without the prior approval of the banks.

- *Disposals, acquisitions, capital expenditures*—There will be restrictions on the company's activity in each of these areas without the prior consent of the banks.

- *Inter-company loans and management fees*—This is a key area where banks seek to protect themselves by preventing cash leakages from the entities they lend to. The need for restrictions will depend on whether all the subsidiaries in the borrower group are included in the banks' security arrangements, or whether ringfence structures have been created to protect the interests of individual banks.

- *Dividends, share buybacks or other forms of shareholder distribution*—Restrictions or absolute prohibitions will be incorporated to prevent shareholders extracting funds from the company at the expense of the lenders.

- *Financial assistance*—The company undertakes not to provide guarantees, loans or any form of financial assistance to third parties without the consent of the banks.

- *Negative pledge*—The company agrees not to provide security or permit any encumbrance to exist over any of its assets in favour of any other party.

Financial covenants

Financial covenants are a specific form of undertaking by the company to maintain certain minimum and maximum financial measures and ratios. In return, the banks agree to continue to provide finance. Financial covenants form an important part of any loan agreement and this remains the case for restructuring agreements.

As highlighted previously, strictly, financial covenants are only required when committed facilities are to be agreed. However, financial covenants are also a useful tool for agreeing explicitly objective measures of the expectations of the company and its lenders. They provide discipline for the company and the banks' own monitoring arrangements. For this reason, financial covenants can also be valuable for loan workouts involving uncommitted facilities.

Effective financial covenants should be:

- Relevant to the circumstances of the company.
- Simple to understand and measure.
- Constructed to trigger early in case the company is failing to meet targets.

Financial covenants serve to:

- Establish an objective test of creditworthiness. They can be set to measure progress as well as absolute performance.
- Offer a timely warning of potential distress.
- Restrict the company from undertaking certain activities.
- Provide the company's lenders with the right to terminate their commitment under a loan agreement in the event of non-compliance.
- Bring the bank and company together.

If a financial covenant is breached, banks may:

- Agree to waive the breach either temporarily, or permanently.
- Completely re-negotiate the covenants.
- Leave the facilities on demand.
- Accelerate the facilities by demanding repayment.

As with other undertakings, the scope of the financial covenants in a restructuring agreement will be more wide-ranging and restrictive than would be expected in a standard loan agreement. The 'financial' ratios used as covenants may be both the standard measures used in traditional ratio analysis, as well as operational targets such as quality standards and staffing levels.

The measures will need to be tailored for the circumstances of the transaction. This is because the banks may want to exert greater control in relation to specific issues. For example, where reduction in personnel is a key need for the restructuring, related indicators will be focused on. Furthermore, the company's financial performance is unlikely to meet the normal range of values, particularly in the initial stages of the turnaround. Financial covenants will be tested more frequently than in normal loans (for example, quarterly). They will also involve stepped ratios designed to allow time for recovery, but also demand progressive improvements in the company's finances.

The level at which financial covenants are set is a matter of judgement. The objective is to agree them so that they are effective, whilst not becoming unduly restrictive. Some flexibility in performance should be allowed for to prevent the facility constantly defaulting.

The most frequently employed financial covenants in financial restructuring agreements are set out below. They are normally divided into three types:

- Balance sheet tests.
- Earnings ratios.
- Cash flow measures.

Balance sheet tests

Tangible net worth	Measure	:	Total tangible assets less all current- and long-term liabilities.
	Description	:	This covenant provides a measure of the underlying strength of the business. It requires a minimum margin to be maintained between the value of physical assets and the level of liabilities of the company.
	Parameters	:	Often set at or near existing levels.
Gearing	Ratio	:	$\dfrac{\text{Total debt}}{\text{Tangible net worth}}$
	Description	:	This covenant looks at the extent to which the physical assets of a company have been leveraged, by measuring the balance between debt and shareholders' funds in the business.
	Parameters	:	50% to 125%, but wide variances apply for different industries. For example, a ratio of up to 300% or 400% may be suitable for capital intensive businesses.
Leverage	Ratio	:	$\dfrac{\text{Total debt}}{\text{Total capitalisation}}$ (debt + shareholders' funds)
	Description	:	As for gearing above. However, in this measure it is not unusual for the definition of debt to be adjusted to include operating lease commitments.

	Parameters	:	30% to 60%, but wide variances as for gearing.
Current ratio	Ratio	:	$\dfrac{\text{Current assets}}{\text{Current liabilities}}$
	Description	:	This ratio focuses on the company's liquidity by measuring the margin by which liquid assets cover short-term liabilities. A more 'aggressive' measure, known as the acid test, deducts stock from the value of current assets.
	Parameters	:	Often set at between 1:1 and 1.5:1.
Net working assets	Measure	:	Stock + trade debtors − trade creditors.
	Description	:	Designed to measure the amount of capital required to finance the day-to-day operations of the business. A figure can be set to ensure that there is no material deterioration in a company's terms of trade, or the management of its working capital.
	Parameters	:	Depends on circumstances.

In addition to these measures and ratios, other balance sheet-related covenants may be suitable for a restructuring agreement. For example, covenants may be introduced in relation to the minimum levels of cash or fixed assets (a security covenant that the company should maintain). Conversely, the agreement may provide for gradually reducing maximum fixed asset levels, where a debt-reduction programme is to be implemented.

Earnings ratios

Profit	Measure	:	Minimum level of profit.
	Description	:	More common in workouts where a company is not able to cover interest payments, at least initially.
	Parameters	:	Depends on circumstances.
Interest cover	Ratio	:	$\dfrac{\text{Profit before interest and tax}}{\text{Interest (gross or net)}}$
	Description	:	This ratio measures the ability of a business to meet the cost of servicing its balance sheet debt obligations. The multiple is set to allow the company to meet other obligations, such as tax and dividends.
	Parameters	:	Normally over 2.5:1.
Fixed charge cover	Ratio	:	$\dfrac{\text{Earnings before interest and tax and rents}}{\text{Interest and rents}}$

	Description	:	This ratio is a more specific variation on the interest cover measure, and is applicable to businesses where a material level of property and equipment assets are financed off balance sheet by way of operating leases. There is a wide range of definitions for fixed charge cover and it is important to check the underlying assumptions. This applies particularly in relation to the rent charge, which can be the whole periodic rent bill (standard) or the notional interest on the capitalised amount of operating leases.
	Parameters	:	Depends on definitions. Minimum of around 1.5:1 for the standard cases.
Dividend cover	Ratio	:	$\dfrac{\text{Profit after tax}}{\text{Dividends paid}}$
	Description	:	This ratio is usually designed to ensure that the business does not pay an uncovered dividend and, preferably, that some element of profit is retained within the business to contribute towards financing future growth.
	Parameters	:	Between 1:1 and 2:1.

As in the case of balance sheet measures, other earnings-related financial covenants can be devised to suit the particular circumstances of a transaction. For example, undertakings in relation to profitability and efficiency that may be relevant include: gross or operating margins; overheads or staff costs as a percentage of turnover; return on capital or return on assets.

Cash flow measures

Cash flow leverage	Ratio	:	$\dfrac{\text{Debt}}{\text{EBITDA}}$ (earnings before interest, tax, depreciation and amortisation)
	Description	:	This measures the level of a company's debt in relation to a broad approximation of its gross cash flow. The definition of debt can be adjusted to include operating lease commitments.
	Parameters	:	Normally a maximum of between 3 and 4 times.
Debt service	Ratio	:	$\dfrac{\text{Cash generated}}{\text{Debt service costs}}$
	Description	:	This is one of the most important covenants in any loan agreement. The definitions of cash generation and debt service can vary widely. Typically cash generated will be made up of:

	EBIT + non-cash movements +/− working capital movements − capital expenditure − tax.
	Debt service costs will include:
	capital and interest repayments + dividends.
	Some definitions may include proceeds from an equity issue and exclude certain elements of discretionary capital expenditure.
Parameters	: Not less than 1:1, as this would imply that the company is only meeting its commitments from new debt raised.

As before, there may be a number of other specific restrictions on how cash is spent. The restructuring agreement is likely to incorporate monetary restrictions on the levels of capital expenditure, acquisitions, and disposals which can be undertaken without the consent of the banks.

Term and commitment

During a loan workout, it is critical for the company to convey at least a perception of medium-term stability. The term over which any restructured facility operates should address this issue. The term should also be closely aligned to the strategic objectives of the company's business restructuring plan. Further refinancings or extensions need to be avoided to prevent disruptions.

Generally, restructuring agreements tend to be based on a two- or three-year term. A minimum of 12 to 18 months is essential to provide adequate time to enable a turnaround. Equally, lenders will be reluctant to commit to a project beyond, say, a three-year period.

Where a debt for equity swap is involved as part of a loan workout, the associated debt restructuring may require a longer period. This is partly because by implication the scale of the turnaround required is likely to be more wide-ranging and fundamental. Also the agreement of shareholders is usually required to undertake a capital reconstruction. Any recovery of shareholder value will take considerable time. For their part, the banks may need to support the company over an extended period to assure the shareholders of a reasonable return.

The directors of a company will normally seek finance on a committed basis. Depending on the jurisdictions involved, this might be a legal or regulatory requirement, or simply a preference on the company's part. For example, under certain circumstances the company's auditors may need to provide an opinion about the adequacy of the company's working capital position and access to finance. This requirement is frequently satisfied by the banks confirming that the necessary level of banking facilities will be available on a committed basis for a period of at least 12 to 18 months.

Frequently, however, the need for committed finance is designed to achieve an unqualified audit report. Although helpful, this may not be necessary. Much will depend on the extent to which a company's difficulties are public knowledge. The parties will need to assess the extent to which a qualified audit report will influence a company's customers and suppliers. If the banks do agree to provide committed facilities, the terms of the restructuring agreement will be drafted very restrictively.

A key consideration in this area will be the voting arrangements for the right to demand and accelerate repayment incorporated in a restructuring agreement. A committed facility is likely to encounter frequent breaches of its terms. Such a facility is often likely to resemble one which is provided on an 'on demand' basis. In a financial restructuring involving a number of banks, the rights of individual lenders are usually subordinated in favour of a majority voting arrangement. An effectively structured voting arrangement avoids a small number of lenders acting unilaterally to demand repayment. This can provide considerable reassurance about the stability of a financial restructuring, even if the facilities are provided on an uncommitted basis.

Restrictions on assignment and transfer

The *raison d'etre* of a moratorium and, to a lesser extent, the subsequent restructuring agreement is to provide stability. Both the agreements will seek to achieve this by restricting lenders' rights to take unilateral action. These restrictions will extend to a banks' ability to assign or transfer their commitments.

Traditionally, assignments of loans by banks have been permitted only on the following terms:

- Within their own financial group without reference to any other party.
- To other members of the bank group lending to the company, with the consent of the co-ordinator or the steering committee.
- To outside parties, with the consent of all the banks (and usually, the company, on the basis that its consent is not to be unreasonably withheld).

With the development of new markets in distressed loans, banks are now more reluctant to forego the right to sell or assign loans to third parties. Unrestricted rights to carry this out risks destabilising a loan workout. This is often a focus of negotiation between the participants in loan workouts in countries where the option to sell or assign loans exists.

Remuneration

Banks involved in a loan workout are remunerated from a number of sources. The considerations relating to establishing the appropriate levels of remuneration are covered below.

Interest rate margin

The need to price a loan to reflect the high risks banks are undertaking in a loan workout needs to be balanced against its adverse impact on the company's already strained finances. The major banks involved in the transaction also have a responsibility to ensure that their relatively strong negotiating position is not abused in relation to interest margins and fees.

As a rule therefore, banks should seek to agree commercially acceptable interest rate and fee pricing. The financial restructuring should reduce the risks being undertaken by the banks. Nevertheless, in some cases it may be appropriate to agree to concessional pricing in return for a success fee, or some form of equity incentive at a later date.

Invariably, a general increase in the interest rate margin will be called for with effect from the start of any moratorium, although this may not be implemented until a restructuring agreement is signed. A common rate will be introduced for all facilities, rather than a standard rate of increase in existing margins. Key exceptions to this include:

- Those cases where the risk profile within distinct ringfence groups differs materially, and differential pricing is warranted.
- New financing, which will normally command a premium. This is an anomaly as the new facilities will enjoy priority over the existing exposures, and will therefore carry less risk. However, there is usually a shortage of lenders willing to provide new finance during a loan workout, and this incentive is often necessary.
- Adjustments for facilities that carry less than 100 per cent balance sheet weighting.
- Those instances where the existing interest rate charged for a facility is already higher than the new level proposed. In such cases the relevant bank(s) are permitted to continue to charge the higher rate.

Co-ordinator and agency fees

These are usually dealt with in a side letter, between the co-ordinator and the company. This should be executed as soon as possible after the moratorium date. Other banks will usually not be informed of the detail of these arrangements. The fees are charged monthly, at a fixed rate, and exclude out of pocket expenses. The co-ordinator fee is usually charged during the moratorium only. Once a restructuring agreement has been signed, this arrangement ceases and a more standard agency fee is introduced.

Steering committee fees

These are not always applicable and it is usually left to the steering committee members to raise the issue. Unless a considerable workload is anticipated at the outset, or arises through time, steering committee fees are usually not provided for.

Arrangement fees

These are payable on signing of the restructuring agreement, based upon the level of facilities extended.

Success fees

These are extensively used, particularly when front-end arrangement fees are reduced, or not charged because of cash flow constraints in the company. There are considerable reputational advantages of levying a success-related fee. 'Success' can be defined in a number of ways, the most common being a linkage with one or more of the following events:

- The maturity date for the facilities.
- A predetermined level of disposal proceeds or full repayment.
- A predetermined share price.
- A change of ownership.

SECTION C

THE LOAN WORKOUT PROCESS

24

INTRODUCTION TO DEBT FOR EQUITY SWAPS

Introduction

Debt for equity swaps are a valuable technique that can be used as a key component of a loan workout. They offer many advantages over conventional debt-focused restructurings. Converting sufficient debt into equity readily strengthens a company's finances. One particular attraction of this for lenders is that the company can make orderly disposal of its assets and realise greater value to pay down its debt. As a result, and for other reasons highlighted in this chapter, debt for equity swaps are being used increasingly in loan workouts.

At the same time, debt for equity swaps are highly complex transactions, involving commercial, financial, legal and regulatory issues beyond the normal scope of commercial banking. Perhaps more importantly, they risk focusing attention only on the financial symptoms, rather than the underlying problems of a company. Many of these and other factors mean that debt for equity swaps need to be used only on a highly selective basis.

Financial restructurings involving debt for equity swaps can be divided into three broad components:

- The conversion of an appropriate amount of debt into some form of equity.
- The restructuring of the remaining debt facilities.
- The raising of new funds in the form of debt and, sometimes, equity.

The focus of this section of the book is on the equity component of loan workout transactions only. The principles for restructuring debt, the raising of new funds and resolving inter-creditor issues are addressed elsewhere in the book. This chapter highlights the fundamental concepts underpinning debt for equity swaps, their advantages and drawbacks, and the conditions under which they might be applied as a financial restructuring technique. It also outlines the key parameters that need to be addressed in structuring such transactions. Some of these parameters are explored in greater detail in Chapters 25 to 28.[1]

Debt for equity swaps are much more affected by the variations in legal and regulatory provisions between countries than conventional debt-only restructurings. This is partly because many jurisdictions have strong controls over banks acquiring and holding shares in non-bank companies.

Definition

Debt for equity swaps can be defined as:

> Capital reorganisations in which creditors (usually, but not exclusively, lenders) exchange or convert a proportion of a company's indebtedness for one or more classes of its share capital.

Thus, a debt for equity swap essentially affects the structure of liabilities in the balance sheet of a company. A proportion of a company's obligations to financial or other creditors is replaced with share capital. This may be carried out in a number of ways. For example, the debt may simply be 'converted' into equity, after due legal process. Alternatively, a notional repayment of the debt could be followed by the funds received being used by the creditors to subscribe for shares. This would be purely a book transaction. Moreover, the debt being swapped into equity may be replaced by share capital of equal or lower book value.

Key elements

A capital reorganisation involving a debt for equity swap is likely to be most appropriate when the total enterprise value of a company, represented by its assets plus goodwill, falls below the level of its debt. The main purpose of such a transaction is to reduce the financial risk of the company, usually by reducing debt to a more sustainable level.

Figure 24.1 below illustrates the point, distilled into the most basic elements. Over time, the going concern value of the company has fallen below the book value of its

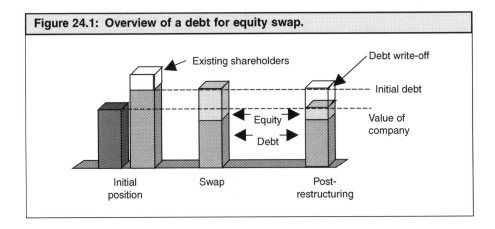

Figure 24.1: Overview of a debt for equity swap.

debt. As a result, the company's existing shareholders have lost all intrinsic value in their shareholdings. In the second stage, a proportion of the company's debt is swapped into equity, with the book value of debt plus (new) equity now equalling the book value of the original debt. However, the total economic value of debt and equity cannot exceed the economic value of the company. Hence, the post-restructuring column shows the value of equity falling to the appropriate level, resulting in an effective write-down in the book value of the original debt.

A country's tax, accounting and legal regimes will influence the mechanics of the balance sheet transformation process. For example, the deemed repayment of debt with lower value shares in a debt for equity swap can be seen as a taxable gain for the company in some jurisdictions. In such a case, a more tax efficient method for achieving the swap will need to be structured.

Different types of liabilities, including accrued interest, term loans, drawn facilities, contingent exposures, or asset-backed loans can be swapped into equity. One or more different types of equity or *quasi*-equity instruments, including ordinary or preference shares, as well as convertible shares or bonds may be used for this purpose.

Advantages of debt for equity swaps

The principal attraction of debt for equity swap transactions is that they reduce financial risk by improving the company's balance sheet structure and cash flow. By the time such a transaction is seriously contemplated, the company's debt servicing burden is usually impossible to meet and its operations are severely constrained by a lack of operating and investment cash. By substantially reducing its debt servicing obligation, a swap transaction provides a release for the company and, with appropriate operational restructuring, can provide a robust financial foundation for its turnaround.

The financial stability provided by debt for equity swaps also has the effect of restoring confidence in the company in the eyes of its key stakeholders. A sounder financial position, combined with a positive signal of support from the company's lenders and the other participants in the swap, can provide a considerable boost in this area. Moreover, a debt for equity swap enables the management team to refocus attention on the business, away from constantly dealing with the company's bankers and other creditors.

Debt for equity swaps have been traditionally undertaken for companies suffering from extreme financial and operational problems. Turnaround strategies for such companies often require a substantial disposals programme, whether it be related to assets or businesses. In such situations, swap transactions also improve the companies' negotiating position by enabling them to avoid distressed sales. Increasingly, lenders are prepared to contemplate extended loan workouts (of beyond five years) involving debt for equity swaps to enable orderly disposal of assets at full value.

As stressed previously, a key ingredient of a loan workout is new finance. Candidates for debt for equity swaps are in critical need of equity capital. When a company's existing equity capital base has been eroded to a negative value (sometimes many times over), existing or new shareholders, and indeed lenders, are unwilling to inject funds simply to repay existing debt. In such circumstances, debt for equity swaps present an attractive alternative to a debt write-off to enable new funds to be raised.

All the above factors improve the prospects for a distressed company, and thereby the potential return for bankers.

In addition, as Figure 24.1 clearly demonstrates, a debt for equity swap is often an explicit recognition of the banks' effective equity position. Although the banks' exposure is recorded as debt, a large proportion of it carries equity risk by the time such a transaction is envisaged. By swapping an appropriate amount of debt into equity, banks explicitly recognise the true underlying position. Moreover, as shareholders, they can participate in returns commensurate with the risk they are bearing. An indirect benefit of such transactions is that the banks can be seen to be supportive of their clients.

In certain countries, an insolvent balance sheet triggers various potential liabilities for a company's directors unless they take corrective action. Often, this may compel a company to commence statutory insolvency proceedings, even though it may not be the most appropriate commercial step. A debt for equity swap addresses this problem by restoring balance sheet solvency.

Finally, in countries with legal and regulatory structures that are not very supportive of creditors' rights, debt for equity swaps can provide an effective mechanism to enhance control over a company's affairs. The rights of shareholders in a company tend to be stronger than those of lenders, particularly outside insolvency. For example, in most countries, the shareholders in a company can replace its management by voting them out at a general meeting. Also, their approval is generally required for most major corporate activity. This role in corporate governance can provide lenders with a valuable tool to ensure that any plans to restructure a company are being implemented effectively.

Disadvantages of debt for equity swaps

Prima facie, the major disadvantage of debt for equity swaps for lenders is the relegation to ranking below the company's unsecured creditors to the extent of the debt conversion. However, provided the amount of residual debt in the company after the restructuring is greater than the value of the banks' security (after allowing for any expected improvement in security values), and provided the other, unsecured, creditors are not substantial, the impact of such a loss on the banks' position may in practice not be immediately significant.

Debt for equity swaps can bring immediate relief to a company's debt servicing burden by substantially reducing its level of borrowings. This can lead to inadequate attention being paid to addressing the company's underlying business-related problems, which are more difficult to resolve. As a result, debt for equity swaps risk being a temporary solution, as unresolved problems of the company continue to cause a deterioration in its performance. Further restructurings would be required after a period if this happens.

Another major disadvantage of swap transactions is that they tend to be considerably more complex than conventional debt refinancings and reschedulings. They generally involve a larger number of parties, often with directly conflicting interests, and complex legal and regulatory issues. This makes them time-consuming and expensive. The complexity and time requirement, combined with the often-critical condition of the company, also makes such transactions risky to deliver.

Additionally, shareholdings can bring with them substantial on-going legal and regulatory obligations. Banks without the administrative infrastructure for dealing with shareholdings can find them onerous, although some of the obligations could be delegated, for instance to a lead or agent bank. In addition to external requirements, banks' internal compliance systems need to be adapted to comply with, for instance, insider dealing and Chinese Wall issues. Banks' dual position as lender and shareholder can give rise to potential conflicts of interest. For example, there can be strong pressure to continue to lend to a company in which an institution holds shares, even when such lending does not meet normal credit assessment criteria.

The need to discharge corporate governance responsibilities associated with influential share stakes can also be challenging. A much more proactive stance than that associated with the position as a lender is necessary. New skills need to be acquired and more wide-ranging monitoring systems established, particularly if a bank becomes a large shareholder in companies pursuant to debt for equity swaps.

Exit-related considerations add further to the complexity of debt for equity swap transactions. It is very difficult to estimate the likely value that might be realised on disposal of the shares, particularly as the timing of such disposals cannot be determined with certainty. The ultimate realisation of value from an equity stake is also more complicated, especially given the banks' continuing relationship with the company and, where relevant, the associated insider dealing implications for companies quoted on stock exchanges. In any event, as part of the negotiations, banks are often required to enter into 'lock-in' agreements that limit their freedom of disposal.

Debt for equity swap transactions typically require longer time-frames than debt-only workouts. This partly reflects the company's serious problems, and also the time required for sufficient value to accrue in the company's equity. A longer workout period adds to transaction risk.

Debt for equity swaps transacted under a voluntary loan workout framework require the consent of the company's existing shareholders. If this consent is not forthcoming, the company's liquidation will probably ensue. Conventional debt-only workouts do not require such consents.

Debt for equity swaps should be entered into only after these issues have been carefully evaluated. Nevertheless, despite these drawbacks, a swap carried out effectively is a very valuable financial restructuring tool.

When is it appropriate?

A debt for equity swap is essentially a financial solution, although it usually has a positive influence on a company's underlying performance by improving confidence and providing a more stable base from which to conduct business. As with any conventional financial restructuring, it would normally be undertaken when the potential returns arising from the transaction compensate for its marginal risk. Debt for equity swaps tend to be high risk transactions, therefore the hurdle rate of required return tends to be high.

In most debt for equity swaps, the following criteria need to be met for the restructuring to be successful:

- Strong core operating business(es), with good prospects, which will deliver the required returns. Or

- Potential for capital appreciation, essentially to gain time and ensure disposals are not made in a depressed market, or from a position of weakness. And
- A strong management team to deliver the turnaround.

In addition, certain transaction-specific conditions need to be fulfilled. The principal amongst these is a commitment from all participants to reach a solution voluntarily. Negotiations relating to debt for equity swaps are particularly difficult and necessarily require substantial compromises from all the participants. There must be a feasible exit route for the shareholders, whether through sales in the stock market or to a trade buyer. The company, or shares in it, must be capable of being sold, or made saleable as part of the restructuring. Lastly, but probably most critically, there needs to be time to structure and negotiate a solution. As indicated above, these transactions tend to be time-consuming and in an unstable environment the possibilities of the restructuring failing are very high. Before contemplating a debt for equity swap, lenders would normally wish to satisfy themselves that any requirement for bridging finance during the period needed to complete the transaction can be controlled.

The nature of the company

Certain other features of a company can influence its attractiveness as a candidate for a debt for equity swap.

For example, a 'people'-based service company, with relatively few tangible assets, will be more suitable for a debt for equity swap. However, in such cases, lenders' negotiating strength will be weaker. The company's management and senior staff will be able to demand more attractive terms given the reliance of the company's performance on their co-operation. Moreover, in the absence of 'hard' security, lenders will have more to lose in case the transaction fails.

Similarly, companies that are quoted on a stock exchange are *prima facie* more attractive candidates for such transactions. They provide the lenders with a potentially ready exit route and, in the later stages of the turnaround, a mechanism to value their shareholdings. Nevertheless, the greater complexity and costs associated with debt for equity swaps of quoted companies needs to be taken into account when evaluating such transactions.

Debt for equity swaps entail considerable costs and the deployment of specialist resources for long periods. They tend to be more expensive than similar debt-only loan workouts. As a result, a company needs to satisfy stricter size and exposure-related criteria to justify such transactions. Moreover, it is more difficult to dispose of shares in smaller companies, unless they have particularly unique features.

Principal transaction parameters

Financial restructurings involving debt for equity swaps are generally formulated with reference to a number of parameters. The most important of these are highlighted below.

- The type of debt that should be included in the swap element of the transaction. For example, should all financial liabilities be included, or only the accrued interest.

Also, are the exposures of all the financial creditors going to be subjected to a swap, or just the unsecured banks?

- Once the pool of debt from which the swap will take place has been determined, the amount, or proportion, that should be swapped into equity needs to be decided. Is all the debt going to be converted into equity, or only a fraction? Also, will all types of debt be treated equally, or will, for example, a higher proportion of accrued interest be converted than the capital exposure? How will the different creditors with different relative exposures be treated?

- What type of equity, or *quasi*-equity instrument should the swapped debt be converted into? Should it be ordinary shares, or preference shares, or convertible instruments, or would a combination of instruments more accurately meet the needs of the participants in the transaction?

- What percentage of the company's new shareholding should the swapped debt represent? Should it be the entire share capital, or should existing shareholders retain an interest?

- What are the legal, regulatory, accounting and taxation implications of the proposed transaction?

Each of these parameters is inter-related with the others and a decision relating to one can have a substantial impact on the rest. The remaining chapters of this section seek to answer these questions by addressing the various issues that should be considered when developing a debt for equity swap transaction.

---

[1] Various issues explored in Chapters 24 to 28 drawn on: S. Chatterji, *Debt for Equity Swaps*, Corporate Finance Guideline, Corporate Finance Faculty of the Institute of Chartered Accountants in England and Wales, Issue 13, June 1999.

25

TRANSACTION APPROACH

Introduction

Given the complexity of debt for equity swaps, it is particularly important that these transactions are approached methodically and controlled effectively. The need to balance the requirements of a large number of participants with different objectives exacerbates the delivery risk of these transactions. The possibilities of failure are considerable without a clear strategy and effective implementation. Moreover, the technical complexity inherent in swap transactions requires the close involvement of professionals representing a wide range of specialisms. The task of co-ordinating this team is considerably facilitated by clear objectives supported by a transparent transaction framework.

Chapter 10 outlined the key steps involved in a conventional loan workout transaction. This framework would also apply to debt for equity swaps, although with some modifications to accommodate equity-related issues. This chapter highlights the activities in a debt for equity swap transaction that distinguish it from a conventional loan workout.

The need for specialist advisors

Once a debt for equity swap emerges as a possible solution for a loan workout, the need arises to augment the skills available in the advisory team. Additionally, the scope of work for the existing advisors needs to be widened. Moreover, the lenders themselves may consider drawing on in-house expertise in this area, if available. This normally happens after the restructuring objectives for the company have been identified, pursuant to a due diligence investigation. In some cases, the need for a swap may become apparent earlier, perhaps from the 'quick and dirty' report, or from the lenders' own initial information review.

The reporting accountants' role in respect of preparing the full report needs to be expanded. Essentially, given its impact on the value of equity at exit, the scope and limits of the turnaround in the company's performance need to be assessed more thoroughly. Also, the reporting accountants may be able to advise on the equity structuring aspects of the transaction if they have the necessary expertise available in-house.

The team of lawyers, hitherto likely to have been banking and debt specialists, should also be supplemented with corporate finance expertise. The corporate finance lawyers' principal role is to advise the lender group on the legal implications of debt for equity swaps in general, and of structuring the options being considered in particular. They should also assist in negotiating and drafting the documents relating to the equity element of the transaction. This will relate to agreements for underwriting a share issue, circulars to the shareholders, and dealing with various regulatory agencies, where relevant. Co-ordination and efficiency is maximised if all legal expertise can be drawn from the same firm of lawyers.

More debatable is the involvement of investment bankers, particularly given the relatively high costs of engaging them. In our experience, lenders are at a considerable disadvantage without investment banking advice if the company and its shareholders have retained their own such advisors. In most smaller transactions, a combination of the corporate finance specialists from the reporting accountants and lenders' legal advisors would generally be able to meet much of the equity structuring, valuation, negotiating, and other specialist needs. Especially for larger transactions, however, we strongly believe that investment banking advice is necessary. Without it the lender group risks being placed in a defensive position, rather than being proactive in negotiations.

Transaction-related considerations

Debt for equity swap solutions are particularly effective in meeting certain restructuring objectives. Given the nature of the technique, these objectives are primarily related to the company's current and future financial parameters. At the same time, a debt for equity swap requires certain preconditions to be met. For example, there needs to be a feasible exit for the lenders' shareholdings. The following considerations should be addressed when approaching debt for equity swap transactions:

Financial structure-related objectives

Debt for equity swaps are likely to be most appropriate when the principal financial structure-related objectives of the loan workout relate to the improvement of one or more of the company's:

- Net worth.
- Gearing.
- Debt serviceability.
- Earnings or cash interest cover.

By reducing the level of debt, a swap can directly alleviate problems relating to these financial indicators.

Term of the workout

The term of the workout period is another consideration. Too short a workout period risks turnaround, and therefore the full potential in the value of the company's shares not being realised. Conversely, an extended workout period involves considerable risks. The uncertainty associated with projections beyond, say, five years is such that other than in highly exceptional circumstances, a workout period beyond five years should not normally be contemplated.

Exit

The practicalities of implementing alternative exit-related options need to be evaluated in detail. Frequently, an erroneous assumption is made that exit will be automatically possible.

Balancing debt and equity interests

In a conventional loan workout, the focus is on how the business will be able to meet its debt servicing obligations. Restructuring objectives tend to be biased toward cash generation, through cost reduction and disposals. This changes when lenders also become shareholders in a company. Restructuring objectives that enhance the company's longer-term earnings prospects and, more directly, maximise its shareholder value also become important considerations under this scenario.

Occasionally, conflicts may arise between the restructuring objectives that seek to reduce a company's debt and those aimed at maximising the value of equity. Lenders need to evaluate their overall exposure to the company in balancing these aims. Given the considerably higher risk attached to shares acquired pursuant to debt for equity swaps, debt-related interests will normally carry greater weight.

Impact on information gathering and assessment

Once equity-related solutions become possible in a loan workout, the scope of the reporting accountants' investigation will need widening. This is because lenders would also need to consider the potential returns from their shareholdings in addition to debt-related matters. This requires an assessment of the medium- and long-term sustainable earnings of the business. In turn, this demands a more detailed understanding of the company's competitive environment. The reporting accountants' final report needs to address these matters.

The robustness of all earnings-enhancing proposals needs thorough testing to ensure that the management's turnaround strategy is viable. Traditionally, the lenders' focus is on cost reduction and cash generation options. Enhancing earnings often needs additional investments and, for example, marketing-related expenditure. Cash constraints during a loan workout make such supporting expenditure difficult. The feasibility of a company's revenue-enhancing strategy given the scarce availability of funds requires particular examination.

Assessing the appropriateness of debt for equity swaps

A debt for equity swap would normally be appropriate where:

- There has been a rapid deterioration in a company's asset values as a result of large write-downs or accumulated losses. Or
- The company is unable to generate sufficient earnings or cash to service its debt obligations in the foreseeable future, having taken into account alternative cash generation options.

As a general rule, a debt for equity swap would only be a long-term solution to the company's problems if the prospects of the underlying businesses are positive. It must be sufficiently profitable and cash generative to service the residual debt fully and to achieve real equity value after the restructuring. Debt for equity swaps are also suitable for providing medium-term stabilisation to facilitate exit through disposal(s) after an improvement in asset values. For example, this would be the case for property companies during a depressed property market.

Debt for equity swaps are often considered a soft option for situations where liquidation is really the appropriate solution. The transaction enables provisions against bad or doubtful debt to be deferred, with the additional hope that the company's prospects will recover in the interim. To be justified, such debt for equity swaps are usually supported by unrealistic earnings or projected valuation for the company. Almost inevitably, they result in greater losses for lenders than if robust action were taken in the first instance. Debt for equity swaps are not a panacea for cases where other options are unavailable or unpalatable. They have to make sense in their own right.

Evaluating debt for equity swap proposals

In undertaking a debt for equity swap, banks become shareholders in the company, as well as generally remaining lenders to it. The transaction should therefore be evaluated by applying parameters appropriate to both debt and equity.

Figure 25.1 below highlights the principal components of risk and return that should be incorporated in evaluating a debt for equity swap.

Risk

The four categories of risk outlined in Figure 25.1 are consistent with those for conventional loan workouts and have been described previously in this book. One of the key characteristics of risks associated with debt for equity swaps is their magnitude. Such transactions tend to have considerably higher risk than conventional debt-only workouts. Operational risk tends to be higher because the total returns from the transaction are much more dependent on a turnaround being successful, as the returns on equity need to be considered. The transactions are also more risky structurally, as the complexity and time needed increase the possibility of failure. Uncertainties relating to the timing and feasibility of exit from shareholdings also compound the

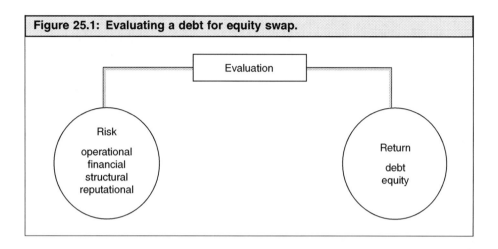

Figure 25.1: Evaluating a debt for equity swap.

problem. Being substantial shareholders in a troubled company has greater reputational implications than being only lenders.

There is scope, on the other hand, to reduce financial risk if sufficient debt is converted into equity. Moreover, it could be argued that debt for equity swaps will usually be contemplated for cases where the lenders already risk making substantial losses. The marginal risk of such transactions may not be as high as that indicated by looking at the transaction in isolation.

Return

The expected return from a debt for equity swap is the present value of returns from debt and equity. Figure 25.2 highlights its key components:

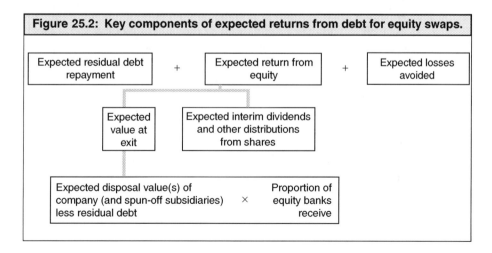

Figure 25.2: Key components of expected returns from debt for equity swaps.

If the residual debt is being serviced on commercial terms and is expected to be fully repaid, the face value of the loan should be taken as the expected return. The present value of any excess interest margins and fees should also be accounted for. Conversely, if concessionary debt servicing terms have been agreed as part of the loan workout, the face value of the debt will need to be discounted appropriately.

A considerable element of the complexity inherent in debt for equity swaps comes from the uncertainty associated with expected returns from the equity component of such transactions. Estimating the future value of the restructured company's equity is a complex exercise. Carrying out such a task accurately when the uncertainties are compounded by a turnaround is extremely difficult. This is made further complicated if different types of equity and *quasi*-equity instruments are used. The expected value of equity can be calculated by using various assets, earnings and cash flow-based models.

Evaluation

Once the risks and marginal returns from the transaction have been estimated, the transaction may be evaluated. The objective of this exercise is to ensure that the returns from the transaction compensate the participants for the risks involved, Also, where more than one proposal is available, their relative attractiveness can be compared. Debt for equity swaps may be evaluated in a number of ways, including by calculating the transaction's internal rate of return, or its risk:reward ratio.

Issues relating to risk, returns, and evaluating loan workout transactions are covered in detail in Chapter 14.

Negotiations

Conventional debt for equity swaps involve the sharing of (potential) loss between a number of stakeholder groups. These usually include the creditors and shareholders of the company, with different interest groupings within each. The outcome of such transactions is heavily dependent on the relative negotiating strengths of the parties involved, rather than on any scientific basis of determination. The importance of careful preparation and execution of negotiations is therefore critical.

Table 25.1 below highlights the likely negotiating position of some of the typical participants in a debt for equity swap.

Once lenders have developed their negotiating strategy, including their initial and fall-back positions, the broad restructuring principles should be agreed with the company and its advisors. In some instances, it may be necessary for the lenders to also negotiate directly with representatives of certain key interest groups, such as bondholders, preference shareholders, or major ordinary shareholders.

It is also important that the lenders formulate appropriate contingency plans in the event that shareholders reject the restructuring proposals.

The specific matters that affect lenders and shareholders in negotiating debt for equity swaps are addressed below.

Table 25.1: Negotiating Positions of Key Stakeholders in a Debt for Equity Swap.	
Lenders	Entitled to the most value left in the company, but with most to lose.
Bondholders	Enhance risk and complexity of the transaction if affected by restructuring terms as they are often a disparate group, with widely varying objectives.
Shareholders	Usually with little or no value left in the company when debt for equity swaps become necessary.
Management	Ostensibly interested in delivering a solution that is fair to all stakeholders. Sometimes, may have substantial shareholdings in the company.
Other creditors	Usually a disparate group, with passive involvement in negotiations; usually unaffected by a successful restructuring.

Lenders

From the point of view of lenders, when negotiating debt for equity swaps it is important to realise that:

- Shareholders and most unsecured creditors will almost certainly have lost substantially all the value of their financial stake in the company; they will have relatively little more to lose if the company fails.

- Secured lenders and creditors would normally be 'entitled' to almost all the value left in the company. At the same time, however, as a group they will usually also have most to lose from the company's liquidation or bankruptcy.

- The agreement of all financial stakeholders affected by the swap, including the unsecured creditors and shareholders, is likely to be required if the restructuring is to be agreed voluntarily. The right to this 'consent' to the transaction has some intrinsic value.

Thus, debt for equity swap negotiations with stakeholders who have little or nothing more to lose essentially involve a trade-off between the lenders' desire to capture as much value of the company as possible, and the shareholders' desire to maximise the value of their intrinsic negotiating position. The principal lever for the latter group is the lenders' fear of losses resulting from bankruptcy of the company.

Shareholders

Ultimately, shareholders' approval will be required for any voluntary debt for equity swap transaction. As stated earlier, the objective of any rational shareholder will be to maximise the value of this 'consent'. Such value is determined by the proportion of the enlarged equity in the company they retain.

In countries with developed investment institutions, shareholder approval would be deliverable by the major institutional shareholders. They tend to take a long-term view and therefore support a company's survival, provided an equitable solution is offered.

To the extent that members of the company's Board are also major shareholders, the approval process is simplified. This is provided they agree with the broad objectives of the restructuring and the impact it will have on the company's future.

It is preferable to obtain irrevocable acceptances of the debt for equity swap proposals from the company's major shareholders as early in the process as practicable. Although this is possible in the case of members of the management and, to a lesser extent, from major non-institutional shareholders, institutional shareholders are usually reluctant to provide such undertakings. In that event, lenders need to ensure that at the very least the institutional shareholders are likely to be supportive before formally presenting the proposals for approval.

If shareholders refuse to support a restructuring plan, the most likely consequence is insolvency (or the implementation of any other contingency plan if one has been formulated). However, any revised proposals that will also require the shareholders' consent will place the lenders in a very weak negotiating position. In any event, confidence in the company will be severely eroded in the interim. It is important, therefore, that lenders, the company, and their respective advisors assess the prospects of a plan's approval before any formal approach to all the shareholders as a group is made.

In many countries, it is normal for the company's Board and its financial advisors to conduct negotiations with shareholders and to represent their interests in discussions with the lenders. Constant feedback is required on the progress of these discussions. In the event that they encounter difficulties from one or more major shareholders, the banks and their financial advisors may need to communicate or negotiate with the dissidents directly.

Negotiating problems in relation to shareholders are usually encountered with one or more of the following groups:

- A major shareholder, or group of shareholders, who hold an influential shareholding in the company and intend to use the stake to leverage their own position.
- Preference or convertible shareholders, who usually have a significant influence on the transaction by the time a debt for equity swap is contemplated, as it is likely that one or more of the instrument's default provisions will have been triggered, giving them substantial voting rights.

Preference and convertible shareholders have two objectives. In the first instance, they seek to maximise the value accruing to all the shareholders in a company. In addition, they seek to maximise their share of the total value allocated to shareholders. All classes of existing shares will usually be converted into ordinary shares as part of a restructuring plan. Preference shares are typically converted to ordinary shares on terms considerably more attractive than envisaged in their original documentation, to reflect their ranking ahead of ordinary shares.

It is not unusual for large stakes of preference shares to be held by a small number of potentially hostile investors. Indeed, 'vulture funds' often target the acquisition of preference shares during restructuring negotiations because of their disproportionate influence.

In the event that lenders encounter shareholders with a declared intention to block a restructuring plan, appropriate action may include:

- Developing alternative plans to circumvent their ability to block the proposals. For instance, a plan could be developed that requires only a simple majority, rather than a super-majority (for example, 75 per cent of shareholders).
- Commencing direct negotiations with the parties.
- Refining the contingency plan to ensure that it could be triggered easily in the event that the restructuring is not approved by the shareholders.
- Considering direct access to the media or other influential third parties with the view of gaining wider support.

Exit-related considerations

The exit strategy needs to be clearly defined and agreed between the lenders and the company at the time of the restructuring. In addition to providing a time-frame for the loan workout, this enables the management to formulate the company's business strategy with the objective of maximising lenders' returns within a defined timescale.

Although it is most likely that the lenders' exit will be linked to a solution which involves both debt and equity (say, the sale of the group to a third party), there may be interim pay-downs of debt through asset or business disposals, or interim sales of the lenders' shares.

As highlighted above, when assessing the exit strategy, lenders should not only consider the projected financial implications, but also the underlying corporate logic. For instance, will the business be suitable for flotation? Are there likely to be potential buyers in that particular industry of sufficient size?

The ultimate exit under a loan workout could involve one or more of the options outlined below.

Debt

- Repayment through:
  - Asset disposals.
  - Surplus from disposal of subsidiaries.
  - Flotation of subsidiaries.
  - Disposal of group companies, without debt.
  - Injection of new equity funds.

- Disposal of subsidiaries or the group, with the debt, to a financially stronger company.
- Refinancing, once the group's finances or its operating environment has stabilised and it has improved its credit rating.

Equity

- Preference shares:
  - Redemption.

- Conversion into ordinary shares (and subsequent disposal).
- Disposal.

■ Ordinary shares:

- Sale to an acquiror of the company.
- Flotation (see below).
- Piecemeal disposal of shares.
- Co-ordinated placing of all the lenders' shares.
- Distribution, if any, on liquidation.

Considerations such as insider dealing and reputational risk constrain the piecemeal disposals of shares in the stockmarket by lenders. This factor should be taken into account when formulating the lenders' exit strategy.

When considering a flotation as a possible exit route, the company's suitability for obtaining a quotation at the target date needs to be assessed. Stock exchange requirements and institutional investor criteria for floating a company tend to be strict. The lenders' investment banking advisors should independently assess the likelihood of an exit through the stockmarket.

In deciding on an exit, the lenders' overall exposure to the company, including debt (which is likely to be of more value) should be considered. This could mean that, in certain situations, lenders may forego an opportunity to maximise realisation from shares in order to protect their debt exposure.

The exit strategy should be constantly reviewed throughout the loan workout period in light of the company's performance, market conditions and demand for the businesses from potential acquirers. Lenders should be prepared to react rapidly to exploit opportunities as they arise.

26

EQUITY INSTRUMENTS

Introduction

Equity instruments can potentially be extremely useful as flexible tools in engineering a financial restructuring. In addition to tailoring the risk and reward profile of the transaction, an almost infinite combination of equity and *quasi*-equity instruments may be designed to meet the other needs of a company's stakeholders. The instruments can also enable a financial structure to be created that more closely complements the anticipated business needs of a company. Nevertheless, approaching equity instruments with less than a complete understanding of their benefits and drawbacks can be highly dangerous. Specialist advice in this area is essential.

Figure 26.1 highlights the impact of a debt for equity swap on lenders with respect to their loss of ranking from such a transaction. It also shows some of the financial instruments involved in such transactions.

This chapter provides an overview of the key equity instruments commonly used in debt for equity swaps. This includes some of the more important characteristics of ordinary and preference shares, with relevance to swap transactions. Almost all equity instruments that lenders receive will be variations, or combinations, or derivatives of these two instruments. The more common rights and characteristics associated with them and their implications are also explored. A selection of other financial instruments that might be used in swap transactions, including those that have embedded in them rights of convertibility into other instruments, are also considered. Issues relating to the choice of appropriate instruments are also highlighted. Finally, the key principles underlying the valuation of equity instruments are outlined.

The characteristics of the various financial instruments described in this chapter have been generalised so far as possible to accommodate differences in equity-related laws between countries. However, the legal framework in some countries may further limit the scope of variation in some of these instruments.

Although the various financial instruments highlighted in this chapter offer attractive opportunities to tailor transactions, using them adds considerably to the costs and the

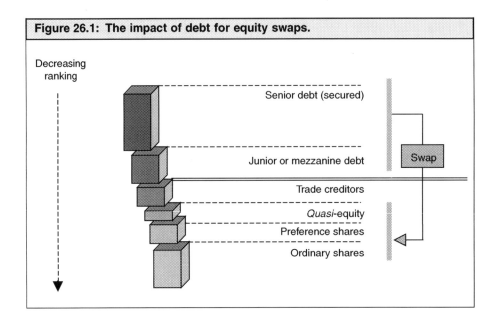

Figure 26.1: The impact of debt for equity swaps.

complexity. On balance, simplicity should be preferred and the use of complex instruments limited to situations that particularly require them.

Ordinary shares

Ordinary shares, also referred to as common stock, are the most basic form of investment in a company. At their simplest, they entitle their holders to a dividend (although this is not guaranteed) and, in the event that a company is liquidated, any surplus remaining after all other claims on the company have been satisfied. Ordinary shareholders are also normally entitled to vote in a company's general meetings. These financial instruments represent the 'ownership' of the company.

The most important characteristics of ordinary shares in the context of debt for equity swaps are as follows:

- *In most jurisdictions, the entitlement to approve major corporate decisions is reserved for the ordinary shareholders.* In particular, ordinary shareholders have the ability to replace a company's management. Although any agreement relating to the debt component of a swap will enable lenders to take action under certain circumstances, having ordinary shares (provided such holdings reach the appropriate thresholds) provides lenders with more direct control over a company's affairs.

- *The value of ordinary shares most closely mirrors any turnaround in the company's performance as it reflects the surplus after all other financial claims on a company have been satisfied.* Ordinary shares are the most direct means for lenders to share in any upside from a company's restructuring. This objective can also be achieved indirectly by swapping debt into financial instruments convertible into ordinary shares. Such instruments are discussed later in this chapter.

- *New ordinary shares would normally rank equally with a company's existing ones, unless ones with special rights are issued.* As a result, the financial interests of the lenders are the most diluted by conversion of debt into these instruments. Other equity instruments, such as preference shares, rank ahead of ordinary shares in a number of respects (see below) and may enable lenders to preserve a degree of priority. However, if a company's existing ordinary shareholders are to be sufficiently incentivised to approve a transaction, they need to have some residual financial interest left in the company. As a result, other things being equal, it is likely that a restructuring involving ordinary shares will be more readily approved by them.

- *It is usual for all types of existing shares in a company to be converted into ordinary shares at the time of a debt for equity swap.* Swapping debt into ordinary shares contributes to the maintenance of a relatively simple capital structure. The results of the financial restructuring are also more transparent.

- *Where a company has ordinary shares quoted on a stock exchange, swapping debt into that instrument provides the easiest access to a secondary market for the lenders' equity holdings.* Additionally, there is normally a need to ensure adequate liquidity in the market for the company's ordinary shares.

- *In some countries, the conversion of debt into ordinary shares requires only the approval of existing ordinary shareholders.* This can be an advantage where existing preference shareholders are hostile to the restructuring. This is the case provided that the terms of the preference shares have not been breached to the extent that preference shareholders become entitled to vote on the restructuring.

Different classes of ordinary shares

Under certain jurisdictions, it may be possible for a company to issue a new class of ordinary shares, for example 'Class A' or 'Class B' shares. Such shares may have different voting entitlements compared to the existing ordinary shares, or offer preferred rights to dividends or capital distributions. These instruments may be used as an alternative to preference shares as part of a swap. Although *prima facie* attractive, the advantages such shares offer are often very limited in reality. For example:

- A preferred ranking for capital distribution is usually only available in the event of insolvency. If a turnaround fails, insolvency is unlikely to provide a distribution to any class of equity holder.

- Most financially distressed companies are unable to pay dividends to ordinary shareholders, at least during the early stages of a workout.

- After a debt for equity swap, lenders usually become substantial shareholders in a company and command significant voting influence without the need for a special class of shares.

Preferred ordinary shares add to the complexity of the transaction. In the case of stock exchange quoted companies, a lack of understanding by the market and their illiquidity usually outweigh any potential advantages. However, there may still be particular circumstances which warrant the need for such shares, especially in the area of voting control.

Stock market quotation

Many debt for equity swaps will be of quoted companies. Therefore, it is likely that the shares received by the lenders will be tradable on a stock market, with the associated liquidity-related attractions. However, the following issues need to be recognised when negotiating for quoted shares:

- The prevailing market value of existing shares will not be an accurate indicator of their underlying economic value. In most circumstances, the intrinsic equity 'value' of a candidate for a debt for equity swap is negligible at best. The share's market value reflects a lack of information, or the optimistic anticipation of a restructuring agreement. It may also reflect an 'option' value in recognition of the rights available to shareholders to participate in a restructuring.

- Although the stock market presents a potentially attractive exit route for lenders, in reality the market in shares of a post-restructured company will often be very illiquid, partly because generally a high proportion of the equity will be held by lenders. Exit from large positions through the market, therefore, can rarely occur through piecemeal disposals. Rather, a co-ordinated placing or re-flotation will probably be necessary.

- Depending on the country, holdings of stock exchange quoted shares can subject lenders to certain potentially onerous legal and regulatory obligations.

- Unless new equity is being raised at the time of the debt for equity swap, the company is unlikely to be able to pay any dividends on its ordinary shares over the medium-term.

Thus, in reality a stock exchange quotation of shares received for swapped debt will not be as attractive as is often perceived. As a general rule, if a company already has quoted shares, or the shares can reasonably be expected to become attractive to investors within the workout period, a quotation is a valuable asset. In other circumstances, the associated costs and benefits need to be evaluated more carefully and the option of seeking a stock exchange quotation deferred.

Preference shares

Preference (or preferred) shares are ones that have defined, but usually limited, rights to the profits and distributions of the capital of a company. They can incorporate rights that offer preference over ordinary shares in a number of areas.

Preference shares can offer a number of advantages to lenders. They can be tailored to meet the lenders' needs whilst taking into account a company's anticipated financial performance over the turnaround period. They also enable the lenders to preserve priority over the ordinary shareholders in the event of a capital distribution. As with the preferred classes of ordinary shares, however, the advantages offered by preference shares can be limited in practice.

A major limitation of preference shares is that, unlike ordinary shares, their value does not directly mirror a company's performance and prospects. As a result, vanilla preference shares are not appropriate instruments for tracking a turnaround in a company's operations, with respect to the value thereby created for shareholders.

Preference shares are structured by incorporating various rights into them. Principal amongst these are:

Dividends or coupons

Preference shareholders would normally be entitled to a dividend ahead of the company's ordinary shareholders. Dividends on preference shares can be cumulative, and the level payable may be fixed, stepped or variable. Variable dividends can include a linkage with prevailing interest rates, earnings (called a participating dividend), ordinary dividends, or a combination of indicators. For most post-restructured companies, dividend rights in preference shares, if incorporated at all, would usually be a variation of a stepped-up coupon in anticipation of a turnaround. It may also incorporate a dividend holiday for a period. An increasing dividend is also a powerful incentive for the company's management to redeem the preference shares, if this is an option.

Although coupons on preference shares are generally attractive, they can at times be impractical in debt for equity swap transactions. In most jurisdictions, any dividend can only be paid out of distributable income or reserves. This will often prove a constraint for a post-restructured company if it has little or no reserves left in its balance sheet. Nevertheless, this drawback can be partly offset by the more advantageous tax treatment of dividends in the hands of investors in some countries, especially if a company in a turnaround situation does not have adequate profits to exploit the tax benefits associated with any interest payments.

Voting

The voting rights on preference shares will usually be restricted to limited circumstances when the entitlements relating to the shares are breached, such as a company's liquidation, dividend arrears, or non-redemption. It may nevertheless be possible in some countries to incorporate voting rights in preference shares, although this is not common. This would be desirable if lenders need a measure of control that would not be available otherwise. On the other hand, non-voting shares may carry certain advantages, including exemption from certain legal, taxation and regulatory provisions.

Redemption

In some countries, redemption rights may be incorporated into preference shares. Such rights are generally highly desired by lenders, as they essentially transform preference shares into *quasi*-debt. The redemption of preference shares can be agreed, for example, on a fixed date in the future, upon certain events occurring, if certain other covenants relating to preference shares (such as dividend payments) are breached, or at the option of the company or holder between certain dates. To safeguard the prospects of redemption, preference shares can sometimes incorporate 'negative control rights' over certain actions of the company, which would deplete its distributable reserves. In most countries, various constraints are imposed on the latitude and flexibility available to incorporate redemption rights if the company's shares are publicly traded.

A Board would normally be reluctant to grant compulsory redemption rights, particularly if the company's financial prospects are uncertain. Fallback alternatives to redemption rights could include incorporating:

- Contingent redemption rights, say, on the disposal of key assets, or businesses.
- Rights to convert into ordinary shares at penal rates as a substitute for redemption (in restricted circumstances).
- Penal coupon rates after a specified date to encourage redemption.

There are two major potential problems associated with incorporating redemption rights in preference shares. Firstly, redemption is generally possible only from distributable reserves in a company's balance sheet. This can be a major drawback in turnaround situations, as the company's reserves tend to be depleted by historic losses. Indeed, if a debt for equity swap has been considered an appropriate situation, a company may show a balance sheet deficit. This problem can be addressed in some jurisdictions by implementing the necessary legal steps to eliminate deficits in distributable reserves as part of the restructuring. Secondly, certain redeemable preference shares, particularly when a company has no control over the event or timing of redemption, are now required to be accounted for as debt, rather than equity, in a company's balance sheet. If this is the case, any advantages relating to the improvement of a company's balance sheet from a debt for equity swap will be lost.

Convertibility

A convertible preference share entitles the holder to convert the instrument into a predetermined number of ordinary shares in the company at some future specified date. These instruments enable the holder to benefit from many of the advantages of preference shares, whilst at the same time retaining the ability to benefit from the advantages of ordinary shares, such as sharing in any growth in value of the company. Additionally, the ability to convert preference shares into more tradable securities, such as quoted ordinary shares, provides holders with an exit route via the stock market.

The terms by which preference shares can be converted into ordinary shares vary. The conversion price may be fixed, that is, at a fixed price per ordinary share. Alternatively, such terms may be variable, with the conversion price varying with the company's performance or asset realisations. The latter is unusual, however, in quoted companies. Stock exchanges are usually keen to ensure that the effects of any future conversion are transparent, and that any uncertainty is minimised.

The price at which preference shares are converted into ordinary shares is usually set at a premium to the price of ordinary shares prevailing at the time the preference shares are issued. This limits the dilution suffered by the ordinary shareholders.

Lenders need to ensure that they retain the right of conversion for as long as possible, in order to maximise flexibility. Any right of the company to enforce conversion should be limited to the most exceptional circumstances. Lenders should also restrict the manner in which the conversion may be effected, to prevent a mechanism that is tax inefficient for the shareholders.

Stock market quotation

In most situations, preference shares will be issued to the lenders as a new class of shares. As such, they will be held by the lenders only, who may be few in number. In addition, any preference shares issued as part of a debt for equity swap transaction will probably be tailored to the needs of the lenders, which might not be consistent with the characteristics demanded by institutional investors (for example, an appropriate coupon, or a rating). Consequently, investors are unlikely to find investing in such shares an attractive proposition. It is rare, therefore, that obtaining a quotation for these shares will be of sufficient benefit to warrant the costs associated with stock market-related obligations. At least initially, convertibility to quoted ordinary shares should enable lenders to access a market-related exit as an alternative. There would be a strong case for obtaining a quotation, of course, if the shares issued to the lenders are of the same class as existing quoted preference shares.

Restrictions

In order to protect the preference shareholders' interests, class rights attaching to them will usually preclude the company from taking certain actions without specific approval from preference shareholders. These restrictions generally protect:

- The preference.
- Dividend and redemption rights.
- Conversion and anti-dilution rights.

In principle, therefore, preference shares are an attractive instrument into which to swap debt. They can be designed to incorporate many features that are attractive to lenders and that mirror some of the characteristics of debt. Various legal, regulatory, accounting and taxation-related constraints can, however, limit the extent to which many of the rights embedded in preference shares can be availed in practice. The likely weak financial situation of a company that has recently been the subject of a debt for equity swap is a further problem. For example, in the event of a liquidation, it is highly unlikely that there would be any capital left for distribution to any shareholders. In that event, the entitlement to preference in distribution over ordinary shareholders is of little intrinsic value. Convertible preference shares can be designed, to an extent, to overcome some of the drawbacks associated with vanilla preference shares.

Given the mix of advantages and disadvantages therefore, in our opinion preference shares should be used selectively. The company's underlying economic and financial condition needs to be carefully evaluated to ensure that the features incorporated in such instruments will really apply. In many circumstances the advantages of the simplicity offered by ordinary shares outweigh those offered in practice by preference shares.

Convertible debt instruments

A convertible debt instrument (convertible bond or debenture) has the features of a normal fixed rate bond, but is convertible into the shares of the issuer or another group company. The conversion right cannot be separated from the debt. The coupon rate on a convertible bond would normally be lower than that for ordinary debt issued by the same borrower. This discount reflects the implicit value of the conversion option. As with preference shares, the conversion price is generally at a premium to the prevailing share price for the company. Other conversion-related features are also similar to those applicable to preference shares.

A swap converting a company's debt into its convertible bonds is not an immediate debt for equity swap. Unless a discount is involved in the swap, there is no reduction in the company's liabilities. A reduction in indebtedness, which is usually a critical component of debt for equity swaps, does not occur.

Convertible bonds can, however, still be valuable in loan workouts. They are suitable for certain situations in particular, including:

- *Where an immediate reduction in a company's debt is not required*, but there is a possibility that it may be necessary in the future. Terms can be designed to trigger a conversion of the bonds into equity upon the occurrence of certain events (for example, the failure to dispose of an asset), or on a predetermined date.

- *When a company is not able to service its interest obligations*, or does not otherwise meet normal credit criteria. Conversion rights can be tailored to compensate the banks for foregoing interest payments, or accepting a low rate of interest, or otherwise taking on equity-type risk.

- In certain circumstances, it may be possible to *issue convertible bonds that entitle holders to shares in a different company* (for example, a subsidiary of the group). Depending on the country, there are usually various restrictions on the circumstances under which such conversion can be carried out. Where possible, this can be an attractive option, for example if a subsidiary is earmarked for disposal as part of the restructuring.

- *Where a company's debt is being converted into a number of instruments*, and a tranche of debt is swapped into convertible bonds. This might enable a better tailoring of the restructuring to the risk:reward preferences of the participants.

In some cases, the use of debt linked with warrants instead of convertible bonds may be a more appropriate option. In this case, the capital of the company will increase, as instead of converting debt into shares, the warrant, if exercised, will require its holder to subscribe cash for shares at a predetermined price.

Warrants

Warrants are essentially long-term call options issued by a company. They enable its holders to subscribe for shares in the company at a predetermined price, often at a premium to the company's prevailing share price. In financial restructuring transactions, they are usually issued to lenders, or sometimes existing shareholders. Warrants enable their holders to acquire (or increase) a stake in the company's enlarged equity, after a target level of valuation is achieved.

This can be valuable in negotiations, particularly if the future prospects of a company are not clear. For example, at the time of a debt for equity swap, lenders may wish to acquire a very large proportion of the enlarged equity in a company to ensure that they are able to recover their original exposure. At the same time, they may be willing to concede to existing shareholders the ability to increase their proportion of the shareholding in the company once a target value of their shareholding is reached. Warrants to subscribe for shares in the company once a specific share price has been attained could be issued to the company's existing shareholders to achieve this purpose. Warrants are similarly useful if there is a dispute over a company's valuation.

Similarly, banks can be issued with warrants so that they can share in any upside in a company's share price, whether immediately or after a target improvement in the price has been achieved. Such warrants can be issued as a component of a debt for equity swap transaction, or in a conventional debt-only workout, for example, where the lenders are not charging a rate of interest that reflects the underlying credit risk of the company.

As indicated earlier, unlike convertible bonds, where the underlying debt is itself converted into shares on prespecified terms, warrants usually provide for shares to be issued for cash. Conditions relating to the use of such cash received by the company, which may include its application to reduce its debt, are agreed as part of the loan workout.

Warrants can be issued with long maturities, of up to 10 or 15 years. A series of warrants might be issued as part of a restructuring, providing for different exercise prices or with different maturities. Warrants issued by stock exchange listed companies can often themselves be traded, either in bearer or registered form. This has the advantage of providing holders with an opportunity to realise the value accrued in their warrants without needing to wait until they are able to exercise them. Finally, warrants can also be issued that entitle the holder to subscribe for shares in a company other than the issuer, for example, a subsidiary.

Other equity instruments

As stressed at the beginning of the chapter, a considerable range of equity and *quasi-equity* instruments can be tailored to meet the specific needs of the participants in a loan workout, subject to conforming with the country's legal and regulatory requirements.[1] The characteristics of a further two instruments are outlined below to illustrate the range of possibilities.

Puttable stock

Here, shares are issued by the company with a put option attached. This would require the company to buy the shares at a specified price at or between agreed dates in the future. This puts a floor under the value of the shares which the debt has been converted into. However, being effectively redeemable ordinary shares, there are usually very strict legal restrictions on the terms under which such instruments can be issued. Also, they may be deemed to be *quasi*-debt and the company may be required to account for them as such. Moreover, the company may not have the financial capacity to meet its obligations in the future under the terms of the put option. Nevertheless, these instruments have been issued in some countries as part of financial restructurings. A variation of the instrument, which might be more appropriate in loan workouts, is stock with an option to put it to another entity. For example, this could be a major shareholder of the company which is financially more strong.

Convertible stock notes

These are debt instruments that meet their interest and principal servicing obligations by the issue of new shares in the borrowing company, rather than cash. They are particularly suitable for companies undergoing loan workouts. In addition to conserving cash, unlike warrants they do not require lenders to subscribe additional cash to acquire shares.

Structuring principles

Given the range of available equity and *quasi*-equity instruments, some basic principles are required that can guide the lenders on the appropriate instrument that should be selected for a debt for equity swap. Fundamentally, three parameters are involved:

- The sharing of value accruing to the equity component of a company's capital structure.
- The allocation of risk between the participants.
- Related to the previous parameters, other features and controls that might be desired, depending on the specific circumstances.

Sharing of value

This is usually the principal focus of any equity structuring exercise, and the main factor that gives rise to the complexity arising in debt for equity swaps. On the other hand, the flexibility offered by the various financial instruments can enable the needs of the participants to be satisfied, thereby preventing the transaction failing.

The two key issues related to the sharing of value that affect the structuring of the equity component of debt for equity swaps are:

- What proportion of the value of a company's equity should each (category of) participant be entitled to.
- Should this proportion be varied, depending on the absolute levels of valuation attributable to the company, or each category of participant?

The latter is important because of some of the reasons highlighted earlier in this chapter. For example, the lenders may find it easier to accept that the existing shareholders in a company should receive a large proportion of the company's enlarged equity provided their original exposure, or some other target valuation of equity, is recovered. Moreover, there might be different classes of lenders and shareholders, and their respective shareholdings may need to be varied depending on the valuation thresholds reached.

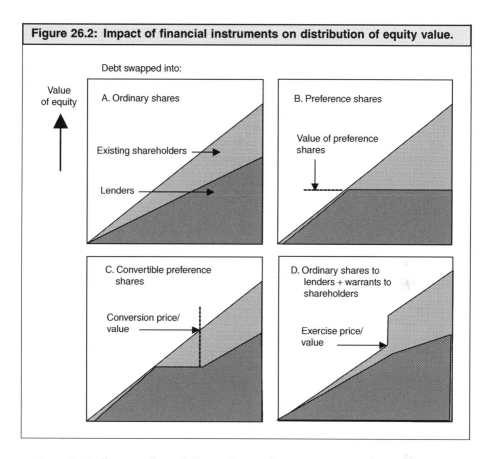

Figure 26.2: Impact of financial instruments on distribution of equity value.

Figure 26.2 illustrates how different financial instruments can be used to achieve some of these aims.

Four different scenarios are highlighted in Figure 26.2 above, each demonstrating the impact of different equity instruments on how the total value of a company's equity is shared after a debt for equity swap. In Box A, the lenders have acquired ordinary shares in exchange for debt. The relative proportion of a company's total equity value that the lenders and original shareholders are entitled to, denoted by the dark and lightly shaded areas respectively, remains constant as the value of the company's equity rises. Box B illustrates the scenario where the lenders have acquired preference shares. Legally, they are entitled to the entire value of the company's equity up to the nominal value of the preference shares. Any surplus over this belongs to the existing shareholders. In practice, some value will accrue to ordinary shares throughout, to reflect their potential prospects in the future.

Box C shows the same preference share, but with a convertibility feature. The lenders who swap their debt for this instrument can start sharing in an increase in the value of the company's equity after a point, depending on the conversion price of the shares. Finally, Box D demonstrates the impact of warrants being issued to the shareholders in a debt for equity swap in which the lenders have converted debt into ordinary shares. Upon the exercise of the warrants, the value of the company increases by the subscription value of the newly issued shares. Also, the lenders suffer dilution, as a result of which their future share of any increase in the value of equity diminishes (demonstrated by a flattening of the line showing the lenders' share).

Figure 26.2 highlights how different financial instruments can help in structuring debt for equity swap solutions. A combination of instruments can be used, or different tranches of the same instrument (for example, more than one series of warrants with different exercise prices) may be issued to develop other variations. These would be bundled into units that are issued by the company in exchange for a given unit of debt. Nevertheless, as stressed previously, a balance needs to be maintained between creating a structure that meets the needs of all the participants in a transaction, and the greater risks and costs associated with more complex structures. In this area, simplicity should be regarded as a key objective in itself.

Other structure-related parameters

The sensitivity of the cash flow projections prepared as part of the restructuring provide a basis for assessing the extent of the risk attached to the equity component of the company's capital structure. If the equity is divided into more than one class of share capital, it would be possible to allocate cash flows to the different financial instruments based on their ranking for capital and income, to assess the riskiness attached to each of them. In reality, however, all classes of equity in most debt for equity swaps are likely to carry very high risk. Therefore, any distinction between them is likely to be relatively marginal. However, this exercise is useful as it helps in estimating and negotiating the required returns from different equity instruments. Liquidity of the instruments will also impact on their riskiness.

Rights attached to the various equity instruments can affect transaction risk by enabling, or preventing, various actions being taken by the company. Voting powers reaching particular thresholds that enable lenders to influence certain actions should be a key consideration when considering the suitability of various types of shares. Additionally, matters such as the income from shares and the feasibility of exit should also be taken into account.

Box 26.1 highlights the use of different financial instruments in a major international loan workout.

Box 26.1

Eurotunnel PLC/SA

Eurotunnel is the operator of passenger and freight rail services using the Channel Tunnel that links the United Kingdom to France. Various

Box 26.1 Continued

problems, including cost overruns in building the tunnel, and delays in its completion, caused it severe financial difficulties. A financial restructuring was agreed with the company's lenders in 1997.

The key objective of this financial restructuring was to reduce the burden of the group's indebtedness by a combination of actions, including the reduction of its debt and fixing, at a lower rate, the cost of servicing the majority of the remaining indebtedness, whilst extending its maturity profile. The restructuring related to Eurotunnel's junior debt of £8.6 billion, which represented 96 per cent of the group's indebtedness. The group's senior debt obligations were unaffected. The transaction was considerably influenced by French financial regulations.

Principal features

- Approximately 55 per cent of existing junior debt converted into a combination of:
  - Equity (in the form of Eurotunnel units).
  - Equity notes convertible into units at a later date.
  - Participating loan notes.
  - A resettable facility.
- Remaining junior debt restructured to bear fixed interest rates over six years at rates significantly below those under existing facilities.
- Maturity profile of financial obligations significantly extended.
- Existing unitholders given the opportunity to subscribe for units to be issued to banks provided the market price of units was equal to or greater than banks' subscription price. Also, they were issued with free warrants that, if exercised, would enable them to retain the majority of equity.

Equity dilution

	Pre-	Post-
Unitholders	100%	54.5%
Junior debtholders (essentially banks)	—	45.5%

The terms of the restructuring allowed for the subsequent increase or further dilution of unitholders' stake, subject to various conditions being fulfilled.

If lenders converted all the equity notes issued to them pursuant to the debt for equity swap, the unitholders would be diluted to only 39.4 per cent of Eurotunnel's enlarged equity. Further dilution, under certain assumptions, down to 24.1 per cent was possible if Eurotunnel could not service all its debt obligations after the restructuring and had to issue new units to meet such obligations.

Box 26.1 Continued

> Conversely, if Eurotunnel's financial performance improved and they exercised all the warrants issued to them as part of the transaction, unitholders could increase their shareholding to up to 55.5 per cent. Two series of warrants were issued, exercisable over different periods. One of the series had an exercise price set at 15.4 per cent higher than the conversion price for debt, the other at the conversion price itself, but on the condition that the concession to the company for using the tunnel was extended. Proceeds from the exercise of the warrants would be used to redeem the equity notes.
>
> *Source*: *Summarised from Eurotunnel circular to unitholders*[2]

Inter-creditor issues

Figure 26.1 at the beginning of this chapter shows that a typical company's long-term funding will comprise various types of capital, each with a different relative ranking or preference in entitlement to capital and income. In practice, there may be lenders or shareholders who have a different ranking from others within each of these layers. One of the principal challenges of a debt for equity swap is to formulate a solution that preserves the relative pre-restructuring rankings of all the financial stakeholders.

The principal means of achieving this is by swapping the debt of a particular ranking for equity with rights entitling the holder to distribution or income in a manner that reflects such a relative ranking. However, it may be impractical to do so in the case of companies with complex financing arrangements because numerous classes of shares may need to be issued for this purpose. In such circumstances, a compromise may be found by 'pooling' various creditors with similar rankings into one or more classes for the purposes of the debt for equity swap.

An alternative solution is to recognise higher rankings by providing for a disproportionately greater value in the final outcome to accrue to that creditor. This may be achieved by requiring the higher ranking creditors to convert a lower proportion of their debt.

Valuing equity instruments

Given the importance that the value of equity can have on the overall return from a debt for equity swap, valuing equity instruments is a critical exercise. Moreover, the methodology adopted must be robust, as the valuation models and their underlying assumptions must withstand challenges during negotiations. Valuation of equity is a difficult exercise. It is particularly problematic in a turnaround situation, given the high degree of uncertainty associated with potential outcomes. Therefore, although the valuation exercise needs to be robust, it is important to trade-off the costs associated with highly complex models that produce results of spurious accuracy against the advantages they offer.

Equity valuation is generally carried out on behalf of the lenders by the reporting accountants, or the investment banking advisors. Depending on the objective of the exercise, the value of a company's equity at the time of an anticipated exit, or at present, will be calculated. The valuation is usually presented as a range, or matrix, of high–medium–low values achievable with probabilities attached to each projected outcome. The range of valuations obtained is a product of different underlying assumptions. Additionally, more than one valuation methodology should be used to ensure that they produce consistent results.

Lenders need to ensure that an appropriate methodology is being applied to the case. Although standard earnings and discounted cash flow-based valuations may be the foundation for most equity valuation techniques, certain situations may require them to be adapted. For example, where a break-up, or the disposal, of substantial parts of a group of companies is being considered, it might be more appropriate to value each unit separately, on a standalone basis, rather than consider the valuation of the group as a whole. Similarly, where parts of a business are likely to be liquidated, a combination of asset-based and earnings or cash flow-based techniques is warranted.

The valuation of convertible instruments and derivatives such as warrants is highly sensitive to the model and the underlying assumptions used. Various generic and proprietorial models are available for this exercise. The parameters used and the valuation process itself are usually not very transparent. Considerable expertise is required to ensure that the exercise is carried out in a manner that takes into account the lenders' interests. Of all the areas in debt for equity swap transactions, this is one in which it is critical that experienced professional advice is sought.

[1] P. Rivett and P. Speak (eds.), *The Financial Jungle—A Guide to Financial Instruments*, Coopers & Lybrand Deloitte, 2nd edition, 1991.

[2] Eurotunnel: Financial restructuring proposals, circular to unitholders, May 1997.

27

OTHER TRANSACTION PARAMETERS

Introduction

The key to designing successful debt for equity swaps is to develop financial structures that meet the risk, return and other preferences of the participants. Numerous variations and combinations of equity instruments can be used to achieve this. In addition, the two principal variables that influence the financial impact of a debt for equity swap are:

- The amount, or proportion, of a company's debt that is converted into equity (or, the 'swap ratio').
- The proportion of the company's enlarged equity that the lenders receive in exchange for the swapped debt.

The factors influencing these parameters, and their impact on the transaction's structure, are explored in this chapter.

Proportion of debt converted into equity

The amount of debt to be converted into equity is probably the most sensitive issue in debt for equity swap negotiations. It often takes the longest time to resolve. The conflict between the interests of the company and its shareholders on the one hand, and the lenders on the other, is the most transparent in this area. This is because the share of a company's enlarged equity that lenders receive tends to be relatively insensitive to the swap ratio, as existing shareholders' minimum needs must be satisfied. As a result, a higher swap ratio tends to reduce the likely return for the lenders. On the other hand, the more of their debt that the lenders convert, the higher is the potential value accruing to the shareholders.

This problem is compounded in some jurisdictions if the lenders are automatically required to make a provision against any debt that has been converted into equity.

The greater the swap ratio is, the higher the loss that the lenders have to recognise immediately.

This conflict of interest is also present in the perception of risk. The higher the swap ratio, the lower the financial risk of the company. Management needs to service a lower debt burden and, as a result, the value of the company's shares increases. The lenders, however, are thereby relegating a higher proportion of their exposure to the company to claims behind the company's creditors who may currently rank after them.

In reality, however, the lenders' traditional argument in this matter is relatively weak. A properly structured swap transaction essentially crystallises the lenders' effective equity risk position, enabling them to share in the commensurate potentially higher returns.

Principal determinants

The amount of debt swapped for equity will be an outcome of negotiations, but should enable the loan workout's objectives to be met. Factors that influence this issue include:

- If there is a balance sheet deficit, it is very likely that the company's net worth will need to be restored. In this case, the target post-restructuring net worth of the company needs to be evaluated, for example, by making financial projections for a number of future accounting periods. This will directly impact on the amount of debt that should be swapped for equity.
- The appropriate level of post-restructuring gearing will vary considerably between situations and the overall objectives of the loan workout. If a sustainable restructuring, perhaps involving the raising of new debt or equity funds is envisaged, the balance sheet indicators may be required to reflect industry norms. In most workout cases, however, this may not be necessary. For instance, a restructuring which anticipates the short- or medium-term disposal of a substantial part of the business should be able to sustain a higher initial gearing.
- If debt servicing is a temporary problem, it may suffice to convert some of the company's debt into low or zero coupon bonds, say with warrants, or even to simply agree an interest holiday.
- As highlighted previously, a high swap ratio may be necessary to attract new debt or equity. If so, the lenders need to consider how much new debt or equity could be raised, on what basis and whether the trade-off is acceptable.

Generally, the principal objective of loan workouts is to re-establish financial stability to a group's operations. The swap ratio is the principal determinant of financial stability in a restructuring. It directly affects how much residual debt remains on the company's balance sheet. It is therefore important to ensure that the lenders' natural desire to preserve as much debt as possible does not defeat the main purpose of the restructuring.

Inter-creditor issues

The residual debt and, therefore, the swap ratio for each lender should reflect its relative strength at the moratorium date. For this purpose, relative strength is determined by reference to how much would be recovered by each lender in liquidation, as estimated by the reporting accountants. Therefore, a lender that is expected to recover a higher proportion of its exposure at the start of the moratorium should retain a higher proportion of its debt after the restructuring. The example below illustrates this concept.

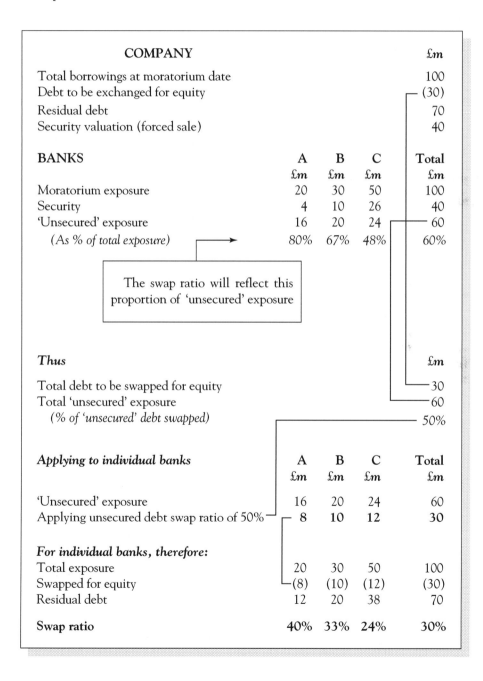

COMPANY				£m
Total borrowings at moratorium date				100
Debt to be exchanged for equity				(30)
Residual debt				70
Security valuation (forced sale)				40

BANKS	A	B	C	Total
	£m	£m	£m	£m
Moratorium exposure	20	30	50	100
Security	4	10	26	40
'Unsecured' exposure	16	20	24	60
(As % of total exposure)	80%	67%	48%	60%

The swap ratio will reflect this proportion of 'unsecured' exposure

Thus	£m
Total debt to be swapped for equity	30
Total 'unsecured' exposure	60
(% of 'unsecured' debt swapped)	50%

Applying to individual banks	A	B	C	Total
	£m	£m	£m	£m
'Unsecured' exposure	16	20	24	60
Applying unsecured debt swap ratio of 50%	8	10	12	30

For individual banks, therefore:				
Total exposure	20	30	50	100
Swapped for equity	(8)	(10)	(12)	(30)
Residual debt	12	20	38	70
Swap ratio	**40%**	**33%**	**24%**	**30%**

Thus, the amount of debt swapped for equity by each bank will be proportional to their anticipated loss in the event of liquidation.

Foreign exchange considerations

Exposures in foreign currencies need to be treated with particular care in financial reorganisations. Foreign exchange rate variations between the moratorium date and the issue of equity instruments to the lenders in exchange for debt can affect the relative exposures of the creditors and distort the type of solution outlined above.

It is important to maintain fairness of treatment between the lenders, principally by ensuring that the movements of exchange rates after their relative positions are notionally crystallised on the moratorium date do not favour only some of the participants.

In order to do so, the relative positions of the lenders on three key dates need to be taken into consideration when determining:

- The respective amount of debt that each lender would need to swap into equity.
- The residual debt retained by each lender after the restructuring.

The key dates are:

- *The moratorium date.* Followed by
- *The 'strike date'*—Being the date on which the participations in the subscription of shares issued in exchange for debt are fixed. Followed by
- *The 'allotment date'*—The date on which consideration for the shares is passed.

In instances where debt denominated in a number of currencies is exchanged for shares issued in only one currency, two problems arise as a result of differential foreign exchange rate movements between respectively:

- The moratorium date and the strike date.
- The strike date and the allotment date.

In order to preserve the relative position of lenders between the moratorium date and the strike date, two key ratios need to be fixed for all lenders:

- *The swap ratio*, being the proportion, in this case in the original currency, of post-conversion debt to pre-conversion debt. This ratio needs to be the same for all lenders in a similar recovery position.
- *The 'moratorium ratio'*, being the proportion of equity that each lender would have received if the debt for equity swap had occurred at the moratorium date, in adherence to the principles illustrated in the example above. This ratio needs to be maintained for each lender as at the strike date.

Relative foreign exchange rate movements between the moratorium date and the strike date will cause the currency swap ratio and the moratorium ratio to move relative to each other. These movements are reconciled by adjusting the price at which each lender subscribes for shares. Thus, each lender may be subscribing at a different price per share at the base currency. The following example, in which UK sterling has been used as the base currency, illustrates the concept:

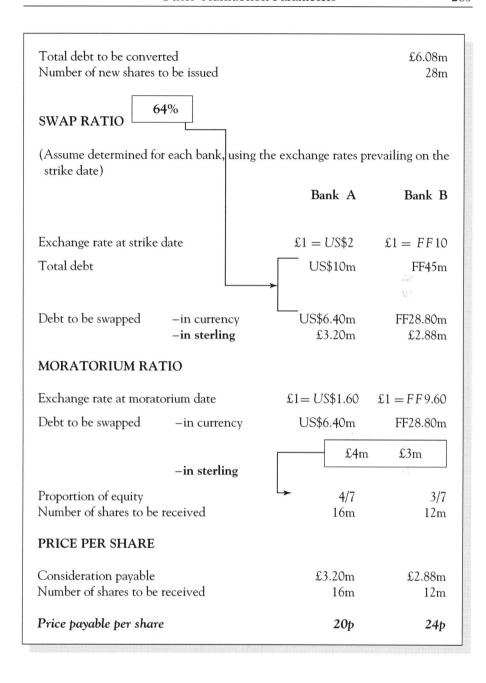

		Bank A	Bank B
Total debt to be converted			£6.08m
Number of new shares to be issued			28m
SWAP RATIO 64%			
(Assume determined for each bank, using the exchange rates prevailing on the strike date)			
Exchange rate at strike date		£1 = US$2	£1 = FF 10
Total debt		US$10m	FF45m
Debt to be swapped	–in currency	US$6.40m	FF28.80m
	–in sterling	£3.20m	£2.88m
MORATORIUM RATIO			
Exchange rate at moratorium date		£1= US$1.60	£1 = FF 9.60
Debt to be swapped	–in currency	US$6.40m	FF28.80m
	–in sterling	£4m	£3m
Proportion of equity		4/7	3/7
Number of shares to be received		16m	12m
PRICE PER SHARE			
Consideration payable		£3.20m	£2.88m
Number of shares to be received		16m	12m
Price payable per share		*20p*	*24p*

Whilst lenders may pay different prices for their shares in the base currency, depending on the level of exchange rate movements, in practice these variances per share are likely to be minimal. The differences in consideration in the base currency do not imply greater or lesser cost or risk, because the currency amount paid by each lender stays constant throughout. Also, the swap ratio in currency terms remains the same for all lenders. Although this technique does preserve the relative position of lenders, the fact that different prices may be payable for a company's shares in the base currency can cause complications. It is critical that the underlying principles for arriving at the share prices are properly explained to all the participants in the transaction. Moreover, the legal and, if relevant, local stock exchange implications of differential pricing should also be carefully assessed.

The distortive impact of the currency movements between the strike date and the share allotment date are simpler to resolve. This revolves around the conversion of foreign currency debt into the base currency for subscription for shares. Exchange rates prevailing at the strike date are used for this purpose. An actual conversion of currency, however, should be avoided on the strike date in case the restructuring does not proceed eventually. Thus the lenders' exposure to exchange rate movements between the strike date and the date of allotment of shares, when actual payment for the shares is made, remains unhedged. The lenders need to consider whether, or how, to address this risk.

Limit to conversion

Factors such as the balance sheet structure of a company and its ability to service its debt should be the principal determinants of the amount of debt that is swapped for equity. Nevertheless, the lenders need to be careful that the conversion process is not limitless. After a certain point, the deterioration in position suffered as a result of the swap outweighs the benefits of the transaction. One of the most important parameters in this area is the value of the lenders' security.

Essentially, the lenders should avoid swapping their debt into equity to the extent that the residual debt remaining after the swap is lower than the value of their security. This is to prevent promoting other creditors in the event of the company's liquidation after the conversion. Figure 27.1 below illustrates the concept.

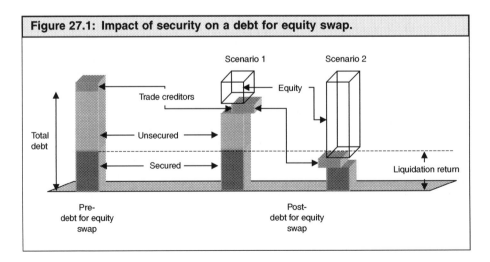

Figure 27.1: Impact of security on a debt for equity swap.

In the illustration above, the company's trade creditors are being promoted as a result of a debt for equity swap. However, in the first scenario the swap is not deep enough to promote creditors to the extent that they share in the lenders' security. In the second scenario, the swap ratio is higher. As a result, if the company is liquidated after the restructuring is agreed, the lenders will receive a lower return than they would have if liquidation occurred without a debt for equity swap having taken place.

Non-debt exposures

'Soft', or contingent exposures, such as interest or currency swaps, performance bonds, and guarantees pose a particular problem in debt for equity swaps. It is not possible to determine at the time of the restructuring the magnitude of debt that would result if and when they crystallise.

There are essentially two methods of dealing with non-debt exposures in debt for equity swap transactions:

- Certain exposures, such as swaps and financial letters of credit, can be closed-out and the resulting exposure converted to a loan. Additionally, in some instances there may be strong indications that certain other exposures will crystallise in the near future. In these cases, the amount of debt the particular lender converts should be adjusted upwards accordingly.

- Otherwise, the loss-sharing arrangements in the restructuring agreement should address the impact of the non-conversion of non-debt exposures. These provide that all the lenders will be entitled to share in any post-enforcement distributions based on their pre-debt for equity swap relative exposures. As a result lenders with non-debt exposures do not gain any advantage.

Proportion of equity for lenders

The swap ratio determines the size of the company's enlarged equity 'cake' that is available for sharing between its lenders and other financial stakeholders. The proportion of equity that lenders get is a reflection of the share of the 'cake' that lenders can retain for themselves.

A debt for equity swap would usually be contemplated in situations where the total value of a company, even on a going concern basis, is less than the face value of debt. Existing equity holdings are therefore likely to be worthless. It would follow that lenders should be entitled to the entire diluted equity capital of the company after a debt for equity swap, irrespective of the amount of debt converted.

However, in reality, it is unusual for existing shareholders' interests to be diluted to zero in voluntary loan workouts, since any dilution is normally subject to their approval. If their agreement to a restructuring is not secured, the alternative is usually some form of insolvency procedure and larger losses for lenders. Shareholders will be no worse off. Consequently, in the absence of any legal recourse, the shareholders would need to be incentivised sufficiently to approve the transaction. The residual stake of existing shareholders will also be influenced by any new funds that they may be injecting into the company as part of the loan workout.

In addition, in the case of a publicly quoted company, it may be desirable to maintain, or even encourage, a healthy market in the company's shares to facilitate an eventual exit by the lenders. This can generally only be achieved by leaving a sufficiently high proportion of shares with existing shareholders.

The lenders' aim would therefore be to secure the maximum share of the diluted share capital of the restructured company given the constraints outlined above. The outcome will usually be a product of intensive negotiations.

Principal determinants

In addition to their relative negotiating strength, the following factors could affect the proportion of a company's enlarged equity the lenders negotiate for:

- *Prospects of any additional equity injection.* If this is forthcoming as part of the restructuring, or is anticipated soon after, then greater value will need to be left in non-lender hands. This is needed to preserve the confidence of existing and potential shareholders and, particularly in the case of a publicly quoted company, to ensure a healthy market in its shares.

- *Precedents.* The outcome of similar restructurings completed recently will influence negotiations and, therefore, the eventual outcome.

- *Stock exchange requirements.* Most stock exchanges require a minimum percentage of a publicly quoted company's shares to be freely floating. Given the long-term and concentrated share holdings of the lenders after a debt for equity swap, their stakes might fall outside the definition of a free float. In practice, the stock exchanges in many countries may not enforce this requirement strictly in restructurings.

- *Market value of shares.* As previously explained, by the time most conventional debt for equity swaps are considered, there is unlikely to be any intrinsic value left for a company's shareholders. However, for stock exchange quoted companies, the market price of their shares can be used as a negotiating point on behalf of their existing shareholders. This is usually an artificially inflated valuation, attributable to factors such as:

  - An illiquid or thin market.
  - The absence of perfect information.
  - Anticipation of a (favourable) conclusion to the restructuring negotiations.

  The current market value of the shares should not therefore be accepted as a factor which affects the equity entitlement of a company's existing shareholders. Instead, the value projected to accrue to the existing shareholders (as determined by exit valuations based on more reliable information) should form the basis for negotiations.

- *Lenders' exit strategy.* If there is a strong possibility that the lenders will exit through the stock market, it may be in their interest to maintain a liquid market in the company's shares, by leaving a high proportion of the shares with the public.

- *Number of existing classes of equity or debt.* These are in cases where the company's financial arrangements are complex, for example, there exists a combination of different types of debt, bonds, preference shares and ordinary shares. Each of the individual classes of stakeholders will need to be involved in the debt for equity swap. Clearly, irrespective of the strength of each party's actual position, each will require a stake going forward. This will inevitably reduce the proportion of equity that is available to the lenders.

- *Amount of debt converted.* The higher the proportion of debt swapped into equity, the stronger the lenders' negotiating case should be.

- *Asset-owning or service-based companies.* Lenders will generally be in a weaker nego-tiating position in transactions involving service-based companies, especially if the key employees are also significant shareholders.

- *Local stock exchange or other regulations* seeking to protect the interests of shareholders, which seek to avoid excessive dilution of their interests. The level of protection accorded to minority shareholders can vary considerably between jurisdictions.

- *Different financial instruments can be used to vary the level of dilution of existing shareholders* for different degrees of success in the turnaround. For instance, preference shares or warrants can provide a substantially higher proportion of equity to existing shareholders after the lenders have recovered their original exposure to the company.

In addition to the above, the impact of shareholding thresholds, which provide the lenders with the power to influence different decisions, should be taken into account. Often, such shareholding thresholds are useful in preventing the blocking of key restructuring actions, such as disposals of major assets or subsidiaries, by dissident shareholders. Certain shareholding thresholds can also trigger regulatory or legal obligations, for instance filing of returns or disclosing movements in shareholdings.

Figure 27.2 below highlights the key shareholding thresholds in the United Kingdom and their implications. The lenders will use these thresholds as targets when negotiating their share of the enlarged equity in a company.

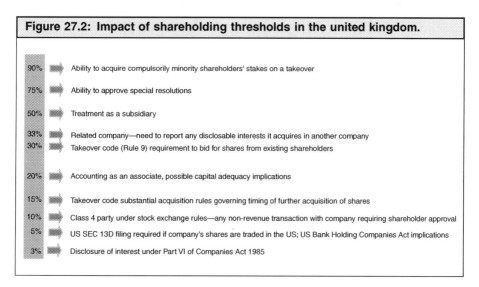

Figure 27.2: Impact of shareholding thresholds in the united kingdom.

90% → Ability to acquire compulsorily minority shareholders' stakes on a takeover

75% → Ability to approve special resolutions

50% → Treatment as a subsidiary

33% → Related company—need to report any disclosable interests it acquires in another company
30% → Takeover code (Rule 9) requirement to bid for shares from existing shareholders

20% → Accounting as an associate, possible capital adequacy implications

15% → Takeover code substantial acquisition rules governing timing of further acquisition of shares

10% → Class 4 party under stock exchange rules—any non-revenue transaction with company requiring shareholder approval

5% → US SEC 13D filing required if company's shares are traded in the US; US Bank Holding Companies Act implications

3% → Disclosure of interest under Part VI of Companies Act 1985

The proportion of a company's equity that the lenders eventually hold out for will be a matter of judgement. It is usually the most visible and, therefore, the most sensitive aspect of the restructuring on the part of the shareholders. In making the decision, lenders will take into account factors such as their relative negotiating position, the risk:reward ratio of the liquidation return compared with potential returns on a successful restructuring, the attractiveness of any contingency plans, and the probability of shareholders voting against the loan workout proposals.

28

OTHER
TECHNICAL ISSUES

Introduction

Much of the complexity associated with debt for equity swaps comes from the need to comply with rules governing their accounting, taxation and implementation, both on the part of the company and its lenders. In addition, the shareholdings arising from such transactions can give rise to continuing compliance and reporting obligations for the lenders, particularly if they become major shareholders in a company. The impact of these matters must be fully considered at the time the restructuring options are being evaluated.

In this chapter, the following technical issues are considered:

- Accounting.
- Taxation.
- Legal and regulatory.
- Mechanics of implementation.

The focus is on considering these issues from a lenders' point of view. However, matters addressed in this chapter vary considerably between countries. Moreover, treatments can at times conflict between jurisdictions. Therefore, it is critical that the readers familiarise themselves with their local accounting, taxation and legal frameworks affecting debt for equity swaps. Also, transactions involving a company with operations in more than one country, or a lender group involving banks from different jurisdictions, may need to comply with the laws and regulations in all the jurisdictions involved.

Accounting-related matters

The accounting impact of debt for equity swaps on the balance sheet of companies is usually the principal area of focus. However, the accounting treatment of such transactions for the lenders can have important implications. The accounting issues for lenders revolve around the impact of the swap on their loan-loss provisions and the on-going valuation of the shares acquired in exchange for debt.

Loan-loss provisions

There are two principal methods of accounting for equity acquired in exchange for debt:

- *Writing-off, or fully providing against the value of the equity.* This is clearly the most prudent approach and is required under the internal regulations of many banks. However, this policy may not always accurately reflect the underlying commercial substance of a debt for equity swap transaction. This is particularly so if the principal objective of a transaction is to restore some value to the company's equity. The risk is that this accounting approach acts as a disincentive for banks to convert the necessary level of debt into equity, and thereby fail to agree to a robust financial restructuring. There is also a possibility that once fully provided, there would be little incentive for lenders to take a proactive role in maximising the value of their equity holdings.
- *Valuing the shares at the lower of cost and net realisable value.* For this purpose, cost is the face value of debt converted and net realisable value is assumed to be the estimated realisation at the proposed exit date. The reporting accountants' valuation of the company's equity is usually used for this purpose. For short-term holdings, say, realisable within one year, the market value (if any) of the shares is likely to be the appropriate indicator of their realisable value. This is providing the market for the company's shares is relatively liquid. The risk associated with this approach is that there is pressure to take an optimistic view on realisable value and hence use a debt for equity swap transaction to delay making necessary provisions against problem loans.

The lender's host country or internal regulations will often restrict the options available for the accounting treatment of shares acquired in distressed clients. It is important, however, to ensure that the accounting method adopted does not distort the substance of the transaction. A swap based on the fundamental financial and business issues will ultimately benefit all the parties involved.

Accounting as a subsidiary or an associate

In certain circumstances, a lender may acquire a holding greater than or equal to 20 or 50 per cent of a company's voting share capital. Under normal circumstances, such investments would need to be accounted for as associates or subsidiaries of the lender, respectively. This can potentially have negative implications, for example losses of the company being rescued would need to be consolidated in the banks' accounts. In most jurisdictions, however, provided it can be clearly demonstrated that the holding is temporary and has arisen as part of a company's support operation, such holdings will not need to be equity accounted or consolidated.

Taxation

The principal tax-related issue normally affecting the lenders in debt for equity swap transactions is the treatment of any loss suffered as a result of exchanging debt for shares which are likely to be worth considerably less than the debt's face value. To maximise tax efficiency, such 'loss' should be available as a tax shelter at the time of the transaction. In certain jurisdictions, however, losses arising from such exchanges may not be recognised for tax purposes until the disposal of the shares.

To create a structure that will secure tax relief at the time of the debt for equity swap transaction, the following factors may need to be addressed:

- The reorganisation must not be structured such that the company 'repays' the outstanding debt and the lenders use the notional proceeds of the repayment to subscribe for the company's shares. Instead, the transaction needs to be an 'exchange' of debt for shares.
- If a proportion of the shares allocated to lenders relates to rolled-up interest, a further advance may need to be made to the company to notionally repay the interest, with this new 'debt' then being exchanged for shares. The direct exchange of accrued interest for shares is often tax inefficient.

The tax efficiency of the transaction, both in the company's and lenders' interests, is a key consideration in structuring debt for equity swap transactions. Often considerable value can be released from the company's accumulated losses by structuring the transaction effectively.

Selected legal and regulatory issues

Legal and regulatory provisions affect debt for equity swaps throughout the transaction and subsequently, until lenders have disposed of their shareholdings. Firstly, there is the need to ensure that the transaction is structured in compliance with all local legal and regulatory provisions. In addition, lenders must ensure that they are not in breach of laws and regulations that apply to them as a result of them being:

- Substantial shareholders in a company.
- Financial institutions holding shares in a non-financial entity.

Laws and regulations relating to the shareholdings held by the lenders in general, and the banks in particular, include:

- Obligations under corporate legislation, or local stock exchange regulation, to disclose acquisitions and movements in shareholdings above a certain threshold.
- The need to comply with local insider dealing legislation.
- In certain circumstances, local and regional mergers regulation may be triggered as a result of the lenders acquiring a substantial shareholding in a company. Dispensation may need to be applied for.
- In some countries there are rules that restrict banks holding shares in non-bank companies. Dispensation is usually available if the shares are acquired to facilitate a rescue.

- Lenders may become a 'connected party' with the company and may, as a result, become subject to additional legal and regulatory provisions that govern their dealings with it.

Capital adequacy

As a general rule, a debt for equity swap should have no effect on existing Basle capital adequacy requirements of individual lenders as both loans to, and shareholdings in, non-lender companies will usually be subject to a 100 per cent weighting. However, local regulations may require additional capital to be allocated to equity holdings.

If a lender acquires a 20 per cent or more equity shareholding in a company, the latter may be treated as an associate and adverse capital adequacy requirements may apply—for example, needing deductions from core capital. Generally, temporary equity holdings arising from debt for equity swaps are not required to be treated as associates or subsidiaries for capital adequacy purposes. However, the matter may need to be clarified with local regulatory authorities.

Transaction mechanics

The procedures for completing a debt for equity swap transaction will be governed considerably by local practice and custom. Some of the more important matters are outlined below.

Issuing new shares

A debt for equity swap will usually be effected through the issue of new shares in a company to its lenders. These could be either an existing class of shares, or a new class, sometimes with conversion rights into existing shares. The result would be the dilution of existing shareholders to the agreed level.

The following example illustrates the impact of issuing an existing class of shares:

	Total	Current shareholders	Lenders
PRE-SWAP			
Existing shares in issue	20m	20m	Nil
AT RESTRUCTURING			
Agreed proportion of shares for lenders			*75%*
Issue new shares to lenders	60m		60m
POST-SWAP			
Shares in issue	80m	20m	60m
Percentage holdings		**25%**	**75%**

For non-listed companies, where the number of shareholders is usually small, the issue of new shares to the lenders would be agreed as part of the overall restructuring.

For publicly quoted companies, the issue of new shares is affected by the local stock exchange regulations. In addition, the existing shareholders would normally be offered the opportunity to subscribe for new shares *pro rata* to their existing holdings to meet their pre-emption rights, where such rights exist. If more than one class of new shares are being issued, these would usually be packaged into 'units'. Any shares not taken up by existing shareholders would be subscribed for by lenders in exchange for debt. Pre-emption can be valuable in negotiations as the shareholders will in effect have the opportunity to avoid dilution by subscribing for the company's shares on the same terms as those offered to its lenders.

Generally, lenders will be subscribing for shares at a substantial premium to the prevailing market price, principally to recognise the implicit discount in the value of the debt being converted. As a result, it is extremely rare that the existing shareholders will subscribe for shares at the same price as lenders. If an equity fund raising exercise is conducted at the same time as an exchange, non-lender subscribers would be offered shares at a lower price than that being 'paid' by the lenders.

Other methods of achieving the desired shareholding by the lenders might be possible, such as:

- Acquisition of the appropriate number of shares from existing shareholders for a nominal consideration.
- Deferral or cancellation of the required number of existing shares.

Usually, however, such mechanisms tend to add considerable complexity to the transaction, and are therefore avoided unless there is a particular need to pursue them.

In addition, statutory provisions may also be available to implement a debt for equity swap through the courts. Strictly, however, they fall outside the scope of a 'voluntary' loan restructuring.

Reduction of share capital

Accumulated losses and asset write-downs often leave a distressed company with negative reserves. A deficit in distributable reserves acts as a constraint on the company's ability to pay dividends or redeem preference shares. It may be in the participants' interest to eliminate such deficits. This will enhance the prospects of preference share redemption, or make it easier to attract new shareholders who will expect dividends to be paid.

In most jurisdictions, deficits in reserves may be eliminated by way of a capital reduction approved by the company's shareholders as part of the debt for equity swap. However, such capital reductions can also require the consent of the court.

Swap of debts in subsidiaries

In debt for equity swaps, shares are usually acquired in the parent company of a group. When a loan to a subsidiary is included in the transaction, problems may arise as the lenders are legally required to give consideration to the parent company in exchange for the shares.

The simplest mechanism of addressing this issue is to 'transfer' to the parent company the subsidiary's indebtedness owed to the lender. Alternatively, the parent company guarantee, if one exists, may be called provided there are no cross-default problems. The process is more difficult if there is no parent company guarantee as such transfers of indebtedness can be construed as the subsidiary providing financial assistance to its parent to purchase the latter's shares. This is prohibited in some jurisdictions.

In certain circumstances, a 'good' company may be created to separate viable assets and businesses of a group from those identified for liquidation. It may be easier to facilitate exit by obtaining, say, preference shares in the 'good' company with conversion rights into the shares of the parent company. The lenders' returns from the transaction will then be linked with the prospects of the 'good' company. The conversion option will provide an additional exit avenue if the group as a whole is sold.

PART IV

CASE STUDY

29

PROJECT GLOUCESTER

Introduction

Project Gloucester involved the loan workout, including a debt for equity swap, of a major stock exchange quoted UK freight forwarder.[1] We were closely involved in the transaction as part of the co-ordinator team. Many of the principles and approaches developed during the transaction were later replicated in other corporate rescues in the United Kingdom and, to some extent, elsewhere in the world. The workout provides an excellent basis for a case study as it deals with many of the issues highlighted throughout the book.

We have amended various details of the case, including the company's name (in fact, Gloucester was the code name used for the company during the transaction) and some information about its finances that are not publicly available. Nevertheless, we have sought to ensure that the case study presents the underlying transaction as accurately as possible.

The case study provides an overview of the company's activities and the causes of its financial problems. The key elements of its business and corporate restructuring plan are highlighted. Some of the issues involved in restructuring the company's debt and providing new finance are then examined. Finally, we provide on overview of the debt for equity swap component of the transaction.

Background

In the early 1990s, Gloucester was a leading international business services group with its headquarters in the United Kingdom. It had 157 subsidiaries and associated companies, incorporated in 24 jurisdictions. It operated in over 30 countries and employed some 11 000 people. The group included one of the five largest global freight forwarding operations and the fourth largest provider of electronic security services in the United States, through its subsidiary XQC. Other activities included physical distribution and property investment. In 1990, Gloucester's turnover was £1.4 billion

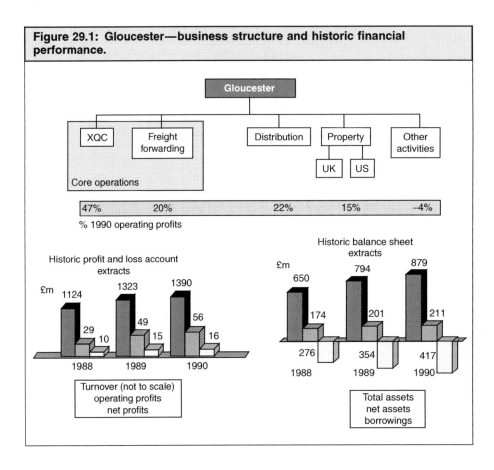

Figure 29.1: Gloucester—business structure and historic financial performance.

and it produced pre-tax profits of £29.4 million. Figure 29.1 highlights the group's business operations and its financial performance leading up to the crisis.

Moratorium

In July 1991, the company approached its principal banks to inform them of liquidity-related problems at the parent company. A moratorium was agreed on 30 July 1991. The initial moratorium agreement was signed by all its participants in October that year. This was subsequently extended a number of times, until a restructuring agreement was signed on 31 July 1992, one year after the calling of the moratorium.

The group's indebtedness

As at the moratorium date, the Gloucester group had banking arrangements with over 70 institutions in 25 countries. The group had total financial indebtedness of £602 million. Table 29.1 provides a breakdown of the group's financial liabilities at the time the moratorium was called.

Table 29.1: Gloucester's Financial Liabilities at the Moratorium Date.

	£m
Loans	367
Debentures	75
Overdrafts	50
Bonds	87
Leasing	17
Other	6
TOTAL	**602**

Lenders included in the moratorium

The moratorium and the subsequent core financial restructuring agreement included all the banks providing loans to the parent company and the group's UK subsidiaries. Notable exclusions were:

- Lenders to XQC, with exposures of approximately £85 million. These loans were excluded because they were to a profitable subsidiary, and did not have any recourse to the parent company.
- Debenture holders linked to a specific UK investment property (approximately £75 million). This exposure had been ringfenced and was considered to be well secured.
- Lenders to overseas subsidiaries on a standalone basis, with total loans of over £200 million. These were excluded from the moratorium because of their relatively small exposures, the fact that they did not have any recourse to the UK parent, and most of the subsidiaries were operating profitably.

In total 29 banks, providing facilities in 20 different currencies, joined the moratorium.

New finance during the moratorium

Very soon after the moratorium was called, Gloucester's main relationship banks provided a £40 million bridging facility pending the disposal of XQC. In the event, offers for XQC fell substantially below expectations. The bridging facility was never repaid and was subsequently included in the financial restructuring. In addition, £9 million of unutilised headroom as at the moratorium date was made available to the company to meet its operating needs.

Other events

The true extent of Gloucester's problems was not apparent at the time the moratorium was called in July 1991. An initial review was conducted by the group's auditors at the time, but this did not reveal any substantive problems. However, the failure to dispose of XQC created major concerns among the company's lenders. This was reinforced when an anticipated upturn in the group's principal markets did not materialise. Over the ensuing period, it became evident that Gloucester's performance had been deteriorating sharply.

The group's Chairman and Chief Executive departed in November 1991. In January 1992, independent reporting accountants were appointed by the banks to investigate the group and to explore the available options.

Causes and impact of the financial crisis

During the decade leading up to the crisis, Gloucester had experienced rapid expansion. Growth was principally achieved through acquisitions, financed mainly by debt. An economic downturn exposed the company to financial strains. This was exacerbated by a loss of confidence in the freight forwarding operations as the company's difficulties became publicised. Underlying this general problem were a number of specific weaknesses in the company's operations and finances. These were identified by the reporting accountants and included matters such as:

- The group's core *freight forwarding* operations were being affected by poor conditions in the United States, a major market. Its European operations were suffering from increased competition. Problems were being compounded by the poor integration of many new acquisitions, some of which had weak management.

- XQC, which had been acquired recently, was failing to meet target business volumes and was suffering from high cancellation rates. A major competitor of XQC had acquired a significant stake in the parent company, and there was uncertainty about its intentions. The reporting accountants also felt that the unit lacked clear strategic direction.

- The group's essentially speculative *property* investments had been affected by a major downturn in the market, particularly in the United States.

- *Other non-core* businesses were generally loss-making. A diverse range of investments, including mining, T-shirt printing and trade financing had been acquired over the preceding years. Most of these were haemorrhaging cash.

- There was a particularly intensive *liquidity squeeze* at the parent company. Much of the group's acquisition-related debt was owed by it. However, in order to protect their exposures, lenders to its various subsidiaries were preventing any cash from being distributed to the parent company. Moreover, some of Gloucester's new freight forwarding operations were absorbing substantial funds. Also, some of the group's banks were withdrawing uncommitted lines of finance.

- The group's core freight forwarding business required a relatively low asset base. Its *financial leverage* was very high. Moreover, the business had high *operational gearing*, with relatively small fluctuations in turnover impacting disproportionately on profitability. In addition to the problems highlighted previously, a combination of adverse market conditions, weak economy and confidence-related factors had severely impacted on Gloucester's profitability by depressing turnover.

The reporting accountants recommended substantial write-downs in the group's reported asset values and various charges to take into account its restructuring needs. The proposed charges, and their impact on Gloucester's 1991 accounts, are illustrated in Figure 29.2 below.

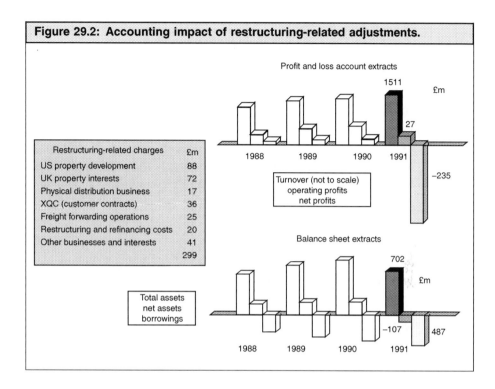

Figure 29.2: Accounting impact of restructuring-related adjustments.

Restructuring-related charges	£m
US property development	88
UK property interests	72
Physical distribution business	17
XQC (customer contracts)	36
Freight forwarding operations	25
Restructuring and refinancing costs	20
Other businesses and interests	41
	299

Thus, after the adjustments proposed by the reporting accountants, Gloucester's consolidated results produced significant net losses in 1991. More importantly, the balance sheet showed a substantial deficit in net worth.

Business restructuring

Gloucester's business restructuring strategy was agreed between the company and its bankers in early 1992, following a presentation of their findings by the reporting accountants. This essentially required the business to refocus and 'hold and develop' its core freight forwarding and XQC operations. In particular, the strategy called for:

- A new *management* team. The group's combined Chief Executive and Chairman had departed earlier during the crisis, after discussions with the company's principal bankers. An interim turnaround specialist and his team were appointed. The plan also provided for the strengthening of the management teams in the group's key operating businesses.

- Short-term exit by way of disposal of Gloucester's *non-core operations*. Proceeds realised would be used to fund the group's working capital needs and reduce debt. Where disposals were unlikely, the businesses would be liquidated.

- The *freight forwarding* business would focus on operations that made a significant return on capital, had strong profit enhancement potential, were of strategic importance to Gloucester's global network, and had small cash requirements. Costs would be reduced and tighter management control systems introduced. Recently acquired subsidiaries would be more effectively integrated into the group's network.

- XQC's activities would be refocused in regions where it had already achieved, or was quickly capable of achieving, critical mass for its monitoring stations. Additional customer contracts would only be acquired in areas where it had a proven competitive advantage and profitability. This would be reinforced by a more effective customer service programme to reduce cancellation rates.

- The business restructuring plan envisaged *exit* for the banks and shareholders by separate trade sales of the core operations. A contingency plan also provided for the flotation of XQC in the US stock markets, or the banks selling their shares in the parent company (acquired pursuant to a debt for equity swap) in the UK stock market.

Financial restructuring

Gloucester's financial restructuring aimed to develop confidence in the company so that the value of its core operations could be enhanced and planned disposals could be carried out in an orderly manner. The key elements of the plan were:

- Interest roll-up on loans to the parent company and the group's UK subsidiaries to alleviate liquidity problems.
- New working capital finance of up to £25 million.
- Placing a significant proportion of the group's facilities on a committed basis for three years.
- Debt for equity swap of £180 million to eliminate the group's balance sheet deficit.

The net impact of the financial restructuring on Gloucester's balance sheet is summarised in Figure 29.3 below.

Some of the key elements of the debt restructuring and debt for equity swap aspects of the transaction are highlighted below.

Figure 29.3: Accounting impact of financial restructuring.				
	As stated £m	Debt for equity swap £m	Extended bank facilities £m	As re-stated £m
Fixed assets	412	–	–	412
Net current (liabilities)/assets	(316)	180	140	4
Long-term liabilities	(203)	–	(140)	(345)
	(107)	180	–	73
Share capital	3	16	–	19
Share premium	35	164	–	199
Other reserves and minority	(145)	–	–	(145)
	(107)	180	–	73

Debt restructuring

The debt restructuring part of Gloucester's financial restructuring was highly complex, given the number of lenders involved with different types of exposures to the group.

Structure of the financial restructuring agreement

For the purposes of the financial restructuring agreement, Gloucester's facilities were grouped into five recourse categories:

1. Facilities extended to the parent company.
2. Facilities extended to the group's UK subsidiaries, with a parent company guarantee.
3. Facilities provided to the UK subsidiaries, without any parent company guarantee.
4. Facilities extended to foreign subsidiaries, with a parent company or a UK subsidiary guarantee.
5. Loans to foreign subsidiaries, without any parent company or UK subsidiary guarantee.

One of the key challenges in this area was to reconcile the interests of the lenders to the parent company and those lending to foreign subsidiaries, many of which were operating satisfactorily.

It was agreed that the banks with exposures to the parent company and UK subsidiaries, comprising recourse categories 1, 2 and 3, would participate in a core financial restructuring agreement. These banks would enter into a three-year commitment with respect to their world-wide facilities. In addition, separate restructuring agreements would be negotiated in each country. Banks with overseas exposures (recourse categories 4 and 5) would be invited to join both the core financial restructuring agreement and the respective local agreements. However, in the event that a bank decided not to participate in both agreements, it would be able to opt out of the UK agreement. In that case, it would not be able to share in the security available to the participants in the core agreement.

New finance for working capital

The banks agreed to meet the group's working capital requirements for a period of up to three years. However, it was agreed that no further new lending would be involved. Instead, the banks consented to release for this purpose £25 million from the anticipated proceeds from Gloucester's planned disposal programme. A few selected banks agreed to extend bridging finance of up to £12 million to accommodate any delays in the receipt of disposal proceeds.

The group's total working capital need was estimated at £30 million. As Figure 29.4 shows, this was based on the company's estimated core working capital requirement of £16 million, with contingent requirements of a further £14 million. The reporting accountants agreed with the company's estimates for its core working capital needs, but felt that the contingent requirements should be lower.

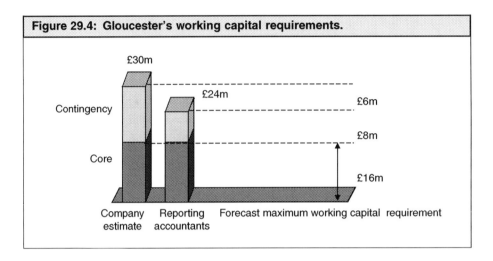

Figure 29.4: Gloucester's working capital requirements.

The bank's commitment to release funds for working capital finance was tiered to reflect the various degrees of certainty with which the funds were required. It was agreed that the banks would provide:

- A commitment to release up to £15 million, to broadly meet Gloucester's agreed core working capital needs.
- A further £10 million (reflecting the contingencies identified by the reporting accountants) would be released, but subject to approval by the steering committee.
- A 'letter of comfort' would be provided for the balancing £5 million, stating that the steering committee will consider approaching the bank group for such release of funds in the event it were necessary.

Roll-up of interest

The group's financial projections suggested that its interest obligations would be covered by earnings at a consolidated level after the restructuring. However, a ringfence around XQC and restrictions on payments of dividends and management fees by a number of foreign subsidiaries meant that interest could not be paid on all parent company loans.

Banks were therefore required to roll-up interest and commission on all UK facilities for three years. This amounted to £39 million. The restructuring agreement provided that accrued interest would be repaid from the proceeds of the disposal of XQC or the freight forwarding operations.

Inter-creditor issues

A major consideration in this area was the relative treatment of banks that were converting debt into equity compared with those that were not. Converting banks were potentially promoting other lenders who were not participating in the swap, such as the providers of guarantees, in the event of the company's collapse. The inter-creditor agreement provided for loss-sharing between the participants in the restructuring. This ensured that the calculation of any post-enforcement distributions would be based on the participants' relative exposures before the swap.

Security and priority

Security for all the facilities under the core financial restructuring agreement comprised mortgage debentures and supplementary legal mortgages from Gloucester and all its material UK subsidiaries. The UK security was held by the co-ordinator on behalf of itself and other participating banks, subject to agreed priorities.

Several layers of priorities were agreed in respect of the UK security pool:

First: £12 million bridging loan plus accrued interest on that loan, extended as part of the financial restructuring agreement.

Second: £40 million new loan and £9 million headroom released during the moratorium.

Third: Accrued interest on the £49 million above and on all the facilities in recourse categories 1 to 5.

Fourth: Moratorium date exposures in recourse categories 1 to 4.

Fifth: Moratorium date exposures in recourse category 5.

Sixth: Any other amount outstanding.

Banks were also permitted to obtain security over the assets of any of Gloucester's foreign subsidiaries they were lending to. This was subject to the agreement of a local moratorium and appropriate sharing arrangements for the security between lenders in that jurisdiction.

Debt for equity swap

The debt for equity swap aspects of Gloucester's financial restructuring were closely inter-linked with the transaction's debt restructuring-related issues. Nevertheless, many of the decisions relating to the swap required separate attention and a sub-committee of the steering committee was established for this purpose. Some of the issues dealt with by the sub-committee are presented below.

Who should convert?

All the banks participating in the financial restructuring were candidates for the debt for equity swap. However, allowance had to be made for the participants who were in a particularly strong position and stood to make no, or very negligible, losses in the event of the company's liquidation. As a result, loans provided by the following groups of lenders were excluded from the swap:

- New facilities provided during the moratorium, which enjoyed a priority in the event of the group's collapse.

- Most banks lending to overseas subsidiaries. These subsidiaries were generally performing satisfactorily and banks lending to them were in a relatively strong position. Moreover, conducting an international debt for equity swap, with lenders in wide-ranging recovery positions, would have considerably added to the transaction's complexity.

- Contingent liabilities that were unlikely to crystallise in the near future.

£280 million of the group's total indebtedness of £651 million constituted the base from which the swap would take place. Loans included were mainly those provided to the parent company and its UK subsidiaries, and also some loss-making non-core foreign subsidiaries.

As highlighted earlier, loss-sharing provisions in the restructuring agreement ensured that the lenders converting debt for equity would not be disadvantaged in the event that Gloucester collapsed during the course of the restructuring.

Amount converted

£180 million of debt from the conversion pool of £280 million was converted into equity, representing a swap ratio of 64 per cent. The principal determinant of this amount was the need to re-establish a satisfactory positive net worth to Gloucester's balance sheet. The group's post-restructuring gearing remained high, at around five times, but it was considered that increasing the amount of debt converted would not have a sufficient impact on leverage to be cost-effective.

Type of shares

The banks converted their debt into ordinary shares in Gloucester. This was partly because they had been able to negotiate a very high proportion of the company's enlarged equity in any event (see below). Also, a transaction involving preference shares would have required a 75 per cent majority approval of existing shareholders. There was a risk that a strategic shareholder, with a substantial stake in the company, would be able to block such a transaction. Moreover, the banks involved preferred a simple structure.

Banks' shareholding

The banks negotiated to acquire 85 per cent of the company's enlarged shareholding in exchange for their swapped debt. This was a matter of intense negotiations and remains one of the highest stakes achieved by banks in a voluntary transaction in the United Kingdom. The sub-committee consulted various specialists on stock market matters to arrive at their negotiating position. A key argument revolved around the fact that the transaction was one of the earliest of its kind in the country. The banks were unwilling to establish a precedent that would see them start from a weak negotiating position in subsequent transactions. Nonetheless, it was perceived that the shareholders' consent to the transaction might not be forthcoming if their residual stake fell below 15 per cent.

Share marketing agreement

The lenders participating in the debt for equity swap entered into an agreement among themselves to regulate their dealing in Gloucester shares. The objective was to preserve value in the shares as a whole by protecting market liquidity, and thereby maximising the possibility of an orderly realisation of shares in the stock market. This is often a concern in debt for equity swaps because banks, who are not natural holders of shares, acquire a substantial shareholding in a company. The resulting 'overhang' can depress the market in the company's shares. In the Gloucester transaction, the banks agreed to regulate their dealings for a period of up to three years by requiring a majority approval of the banks for any disposal.

Evaluation

The banks carried out an exercise to evaluate whether the returns offered by the transaction compensated them for the risks involved. Various techniques were used, but the risk:reward ratio is presented in this section.

Risks

The key risks identified in the transaction were:

- *Business*—Considerable turnaround was being anticipated in Gloucester's freight forwarding operations and there was a high risk that this might not be delivered. Also, publicity about the company's problems had impacted on its business. It was unclear whether there would be any lasting damage to the company's franchise.

- *Structural*—Although the core restructuring agreement would ensure that the banks lending to the parent company and the group's UK subsidiaries provided finance on a committed basis, this was not the case in many of the group's foreign subsidiaries. It was possible that local problems might destabilise the entire group's financing arrangements. Also, there remained considerable uncertainty attached to the timing and feasibility of exit from Gloucester's two core businesses.

- *Financial*—The banks would suffer increased losses if Gloucester collapsed after a restructuring was agreed, because the planned proceeds from disposals would need to be released to meet its working capital requirements. The reporting accountants estimated that on average, the banks participating in the core restructuring agreement would realise 15 per cent of their exposure if Gloucester were liquidated immediately. At the worst point during the restructuring, recovery would fall to only 5 per cent.

Return

The reporting accountants estimated that, on average, banks participating in the core restructuring agreement would receive a return of between 60 and 70 per cent in the event that XQC and Gloucester's freight forwarding operations were sold in an orderly disposal.

Evaluation

Figure 29.5 summarises the risk:reward trade-off for the transaction.

The banks were effectively risking 10 per cent of their exposures, for a potential return of 50 per cent.

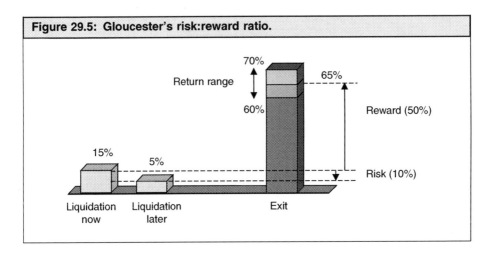

Figure 29.5: Gloucester's risk:reward ratio.

After having given due regard to the risks of the loan workout failing, the banks agreed to proceed with the transaction on these terms. The transaction was also approved by the company's shareholders.

---

[1] *Gloucester Information Pack*, Vol. 1, Synopsis, June 1992.

INDEX

Printed and bound by CPI Group (UK) Ltd, Croydon, CR0 4YY

24/04/2025

14661401-0001